AS YOU LIKE IT

EDITED BY

J. C. SMITH, M.A.(EDIN.), B.A.(OXON.)

Sometime Exhibitioner of Trinity College, Oxford

BLACKIE & SON LIMITED

LONDON AND GLASGOW

BLACKIE & SON LIMITED
16/18 William IV Street,
Charing Cross, London, W.C.2
17 Stanhope Street, Glasgow

BLACKIE & SON (INDIA) LIMITED
103/5 Fort Street, Bombay

BLACKIE & SON (CANADA) LIMITED
Toronto

Printed in Great Britain by Blackie & Son, Ltd., Glasgow

GENERAL PREFACE.

In the WARWICK SHAKESPEARE an attempt is made to present the greater plays of the dramatist in their literary aspect, and not merely as material for the study of philology or grammar. Criticism purely verbal and textual has only been included to such an extent as may serve to help the student in his appreciation of the essential poetry. Questions of date and literary history have been fully dealt with in the Introductions, but the larger space has been devoted to the interpretative rather than the matter-of-fact order of scholarship. Aesthetic judgments are never final, but the Editors have attempted to suggest points of view from which the analysis of dramatic motive and dramatic character may be profitably undertaken. In the Notes likewise, while it is hoped that all unfamiliar expressions and allusions have been adequately explained, yet it has been thought even more important to consider the dramatic value of each scene, and the part which it plays in relation to the whole. These general principles are common to the whole series; in detail each Editor is alone responsible for the plays intrusted to him.

Every volume of the series has been provided with a Glossary, an Essay upon Metre, and an Index; and Appendices have been added upon points of special interest, which could not conveniently be treated in the Introduction or the Notes. The text is based by the several Editors on that of the *Globe* edition: the only omissions made are those that are unavoidable in an edition likely to be used by young students.

By the systematic arrangement of the introductory matter, and by close attention to typographical details, every effort has been made to provide an edition that will prove convenient in use.

THE WARWICK SHAKESPEARE. General
editor, Professor C. H. HERFORD, Litt.D., F.B.A.

Play	Edited by
ANTONY AND CLEOPATRA.	A. E. Morgan, M.A., and W. Sherard Vines, M.A.
AS YOU LIKE IT.	J. C. Smith, M.A., B.A.
CORIOLANUS.	Sir Edmund K. Chambers, K.B.E., C.B., M.A., D.Litt·
CYMBELINE.	A. J. Wyatt, M.A.
HAMLET.	Sir Edmund K. Chambers.
HENRY THE FOURTH—Part I.	F. W. Moorman, B.A., Ph.D.
HENRY THE FOURTH—Part II.	C.H.Herford, Litt. D., F.B.A.
HENRY THE FIFTH.	G. C. Moore Smith, D.Litt., Ph.D., LL.D.
JULIUS CÆSAR.	Arthur D. Innes, M.A.
KING JOHN.	G. C. Moore Smith.
KING LEAR.	D. Nichol Smith.
LOVE'S LABOUR'S LOST.	A. E. Morgan, M.A., and W. Sherard Vines, M.A.
MACBETH.	Sir Edmund K. Chambers.
THE MERCHANT OF VENICE.	H. L. Withers.
A MIDSUMMER-NIGHT'S DREAM.	Sir Edmund K. Chambers.
MUCH ADO ABOUT NOTHING.	J. C. Smith, M.A., B.A.
OTHELLO.	C.H.Herford, Litt. D.,F.B.A.
RICHARD THE SECOND.	C. H. Herford.
RICHARD THE THIRD.	Sir George Macdonald, K.C.B., D.Litt., LL.D.
ROMEO AND JULIET.	J. E. Crofts, B.Litt.
THE TEMPEST.	F. S. Boas, M.A., LL.D.
TROILUS AND CRESSIDA.	Bonamy Dobrée, O.B.E., M.A.
TWELFTH NIGHT.	Arthur D. Innes, M.A.
THE WINTER'S TALE.	C. H. Herford.

CONTENTS.

INTRODUCTION.

I. HISTORY OF THE PLAY.

§ 1. As You Like It was first printed in the collected edition of Shakespeare's plays known as the First Folio, 1623. No Quarto exists, or in all likelihood ever existed, for the play is mentioned by the printers of the First Folio among those which "are not formerly entred to other men". Various points in the text, especially the form of the stage-directions, make it probable that the play was originally printed from an acting copy.

§ 2. Though it was probably put on the boards as early as 1600, no actual performance is recorded during Shakespeare's lifetime, or for long after his death. But Oldys has preserved a tradition that Shakespeare himself acted in the play, in the part of Adam. A younger brother of Shakespeare's, according to Oldys, was alive after the Restoration. In his youth he had often gone up to London to see Shakespeare act, and in his old age was naturally much questioned for reminiscences of his brother, "especially in his dramatic character. But all that could be recollected from him of his brother *Will* in that station" (*i.e.* as an actor) "was the faint, general, and almost lost ideas he had of having once seen him act a part in one of his own comedies, wherein, being to personate a decrepit old man, he wore a long beard, and appeared so weak and drooping and unable to walk, that he was forced to be supported and carried by another person to a table, at which he was seated among some company, who were eating, and one of them sung a song." This description applies accurately to the entrance of Orlando with Adam at the end of the second act.

7

After the Restoration several of Shakespeare's plays were revived, in somewhat mangled forms; but *As You Like It* was not among them. Our usual authorities, at least, say nothing of any such revival; and, as will be seen, there is positive evidence to the contrary. It was not till 1723 that Charles Johnson produced an adaptation of it at Drury Lane, with the title of *Love in a Forest*. In his Prologue Johnson says:

Chas. Johnson's adaptation, 1723.

' In Honour to his Name and this learn'd Age,
  Once more your much-lov'd Shakespeare treads the Stage ";

and declares that his whole ambition is

" The Scene from Time and Error to restore,
  And give the Stage from Shakespeare one play more ".

Evidently, then, Johnson's was the first revival, at least in that generation. To suit the taste of that learn'd Age, Johnson cuts out the purely comic and pastoral characters, introduces the burlesque of Pyramus and Thisbe from *A Midsummer Night's Dream*, makes Oliver kill himself, and marries Celia to Jaques, who, to fit him for playing the cynic in love, is furnished with Benedick's speeches from *Much Ado*. This atrocious medley had a run of a week.

More thorough-going, and even more atrocious, is *The Modern Receipt, or a Cure for Love*, published by one J. C. in 1739. ' J. C.' follows Johnson in his omissions: his additions are all his own. He too marries Celia to Jaques, and their love-making bulks more largely in the play than does the wooing of Orlando and Rosalind.

In 1740 *As You Like It* was restored to the boards, with Quin as Jaques and Mrs. Pritchard as Rosalind, and ran for twenty-five nights. Since then its popularity has rarely flagged. Eighteenth-century critics mention the Jaques of Quin and Sheridan, the Touchstone of Macklin and King, and the Rosalind of Mrs. Barry, Mrs. Pritchard, and Peg Woffington. But the great Rosalind of the century was Mrs. Jordan, who first took the part in 1789. She made Rosalind a mere tomboy—"a tousell'd hoyden"

English Performances.

is Mr. Verity's phrase—but her smile was irresistible. Mrs. Siddons (1785) was the first to bring out the dignity and womanliness of Rosalind, a side of her character to which later actresses have not failed to do justice. In the present century we have the revival by Macready, and the Jaques of Kemble and Hermann Vezin, and the Rosalind of Helen Faucit (Lady Martin) and Miss Rehan of to-day. Lady Martin was perhaps the most famous Rosalind of the English stage. She has written about Rosalind as well as acted her; and readers can still enjoy her tender and vivid conception of the part in the most delightful of her essays.[1]

The play has long been a favourite in Germany. Vincke[2] mentions as many as seven adaptations between 1848 and 1870. All these adaptations take the form of compression, a compression chiefly exercised upon the forest scenes; and exhibit a feeling, as Vincke puts it, that the superstructure is too airy for the massive pedestal. There may be some force in this from a theatre-goer's point of view; but to a reader, at any rate to an English reader, it seems to betray a certain obtuseness as to the real theme and interest of the play. Perhaps the wit suffers in translation. *German and French Adaptations.*

In France there is George Sand's famous adaptation (1856). In her *Comme Il Vous Plaira*, Jaques is the real hero, and ultimately marries Celia, while Audrey at the last moment throws over Touchstone for William. Here, too, the forest scenes are curtailed. Indeed the whole tone of the play is altered, and the centre of interest quite displaced.

II. DATE OF COMPOSITION.

§ 3. External evidence consists of references to the play in record which we can date, and gives a limit before which it must have been written. *(1) External Evidence.*

(1) *As You Like It* is entered in the Stationers' Registers,

---

[1] *Some of Shakespeare's Female Characters.*
[2] *"Wie es euch gefällt"* auf der Bühne: Jahrbuch, vol. 13, p. 186.

under date August 4th, 1600,[1] as a book "to be stayed" (*i.e.* not printed).

(2) In Thomas Morley's First Booke of Ayres, printed at London in 1600, one of the songs of this play ("It was a lover and his lass", act v. sc. 3) is set to music. Morley does not claim the words of his songs; he must have borrowed this from Shakespeare, unless, indeed, they both took it from some older source. But this particular song corresponds, both in its position and in its sentiments, to Corydon's song in Lodge's novel—"A blithe and bonny country lass". This seems to settle the question of authorship, and with it the upper limit of the date.

(3) Negatively, too, external evidence gives a lower limit. *As You Like It* is not included in the list of Shakespeare's plays in Meres's *Treasury of Wit* (1598). Hence, on external evidence alone, the date of composition is fixed to the years 1598–1600; and, as *Henry V.* and *Much Ado* were probably both written during these years, and before *As You Like It*, we are practically confined to 1600.

§ 4. References in the play to events which we can date give a limit after which it must have been written. The allusions in *As You Like It* generally go to confirm the results of the external evidence. Thus (1) the line "Who ever loved that loved not at first sight?" (iii. 5. 81) is a quotation from Marlowe's *Hero and Leander*, which was published in 1598. (2) The expression "like one another as halfpence are" (iii. 2. 323) refers to the halfpence of Elizabeth, in use till 1601. (3) The simile "like Diana in the fountain" (iv. 1. 134) may have been suggested by a statue of that goddess set up in West Cheap in 1596 and in ruins by 1603.

(2) Evidence of Allusion.

But there remain two troublesome references. (4) When Rosalind (iv. 1. 165) swears "by all pretty oaths that are not dangerous", she has been thought to refer to a statute of 1605 to restrain the abuses of Players. (5) Again, in v. 2. 55,

---

[1] The year is not actually given, but is safely inferred from the preceding entry, and from the fact that *Much Ado* and *Henry V.*, which are 'stayed' along with *As You Like It*, were published in August, 1600.

she says, " I have conversed with a magician, most profound in his art, and yet not damnable"; a few lines lower she repeats the caution: " By my life I do; which I tender dearly, though I am a magician ". It is natural to see in this repetition a reference to the statute of 1603, which attached the severest penalties to witchcraft. If these references are not imaginary, they cannot have stood in the play of 1600. They must have been added at some later performance by way of "topical allusions". But even this supposition is not necessary. The first of these passages may refer to some earlier inhibition—perhaps alluded to in i. 2. 77 (see note *ad loc.*); and the statute against witchcraft only re-enacted with increased severity an older statute of 5 Elizabeth.

As to why *As You Like It* was 'stayed' in 1600, no convincing explanation has yet been given. On the strength of various inconsistencies in the first act and the hasty wind-up of the last, Mr. Wright suggests that the play was unfinished. But even if these facts are admitted,[1] they prove not merely that it was unfinished by August 4th, 1600 (in which case we should have expected a Quarto to appear in a month or two), but that it never received Shakespeare's last touches at all. Moreover, the citation from Morley shows that the fifth act was written in that year.

It is more probable that a piratical attempt had been made to publish the play, and that Shakespeare or his company appealed against it. *As You Like It* was then new to the boards, and a printed edition might interfere with its stage success. An extraordinary number of Shakespeare's plays was printed in 1600; from this time onwards he seems to have become very chary of letting his manuscript into the printers'—or pirates'—hands.

§ 5. In the case of *As You Like It*, the metrical evidence yields no definite conclusion as to date. This is due partly to want of facts—only two-fifths of the play is in verse ; partly to the conflicting results of the various tests.[2] All that can be inferred from the metre

(3) Internal Evidence.
(a) Metrical.

---

[1] For a fuller discussion see Appendix B.
[2] On these tests, see the note on Shakespeare's Prosody.

is, that the play falls between *Romeo and Juliet* and *Troilus
and Cressida*. This latitude it shares with *Twelfth Night*, a
play with which it has much in common.

§6. *As You Like It* is entered in the Stationers' Registers
(*b*) Style and along with *Henry V.* and *Much Ado*; and this
Composition. juxtaposition admirably exhibits its place in the
development of Shakespeare's art. With *Henry V.* he finished
his great series of English Histories: with *Hamlet* he plunged
into the world of tragedy. In the "sunshine holiday" between, he wrote those three bright plays—*Much Ado, As You
Like It*, and *Twelfth Night*. They form a group apart; with
little of the verbal cleverness of his first style, and none of
the after-glow which lights up the *Winter's Tale*, yet full of
unspoiled mirth and innocent affection. Only here and there
—in the melancholy of Jaques and the almost too tragic plot
of *Much Ado*—*Hamlet* and *Othello* are foreshadowed. An
excess of symmetry is a trait which *As You Like It* shares
with an earlier group; but this is due to Lodge rather than to
Shakespeare.

III. THE SOURCE OF THE INCIDENTS.[1]

§. 7. The earliest form of the story is found in the *Coke's
Tale of Gamelyn*, sometimes (though wrongly) printed among
Chaucer's *Canterbury Tales*. Whether Shakespeare had
read it is more than doubtful.[2] In any case, the immediate
source of his plot was not the Tale, but Thomas Lodge's
novel of *Rosalind, Euphues' Golden Legacy*. Lodge's story,

---

[1] In this, and the succeeding division of the Introduction, I have dwelt rather
on the constructive than on the imaginative side of Shakespeare's comic art. If
such a method be thought to need justification in a school-book, I might quote
Mr. Pater's words: "The philosophic critic, at least, will value, even in works
of imagination, seemingly the most intuitive, the power of the understanding in
them, their logical process of construction, the spectacle of a supreme intellectual
dexterity which they afford".

[2] See Appendix A. In that Appendix and this part of the Introduction I
owe much to Mr. Stone's article (New Shakspere Society's Transactions, 1880-6,
p. 277), and more to Delius (Jahrbuch, vol. vi. p. 226).

first published in 1590, is based to some extent on the Tale. From it he took the characters of the old knight, his three sons, and the faithful servant Adam; with the incidents of the quarrel in the orchard, the wrestling, and the hero's return and flight. On this simple foundation he erected a pastoral romance. He added the two Dukes (they are Kings in the novel), and their daughters; all the pastoral characters; and all the interest of love and intrigue in Arden—all the main incidents of the play, in short, and all the main characters except Jaques, Touchstone, and Audrey. Moreover, he redacted the rough ballad-style of the Tale into a new and artificial manner. The novel, as its sub-title shows, was written in the fashion set by Lyly's *Euphues* (1579), and thence called Euphuism. It is a style abounding in lengthy homilies, remote fancies, similes from natural history, alliterations and antitheses which sometimes fall to the level of very poor puns: a style described by Drayton as

> "Talking of stones, stars, plants, of fishes, flies,
> Playing with words and idle similes":

and best known from Shakespeare's famous caricature of it in *Love's Labour's Lost*, and Scott's in the *Monastery*.

§ 8. When Shakespeare dramatized the work of a country-man and a contemporary, he seems to have imposed certain restrictions on himself which he did not observe when he drew his material from foreign sources. In the latter case he allowed himself great liberties, altering, omitting, and even (as in the *Merchant of Venice*) combining distinct stories as suited his purpose. But in the case of *As You Like It* and *The Winter's Tale*, which is similarly drawn from Greene's *Pandosto*, he was dealing with a story familiar to many of his audience in its printed form.[1] Accordingly he was content to leave the main features of the story unchanged, to omit only such incidents as resisted dramatizing, and to add only such characters and situations as did not interfere with the known flow of the narrative.

(marginal notes: The Tale of Gamelyn and Lodge's Rosalind. / Rosalind and As You Like It.)

---

[1] Lodge's novel was then in its third edition.

But under cover of this superficial resemblance he practised
a hundred subtle changes. The facts are retained, but their
connection is altered, and with their connection their significance. The external features of the characters remain, but
their acts are attributed to new motives and take on a new
meaning. And over all he throws the splendour of style.
The flat and conventional figures of the novel develop into
full and human characters, and, though isolated phrases are
retained, its academic dialogue is in the main replaced by
the most brilliant natural speech.

§ 9. Only the more obvious changes[1] can be noticed here,
and these may be classed under three heads: (1) Changes
of Time and Place; (2) Omissions and Additions; (3) Changes
affecting Character.

In the novel Rosader and Adam set out for the forest of
Arden: in the play they have no special destina-
tion in view. Otherwise there is no change,
except that Lodge is naturally more precise and prosaic in
his topography.

Changes:
(1 a) Place.

The play compresses into a few days—Daniel counts ten
days with intervals—what in the novel is spread
over a much longer period.

(1 b) Time.

(a) In Lodge there is a long interval between the quarrel
(i. 1) and the wrestling (i. 2): Shakespeare puts them on
successive days.

(b) After the wrestling Rosader stays a while at home, and
that too though he knows of Rosalind's banishment. Orlando
would not be such a laggard in love. He returns at once,
learns Oliver's plot, and leaves the place immediately, in
ignorance of Rosalind's fate.

(c) In spite of this, Shakespeare has followed Lodge in
putting Oliver's banishment after the arrival of the fugitives
in Arden. But this order of events is a concession to
dramatic effect (iii. 1).

---

[1] Minuter changes are referred to in the notes. The differences of names are
these:—Rosader = Orlando; Saladin = Oliver; Torismond = Duke Frederick;
Gerismond=Duke Senior; Alinda=Celia; Corydon=Corin; Montanus = Silvius.
Rosalind, Phebe, and Adam are retained, as well as the assumed names Ganymede and Aliena.

(*d*) For the same reason, he has introduced the pastoral sub-plot before the arrival of Oliver in the forest, and inverted the order of the messages brought to the ladies by him and by Silvius (iii. 5 and iv. 3).

There is one point, however, in his treatment of time, which needs a fuller notice. The most perfect arrangement from the spectator's point of view, and the one which will most easily sustain the dramatic illusion, is that the time supposed to elapse (the ideal time) shall be no more than the time which the play takes to act (the real time). A typical Greek tragedy, like the *Oedipus Tyrannus*, comes near to fulfilling this condition. But such a congeries of dramatic moments is rare, and is unsuited for that development, as opposed to the mere presentment, of character which is the peculiar feature of Shakespearian tragedy. Shakespeare 'cuts the knot' by using *two different time-systems at once*. By one series of time-notes the action is hurried on, as if it were compressed into a few days; by another it is protracted over weeks or months. This phenomenon is not very noticeable in *As You Like It*. But it is there. Compare now these three passages:

(1) *Oli.* Good Monsieur Charles, what's the new news at the new court?

Cha. There's no news at the court, sir, but the old news: that is, the old duke is banished, &c.

. . . . . .

Oli. Where *will* the old duke live?

Cha. They say he is *already* in the forest of Arden

(i. 1. 85–100)

(2) *Duke F.* Ay, Celia, we stay'd her for your sake,
Else had she with her father ranged along.

Cel. I did not then entreat to have her stay;
It was your pleasure and your own remorse:
I was *too young* that time to value her (i. 3. 60–64).

(3) *Duke S.* Hath not *old custom* made this life more sweet
Than that of painted pomp? . . . .
Here feel we but the penalty of Adam,
The seasons' difference, &c. (ii. 1. 2–7).

Double Time.

In the first of these passages the impression conveyed, and meant to be conveyed, is that the usurpation is quite recent. This impression is created to account for the unsettled state of Duke Frederick's feelings, and the causeless fit of passion in which he banishes Rosalind. But once this is accomplished, Shakespeare allows the usurpation to slip back into the past, in order that, when the action shifts to Arden, the exiles may figure as habitués of the forest, fit to support the contrast between the country and the court.

(*a*) The novel opens at the old knight's death-bed. Shakespeare gives all that is necessary to understand the story in Orlando's opening speech.

Omissions and Additions.
2 (*a*) Incidents Omitted.

(*b*) He also omits as not essential a tourney which precedes the wrestling.

(*c*) After the wrestling, Rosader returns home with a rabble of young men, breaks into Saladin's house and feasts his gay companions. After a time he is seized in his sleep and put in irons, from which he is released by Adam, and holds the house till the sheriff comes against him. This episode is closely imitated from the *Tale of Gamelyn*. In the play Orlando returns alone, and is simply warned by Adam.

(*d*) Saladin is thrown into prison by Torismond—a detail which Shakespeare omits to expedite the action.

(*e*) In the novel Aliena is carried off by a band of robbers, from whom she is rescued by Rosader and Saladin. In this exploit Rosader receives a wound: in the play Orlando is wounded in rescuing his brother; and the meeting of Oliver and Celia, which is the object of this episode, is simply effected by making Oliver the messenger. Robbers would be out of place in the philosophic shades of Arden.

(*f*) At the end of the novel news comes that the twelve peers of France have revolted against the usurper: Gerismond sets out to join them with Rosader and Saladin; Torismond is defeated and slain. To end the play lightly, without breaking up the harmony of the wedding scene, Shakespeare has done poetic justice by the milder method of converting Frederick.

Various incidents, for various dramatic reasons, are narrated instead of being represented, *e.g.* the wrestling with the Franklin's sons, the rescue of Oliver, the wooing of Celia, and Frederick's conversion. [See notes.] *(2 b)* Incidents Narrated.

The purely reflective part of Jaques, and the purely comic parts of Touchstone, Audrey, and William, are additions of Shakespeare's own. They are so contrived that, without breaking in on the main action, they lend its humour breadth and depth, and help beyond anything else to turn the pastoral into a comedy. Several minor characters are also added or named for the first time by Shakespeare, viz. Dennis, Le Beau, Amiens, the First Lord, and Sir Oliver Martext. The short lyrical scenes (ii. 5, iv. 2, v. 3) are also new, as indeed are all the songs. *(2 c)* New Scenes and Characters.

Besides these new characters, and the situations in which they figure, Shakespeare has added a number of scenes or parts of scenes to which no counterpart will be found in the novel: *e.g.* i. 1 up to Oliver's entrance, i. 2 to the beginning of the wrestling, i. 3 to the entrance of the Duke, and the whole of ii. 1. These scenes are added to exhibit not merely the external circumstances of the various characters, but their feelings and motives at the time when they are merged in the action.

It is naturally in the treatment of character that Shakespeare has allowed himself most liberty. He has absolutely transmuted the hero and the heroine, *(3)* Changes of Character. with what a gain of dignity and manliness to Orlando and of womanliness and wit to Rosalind, only a detailed comparison, such as is partly attempted in the notes, can show. But in two cases his treatment is so characteristic, and has provoked so much criticism, that the question must be summed up here. The characters in question are Oliver and Duke Frederick.

At first sight there is little to choose between them and the Saladin and Torismond of the novel. Yet with a minimum of change Shakespeare has Saladin and Torismond. given a new interpretation of their conduct. Saladin's enmity to Rosader is due to pure greed and envy. Rosader has inherited the largest share of their father's estate, and to deprive him of this Saladin plots his murder in cold blood, bribes the wrestler to kill him, and sends him to meet his fate on the plea that he must support the honour of the house. Torismond is a companion figure, in drawing whom Lodge seems to have had in his mind the conventional pictures of the Greek Tyrannus. He is first introduced while holding a tournament, intended to divert the people's thoughts from dwelling on their banished king. He banishes Rosalind for fear that one of the peers may fall in love with her and aspire to the throne. When his own daughter intercedes, he banishes her as well, "rather choosing", says Lodge, "to hazard the loss of his only child than anyways to put in question the state of his kingdom". Finally, when he hears of Rosader's flight, "desirous to possess such fair revenues", he seizes on the pretext to confiscate Saladin's property: "by thy means", he says, "have I lost a most brave and resolute chevalier".

Oliver's hatred for Orlando has its root, not in greed—for Orlando has no wealth to covet—but in a far subtler cause, a blood diverted from the course of nature. The boy whom he has neglected as an encumbrance—this boy he sees growing up in spite of him to outshine him even in the eyes of his own dependants. He cannot deny Orlando's graces even to himself, but he will not own that he is in the wrong. His plot with Charles is concocted in the heat of resentment, and, when this redounds to Orlando's glory, his final treacherous attempt is the last effort of a baffled will.

Oliver and Duke Frederick.

The Duke's actions, too, are based on temperament rather than on circumstance. He is twice expressly styled the 'humorous' Duke. He is at the mercy of his own moody passions. In a fit of temper, provoked by the sight of his old enemy's son, he banishes Rosalind, alleging no special reason because he has none to allege. When he finds that Celia too has fled, he has a touch of repentance, succeeded by another access of violence in which he banishes Oliver. His final conversion is quite in keeping with his previous acts.

The meeting of the two 'tyrants', in which this part of the

plot culminates, is brought about by new means which connect it directly with the main plot. Celia is not banished; she runs away: Orlando is suspected—here the time-change noted above (1 *b*) comes in—and Oliver is sent for. With a fine poetic justice, the perverse wilfulness of Oliver is broken by a tyranny still more masterful, and all his fortunes are made to depend on his recovery of that brother whom he had driven from house and home.

If it be felt after all that Oliver hardly deserves his final good fortune, that there is little in his previous conduct to prepare us for his conversion, we can only recur to the conditions under which Shakespeare was working, and reply that he has probably done his best with his materials.

IV. CRITICAL APPRECIATION.

§ 10. So far we have followed the process of creation: it remains to look at the product as an artistic whole. As such it must be judged on its own merits, without regard to its origin, and in its entirety. The separate characters are nothing except as parts of the play, and have no value except in their places there. No doubt there is an interest of character as well as an interest of situation, but in drama, at least, the two cannot be dissociated. Moreover, the various characters and situations are not all on the same level of interest, and a true judgment on the whole will only emerge when they are seen in their right relations. Here criticism must reverse the method of creation, and separate the different strands which the poet has woven together.

§ 11. Every true plot, however short, is made up of two movements, a movement of Complication and a The Dramatic movement of Resolution. These two movements Climax. may vary in relative length, but in a well-constructed play they often fairly divide the action, and the point at which the Complication ends and the Resolution begins may be called the Dramatic Climax. In *As You Like It* this climax will be found in the second scene of the third act, *i.e.* as nearly as possible in the mathematical centre of the play.

This is the famous Forest Scene, where Rosalind in the guise of a youth meets Orlando, and proposes that he shall woo her in masquerade. This scene is the key to the whole action of the play: to this all the previous movements lead up, and from this all the subsequent movements flow. The first hint of it is found in Lodge, in the Wooing Eclogue sung by Ganymede and Rosader. But it remained for Shakespeare to see the dramatic possibilities of the situation. The Wooing Eclogue is jejune compared to the interplay of jest and earnest, of wit and tenderness which forms the texture of the Forest Scene; and even in form it is too mere a frolic to foster that real ripening of affection which Shakespeare makes us see beneath the frolic.

§ 12. It is from this point that we can most profitably
The Main   analyse the structure of the play. Here is the
Theme.   simple and essential plot. Two undeclared
lovers meet: the lady in disguise challenges her lover to woo her as his mistress: their courtship is thus carried on in masquerade till she is assured of his affection, when she discloses herself, and all ends happily. This issue is predetermined almost from the first, so that our attention is directed less to what will happen than to the way in which the theme will work itself out. Hence the play is in form a Comedy of Dialogue rather than a Comedy of Incident. But the real interest lies neither in dialogue nor in incident. The incidents are contrived to bring the lovers together; the dialogue is not a mere run of repartee beginning and ending in a laugh, but is devoted to the expression of the main theme. And that theme is love. *As You Like It* is the comedy of happy love, as *Romeo and Juliet* is the tragedy of star-crossed love.

The hero, indeed, is little more than the ideal lover—the
The Hero.   successful lover, that is, for he is not burdened
             with that weight of passion which in itself foredooms Romeo. Shakespeare has bestowed on Orlando all the solid graces of his part. He is young, manly, gentle, and unfortunate; and perhaps his misfortunes tell as much in his favour as his manliness, or gentleness or youth. When

his luck turns we begin to feel his deficiencies. In the forest scenes he is little but a passive interlocutor, and the burden of the dialogue falls on Rosalind. Shakespeare has given him the victory over Jaques, but his wit is rather of the *tu quoque* order: "Farewell, good Signior Love"; "Adieu, good Monsieur Melancholy": a schoolboy style of retort. If the lover in luck fails to hold our interest, it is perhaps the penalty inseparable from his age and his part, a part in which Scott has owned to frequent failure, and even Shakespeare has not always succeeded.

But his partial failure with the hero only brings out the more fully his consummate success with the heroine. She is a good example of the truth The Heroine. that character and situation cannot be dissociated. Rosalind is created for the situation, and the situation for Rosalind. "She is wit and womanliness", as Mr. Verity says, "in equal proportions"; and it is precisely this combination that makes her Rosalind. Beatrice is as witty, and Imogen more womanly, but nowhere else in the range of Shakespeare's women are the two qualities so brought together that love stimulates wit, and wit lends itself to love. Her full character and powers are not disclosed at once: in the earlier scenes, her repartees are not perceptibly above the level of Celia or the Clown; it is not till she is safe in the forest, and learns that Orlando is near and loves her, that fancy catches fire from feeling, and rises in brilliant coruscation. This is the peculiar quality of her wit. It is neither boisterous nor personal. She does not 'speak poniards', like Beatrice, but deals in bright generalities 'that give delight and hurt not'. When she wishes to wound it is not irony that she uses. Her gaiety is the flower of youth and of a brave and high spirit, a part of her inheritance of noble birth which sustains her in adversity and is never forgotten in her masquerade. Shakespeare has disdained for her sake the obvious farcical opportunities which the situation offers, and some of which he has worked out in *Twelfth Night*. But the charm of Viola is of a dependent kind, to which a little ridicule is not fatal. It may be thought that she keeps Orlando too long in suspense; but it must be remembered that till their second meeting there has been no word of love between them, that she has to assure herself of his feelings and her own, and that the wooing is a real wooing to her—and, in short, the situation has charms of its own which no witty woman could forego.

§ 13. To this simple theme everything else is accessory. Some of the accessories are needed to explain how the lovers first come to fall in love, and how they meet again in new scenes and amid new circumstances; others describe these scenes and circumstances, the natural and social *milieu* of the action; others again serve to strengthen the main plot by way of comparison or to bring into relief by force of contrast. According as they fulfil one or other of these functions, they may be distinguished as (*a*) Preliminaries, (*b*) Background Scenes, and (*c*) Sub-plots.

Accessories.

Some of the preliminaries fall outside the actual play, being presupposed in the conditions in which the action opens. In treating these presuppositions, storytellers have always allowed themselves more freedom than in the actual conduct of the tale. The Greek tragedians were notoriously careless of probability in τὰ ἔξω τοῦ δράματος, things outside the action; and, to take a modern instance, it would need another 'Egoist' to explain how Clara Middleton becomes engaged to Sir Willoughby. In our play it may be observed that Shakespeare gives no reason for the peculiar terms of Sir Rowland's will, on which so much depends; nor does he anywhere explain for which of his virtues the people allowed their amiable Duke to be banished by his 'humorous' brother. These things are ἔξω τοῦ δράματος.

(a) Preliminaries.

The preliminary scenes within the play are those parts of it which lead up to the wrestling at which the lovers meet, explain the ground of their sudden attachment, and give the cause of their banishment and flight. Oliver and Duke Frederick are essentially preliminary characters, though Oliver reappears in one of the sub-plots. The fate of each is itself a play in miniature, with its proper complication and resolution. In both there is the same motive of fraternal enmity (Shakespeare loves thus to heighten an effect by reduplication), and the two denouements are not dissimilar. Adam also belongs to the preliminaries, and drops out of the action at the end of Act II.

§ 14. To the background belong all those scenes and characters which contribute nothing to the action of the play. These scenes are descriptive rather *(b) Background Scenes.* than properly dramatic, and the import of the characters lies less in what they do than in what they say. They give the natural and social surroundings in which the main action moves, and impart to it the breadth and atmosphere of life. The natural surroundings are suggested in a series of brief touches which yet leave a complete picture in the mind; and their spirit has passed into the quiet wisdom of the Elder Duke, and finds tuneful expression in the songs of Amiens and the Foresters. These songs are a notable feature of the play. The forest would be dead without them. They are all 'old and plain'; no luscious madrigals or quaint eclogues such as Lodge delights in, but songs of the greenwood and the holly, of the chase and country love. The themes are all the better for being old-fashioned; they awake echoes of Robin Hood, and their music and associations help not a little to convey that open-air feeling which pervades the play, and which mere description cannot always impart. Here the sylvan predominates over the pastoral: we are in Sherwood, not Arcadia.

The banished Duke belongs essentially to the background. Positive function he has none, except to give away the bride. But his tone and temper make *The Elder Duke.* him an excellent mouthpiece of the moral advantages of banishment. His cheerful reflections bring out the optimist side of that contrast between the country and the court, the natural and the artificial, which is implied throughout the play, and which gives point to the invectives of Jaques and to the humour of Touchstone. The character and circumstances of this exiled moralist inevitably suggest a comparison with Prospero which he is ill fitted to sustain. The adversity which he has tasted is merely material; the iron of ingratitude has not entered into his soul. It is remarkable that he nowhere alludes to his brother's conduct or to the occasion of his own banishment. And apart from this moral difference, he has not the high speculative outlook of Prospero. But this only proves that his reflections are in keeping with the general tone of the play, which, delightful as it is, does not touch any deep moral problem, but dwells lightly on the surface of life.

Jaques is by far the most important of all the background characters. He answers to that description fairly,
Jaques.
but he does absolutely nothing to forward the action of the play. "He is the only purely contemplative character in Shakespeare", says Hazlitt; "he thinks and does nothing." But though he does nothing to advance the *plot*, his removal would entirely alter the *composition* of the whole. He is a foil to half the other characters—to the Duke in his melancholy, to the lovers in his philosophy, and to Touchstone in his humour.

In a sense, it is true, the character of Jaques is a satire on a contemporary affectation.[1] He represents the travelled Englishman, who has come back from the Continent with a soured temper and an empty purse. But Shakespeare, when he wrote *As You Like It*, had long outgrown the mere satirist of *Love's Labour's Lost*. He uses contemporary allusions only to deck some general trait. In Jaques' case the trait is certainly one which has clung to the national character, and makes Kreyssig see in him the father of all those who overrun Europe with guide-books. But there is more in it.

Jaques is a non-combatant in the battle of life. He has tasted pleasure in his youth, he has spent his patrimony in foreign travel, and now in his old age he has retired on his experience. His sole occupation now is to watch the combat he has quitted. Seen from the outside, life is to him a mere dramatic spectacle. Perhaps his point of view is not the best, for he finds more to cry than to laugh over. He sees

---

[1] For a similar affectation compare King John, iv. 1. 13:

"Yet I remember, when I was in France,
Young gentlemen would be as sad as night,
Only for wantonness."

life in its mean, ludicrous, and pathetic aspects; and, indeed, is so much in love with his rôle of spectator, that all the actors must seem to him by comparison mean, ludicrous, or pathetic. And thus he is set off against the Duke, the lovers, and the fool. Lying under the trees, weeping over the wounded deer, and sucking melancholy from the songs of Amiens, he brings out (in contrast to the Duke) a new variation on the theme of the country and the court. He has followed the Duke's fortunes, and calls himself a fool for his pains. For here, in the forest, where the Duke finds the sweet and bracing influences of Nature, Jaques sees the struggle of life repeating itself in folly, selfishness, and misery.

He is sufficiently interested in the lovers to want to convert them to his way of thinking. But they have no time for such vanities, and flout him somewhat rudely off the stage.

It is a holiday for him when he finds the fool. Touchstone's mock wisdom is a new and exquisite experience. Jaques has found his vocation. He will don motley and reform the world with words. He follows Touchstone about, listening to him from behind the trees, and showing off his paces to the Duke with the patronizing admiration of the amateur for the professional.

At last, when the old Duke is restored, he goes to seek out the penitent usurper in his cell, there to continue his study of human nature. He is essentially a creature of idleness, and with the return to active life his function ends. The whole scope and purpose of this character is much in dispute, and we must try to judge him solely by what he says, and what the others say of and to him. In fine, it is a mistake to take him more seriously than he takes himself.

The whole of these background scenes and characters are done with an elaborateness that almost amounts to a fault. It is a fault—and one into which Scott, for instance, has often fallen—to make those persons first in interest who are only second in the action; and though such an error may be readily pardoned in a novel, it is not so easy to forgive in a play, where the main action is after all the main thing. If

As You Like It escapes this charge, it is due to the paramount personality and charm of Rosalind.

§ 15. The main action is further strengthened by no less

(c) Sub-plots.
(1) Oliver and Celia.

than three sub-plots, by the introduction of which Shakespeare avails himself of the principles of comparison and contrast. The loves of Oliver and Celia run parallel to those of Orlando and Rosalind ; but enough has been said about Oliver in an earlier section. As Celia's chief function is to set off Rosalind, so her main charm lies just here, in her loyal and admiring love for her cousin, taller, wittier, and more beautiful than herself. It is an intimate and sisterly affection above any other of the kind which Shakespeare has depicted, and enhances her as much as it enhances Rosalind. But there is never any doubt as to the real heroine. Celia's humour—and she has plenty of fun, though not the sparkle and range of Rosalind—only comes out when they are alone together, and plays in affectionate banter about her cousin. And there is some truth in what she says, that the love she gives is more perfect than that which she receives ; but such is the birthright of heroines.

Ganymede and Aliena only play at shepherds. It is in

(2) Silvius and Phebe.

the sub-plot of Silvius and Phebe, and in the small part of Corin, that Shakespeare has chiefly utilized the pastoral element in his original. The taste for pastoralism had revived in Spain and Italy in the middle of the 16th century, and gradually spread to England, where it strongly affected the work of some of Shakespeare's predecessors, such as Spenser, Sidney, and Lodge. In certain eras of civilization — the Alexandrian, the Augustan, the Elizabethan, and our own—these Arcadian fancies have been a spell on quiet imaginations that find the times out of joint. But the pastoral world, with its classical machinery and conventional subjects, is too unreal for the purpose of Comedy, and when it is made to support the main weight of the plot it is prone to degenerate, as it did in Fletcher's hands, into sentimentalism. Shakespeare seems instinctively to have hit its proper place in Comedy. He uses it, much as he uses

the fairy-world in *A Midsummer Night's Dream*, as sub-
sidiary to the natural human interest of his main action.
The characters here are sketched in a light and conventional
manner. Silvius is merely the love-sick swain, Phebe the
country belle. Corin belongs to a somewhat different world,
the world of the *Shepherd's Calendar* rather than that of the
Arcadia. He is a real shepherd, Shakespeare's compliment
to honest labour.

In his handling of these secondary personages, it is admirable to observe with what boldness Shakespeare has blended
different manners of art, and even different planes of reality,
passing from sentiment to comedy, and from comedy to
farce. But he is careful to keep the extremes apart. An
encounter between Silvius and Touchstone would either
make the one ridiculous or the other offensive.

In an Elizabethan comedy there are regularly one or two
characters whose chief function—whatever else (3) Touchstone
they may incidentally do—is to raise a laugh. and Audrey.
The taste of the audience demanded it, and Shakespeare
acquiesced. The stuff of which these parts are made is at
bottom the same everywhere: the point for criticism to
observe is how Shakespeare makes a virtue of this necessity,
how he gives to each of his clowns or fools the touch that
individualizes them and tones them into harmony with the
play of which they form a part. In the earlier comedies
these parts are usually assigned to clownish servants, such
as Launce and Speed in the *Two Gentlemen of Verona*, or
Launcelot Gobbo in the *Merchant of Venice*. It was a happy
innovation to make the clown of *As You Like It* a professional jester. In the earlier scenes his wit is perhaps too
strictly professional; some of his jokes have a very ancient
tang. But when this excrescence of an artificial society is
transplanted by his own good-nature to the forest, he blooms
into an incongruous epitome of all the contrasts of the play.
Wisdom is a matter of comparison, and the fool is a philosopher in the fields. His solemn moralizings on life and time
are an admirable burlesque of Jaques, all the more exquisite
because Jaques does not see it. But it is naturally on the

two serious themes of the play that his wit is chiefly exercised. On the subject of love he encounters Rosalind, with his sympathetic reminiscences of courting-days and his gross parody of Orlando's poem. But Rosalind's affection is far too robust and natural to take any harm from mockery. " Peace, you dull fool!" she says, and Touchstone discreetly retires, in good order, if not with the honours of war.

On the oft-quoted antithesis between the country and the court, he sums up to Corin with a nicety that leaves not a straw to choose between them. His marriage with Audrey is his happiest effort, and his last word on both subjects. For an ex-courtier to marry an arrant rustic is the feat of a practical philosopher, and a fair retort on Rosalind. She has made wit the vassal of love; Touchstone forces love itself into the service of wit.

§ 16. Like all the plays of Shakespeare's middle period, *As You Like It* possesses the charm of lucidity. It is free from the verbal extravagances which he affected earlier; and the thought is nowhere really hard. Beyond this, we can only say that the verse is good of its kind. It is not a kind that admits of more than a quiet excellence. The lines are not surcharged with feeling, or eloquence, or imagination. They are intrusted with the sentiment, the reflection, and not a little of the action of the piece. But the sentiment is not very passionate, nor the reflection very profound, and the verse is correspondingly deficient in the higher qualities of harmony. Oliver's narrative to the ladies has vivid descriptive touches; the speeches of Jaques and the Duke are famous specimens of declamation. Sweeter are the lines given to Silvius; but perhaps the finest versification in the play is Orlando's speech when he comes upon the banqueters—

> " But whoe'er you are
> That in this desert inaccessible,
> Under the shade of melancholy boughs,
> Lose and neglect the creeping hours of time ", &c.

In point of style, as in point of structure, the main charm

of the play must always lie in the brilliant prose scenes.   The
peculiar excellences of Shakespeare's middle style—clearness, brightness, and equivalence to the matter
—are even more essential in prose than in verse,   (*b*) Prose.
and in this group of tragedies and comedies, from the *Merchant of Venice* to *Hamlet,* his handling of prose is a stylistic
achievement not inferior to his management of metres.   So
much has been done for prose since then, and so little for
blank verse, that it is hard to realize that it is an achievement at all except by comparison with earlier styles.   The
prose of these plays may not possess—it does not need—the
massive and voluminous periods of later masters; but for
lucidity, point, and a certain easy speed it stands alone in
the literature of that age.   Its structure is radically English
and not Latin, but though vernacular it is not vulgar.   Its
only fault, if it be a fault, is an excessive fondness for the
iambic rhythm; but that could hardly be avoided by a poet
whose ear was attuned to that rhythm, and is hardly noticed
by a reader for the same reason.

§ 17. As there is no separate Quarto, the First Folio forms
the sole basis of the text.   Whatever may be the
general merits of the Second Folio (1632), it is   Text.
not an independent authority in the case of *As You Like It.*
In the present edition the Globe text has been followed.
The few divergences are mostly of a conservative kind.   But
wherever the reading adopted differs in any important particular from that of the First Folio, the difference has been
recorded, with the name of the original corrector.

DRAMATIS PERSONÆ.

DUKE, living in banishment.
FREDERICK, his brother, and usurper of his dominions.
AMIENS, } lords attending on the banished duke.
JAQUES, }
LE BEAU, a courtier attending upon Frederick.
CHARLES, wrestler to Frederick.
OLIVER, }
JAQUES, } sons of Sir Rowland de Boys.
ORLANDO, }
ADAM, } servants to Oliver.
DENNIS, }
TOUCHSTONE, a clown.
SIR OLIVER MARTEXT, a vicar.
CORIN, } shepherds.
SILVIUS, }
WILLIAM, a country fellow, in love with Audrey.
A person representing Hymen.

ROSALIND, daughter to the banished duke.
CELIA, daughter to Frederick.
PHEBE, a shepherdess.
AUDREY, a country wench.

Lords, pages, and attendants, &c.

SCENE: *Oliver's house; Duke Frederick's court; and the Forest of Arden.*

AS YOU LIKE IT

ACT I.

Scene I. *Orchard of* Oliver's *house.*

Enter Orlando *and* Adam.

Orl. As I remember, Adam, it was upon this fashion bequeathed me by will but poor a thousand crowns, and, as
thou sayest, charged my brother, on his blessing, to breed
me well: and there begins my sadness. My brother Jaques
he keeps at school, and report speaks goldenly of his profit:
for my part, he keeps me rustically at home, or, to speak
more properly, stays me here at home unkept; for call you
that keeping for a gentleman of my birth, that differs not
from the stalling of an ox? His horses are bred better; for,
besides that they are fair with their feeding, they are taught
their manage, and to that end riders dearly hired: but I, his
brother, gain nothing under him but growth; for the which
his animals on his dunghills are as much bound to him as I.
Besides this nothing that he so plentifully gives me, the
something that nature gave me his countenance seems to
take from me: he lets me feed with his hinds, bars me the
place of a brother, and, as much as in him lies, mines my
gentility with my education. This is it, Adam, that grieves
me; and the spirit of my father, which I think is within me,
begins to mutiny against this servitude: I will no longer
endure it, though yet I know no wise remedy how to avoid it.

Adam. Yonder comes my master, your brother.

Orl. Go apart, Adam, and thou shalt hear how he will
shake me up.   24

Enter OLIVER.

Oli. Now, sir! what make you here?

Orl. Nothing: I am not taught to make anything.

Oli. What mar you then, sir?

Orl. Marry, sir, I am helping you to mar that which God
made, a poor unworthy brother of yours, with idleness.

Oli. Marry, sir, be better employed, and be naught awhile.

Orl. Shall I keep your hogs and eat husks with them?
What prodigal portion have I spent, that I should come to
such penury?

Oli. Know you where you are, sir?

Orl. O, sir, very well: here in your orchard.   35

Oli. Know you before whom, sir?

Orl. Ay, better than him I am before knows me. I know
you are my eldest brother; and, in the gentle condition of
blood, you should so know me. The courtesy of nations
allows you my better, in that you are the first-born; but the
same tradition takes not away my blood, were there twenty
brothers betwixt us: I have as much of my father in me as
you; albeit, I confess, your coming before me is nearer to his
reverence.

Oli. What, boy!   45

Orl. Come, come, elder brother, you are too young in this.

Oli. Wilt thou lay hands on me, villain?

Orl. I am no villain; I am the youngest son of Sir Rowland
de Boys; he was my father, and he is thrice a villain that
says such a father begot villains. Wert thou not my brother,
I would not take this hand from thy throat till this other had
pulled out thy tongue for saying so: thou hast railed on
thyself.

Adam. Sweet masters, be patient: for your father's remembrance, be at accord.   55

Oli. Let me go, I say.

Orl. I will not, till I please: you shall hear me. My father charged you in his will to give me good education: you have trained me like a peasant, obscuring and hiding from me all gentleman-like qualities. The spirit of my father grows strong in me, and I will no longer endure it: therefore allow me such exercises as may become a gentleman, or give me the poor allottery my father left me by testament; with that I will go buy my fortunes.   64

Oli. And what wilt thou do? beg, when that is spent? Well, sir, get you in: I will not long be troubled with you; you shall have some part of your will: I pray you, leave me.

Orl. I will no further offend you than becomes me for my good.

Oli. Get you with him, you old dog.   70

Adam. Is 'old dog' my reward? Most true, I have lost my teeth in your service. God be with my old master! he would not have spoke such a word.

[*Exeunt Orlando and Adam.*

Oli. Is it even so? begin you to grow upon me? I will physic your rankness, and yet give no thousand crowns neither. Holla, Dennis!

Enter DENNIS.

Den. Calls your worship?

Oli. Was not Charles, the duke's wrestler, here to speak with me?

Den. So please you, he is here at the door and importunes access to you.   81

Oli. Call him in. [*Exit Dennis.*] 'T will be a good way: and to-morrow the wrestling is.

Enter CHARLES.

Cha. Good morrow to your worship.

Oli. Good Monsieur Charles, what's the new news at the new court?

B   (M 7)

Cha. There is no news at the court, sir, but the old news: that is, the old duke is banished by his younger brother the new duke; and three or four loving lords have put themselves into voluntary exile with him, whose lands and revenues enrich the new duke; therefore he gives them good leave to wander.

Oli. Can you tell if Rosalind, the duke's daughter, be banished with her father? 93

Cha. O, no; for the duke's daughter, her cousin, so loves her, being ever from their cradles bred together, that she would have followed her exile, or have died to stay behind her. She is at the court, and no less beloved of her uncle than his own daughter; and never two ladies loved as they do.

Oli. Where will the old duke live?

Cha. They say he is already in the forest of Arden, and a many merry men with him; and there they live like the old Robin Hood of England: they say many young gentlemen flock to him every day, and fleet the time carelessly, as they did in the golden world. 104

Oli. What, you wrestle to-morrow before the new duke?

Cha. Marry, do I, sir; and I came to acquaint you with a matter. I am given, sir, secretly to understand that your younger brother Orlando hath a disposition to come in disguised against me to try a fall. To-morrow, sir, I wrestle for my credit; and he that escapes me without some broken limb shall acquit him well. Your brother is but young and tender; and, for your love, I would be loath to foil him, as I must, for my own honour, if he come in: therefore, out of my love to you, I came hither to acquaint you withal, that either you might stay him from his intendment or brook such disgrace well as he shall run into, in that it is a thing of his own search and altogether against my will. 117

Oli. Charles, I thank thee for thy love to me, which thou shalt find I will most kindly requite. I had myself notice of my brother's purpose herein and have by underhand means laboured to dissuade him from it, but he is resolute. I'll tell

thee, Charles: it is the stubbornest young fellow of France,
full of ambition, an envious emulator of every man's good
parts, a secret and villainous contriver against me his natural
brother: therefore use thy discretion; I had as lief thou didst
break his neck as his finger.   And thou wert best look to 't;
for if thou dost him any slight disgrace or if he do not
mightily grace himself on thee, he will practise against thee
by poison, entrap thee by some treacherous device and
never leave thee till he hath ta'en thy life by some indirect
means or other; for, I assure thee, and almost with tears I
speak it, there is not one so young and so villainous this day
living. I speak but brotherly of him; but should I anatomize
him to thee as he is, I must blush and weep and thou must
look pale and wonder.   135

Cha. I am heartily glad I came hither to you. If he come
to-morrow, I 'll give him his payment: if ever he go alone
again, I 'll never wrestle for prize more: and so God keep
your worship!

Oli. Farewell, good Charles. [*Exit Charles.*] Now will
I stir this gamester: I hope I shall see an end of him; for my
soul, yet I know not why, hates nothing more than he. Yet
he 's gentle, never schooled and yet learned, full of noble device,
of all sorts enchantingly beloved, and indeed so much in the
heart of the world, and especially of my own people, who best
know him, that I am altogether misprised: but it shall not
be so long; this wrestler shall clear all: nothing remains but
that I kindle the boy thither; which now I 'll go about.   148
[*Exit.*

SCENE II. *Lawn before the* DUKE'S *palace.*

Enter CELIA *and* ROSALIND.

Cel. I pray thee, Rosalind, sweet my coz, be merry.

Ros. Dear Celia, I show more mirth than I am mistress
of; and would you yet I were merrier? Unless you could

teach me to forget a banished father, you must not learn me
how to remember any extraordinary pleasure.   5

Cel. Herein I see thou lovest me not with the full weight
that I love thee. If my uncle, thy banished father, had
banished thy uncle, the duke my father, so thou hadst been
still with me, I could have taught my love to take thy father
for mine: so wouldst thou, if the truth of thy love to me were
so righteously tempered as mine is to thee.   11

Ros. Well, I will forget the condition of my estate, to rejoice
in yours.

Cel. You know my father hath no child but I, nor none is
like to have: and, truly, when he dies, thou shalt be his heir,
for what he hath taken away from thy father perforce, I will
render thee again in affection; by mine honour, I will; and
when I break that oath, let me turn monster: therefore, my
sweet Rose, my dear Rose, be merry.

Ros. From henceforth I will, coz, and devise sports. Let
me see; what think you of falling in love?   21

Cel. Marry, I prithee, do, to make sport withal: but love
no man in good earnest; nor no further in sport neither than
with safety of a pure blush thou mayest in honour come off
again.

Ros. What shall be our sport, then?

Cel. Let us sit and mock the good housewife Fortune from
her wheel, that her gifts may henceforth be bestowed equally.

Ros. I would we could do so, for her benefits are mightily
misplaced, and the bountiful blind woman doth most mistake
in her gifts to women.   31

Cel. 'T is true; for those that she makes fair she scarce
makes honest, and those that she makes honest she makes
very ill-favouredly.

Ros. Nay, now thou goest from Fortune's office to Nature's:
Fortune reigns in gifts of the world, not in the lineaments
of Nature.

Enter TOUCHSTONE.

Cel. No? when Nature hath made a fair creature, may she not by Fortune fall into the fire? Though Nature hath given us wit to flout at Fortune, hath not Fortune sent in this fool to cut off the argument? 41

Ros. Indeed, there is Fortune too hard for Nature, when Fortune makes Nature's natural the cutter-off of Nature's wit.

Cel. Peradventure this is not Fortune's work neither, but Nature's; who perceiving our natural wits too dull to reason of such goddesses hath sent this natural for our whetstone; for always the dulness of the fool is the whetstone of the wits. How now, wit! whither wander you?

Touch. Mistress, you must come away to your father.

Cel. Were you made the messenger? 50

Touch. No, by mine honour, but I was bid to come for you.

Ros. Where learned you that oath, fool?

Touch. Of a certain knight that swore by his honour they were good pancakes and swore by his honour the mustard was naught: now I 'll stand to it, the pancakes were naught and the mustard was good, and yet was not the knight forsworn.

Cel. How prove you that, in the great heap of your knowledge?

Ros. Ay, marry, now unmuzzle your wisdom. 60

Touch. Stand you both forth now: stroke your chins, and swear by your beards that I am a knave.

Cel. By our beards, if we had them, thou art.

Touch. By my knavery, if I had it, then I were; but if you swear by that that is not, you are not forsworn: no more was this knight, swearing by his honour, for he never had any; or if he had, he had sworn it away before ever he saw those pancakes or that mustard.

Cel. Prithee, who is 't that thou meanest?

Touch. One that old Frederick, your father, loves. 70

Cel. My father's love is enough to honour him enough: speak no more of him; you'll be whipped for taxation one of these days.

Touch. The more pity, that fools may not speak wisely what wise men do foolishly.

Cel. By my troth, thou sayest true; for since the little wit that fools have was silenced, the little foolery that wise men have makes a great show.   Here comes Monsieur Le Beau.

Ros. With his mouth full of news.

Cel. Which he will put on us, as pigeons feed their young.

Ros. Then shall we be news-crammed.   81

Cel. All the better; we shall be the more marketable.

Enter LE BEAU.

Bon jour, Monsieur Le Beau: what's the news?

Le Beau. Fair princess, you have lost much good sport.

Cel. Sport! of what colour?

Le Beau. What colour, madam! how shall I answer you

Ros. As wit and fortune will.

Touch. Or as the Destinies decree.

Cel. Well said: that was laid on with a trowel.

Touch. Nay, if I keep not my rank,—   90

Ros. Thou losest thy old smell.

Le Beau. You amaze me, ladies: I would have told you of good wrestling, which you have lost the sight of.

Ros. Yet tell us the manner of the wrestling.

Le Beau. I will tell you the beginning; and if it please your ladyships, you may see the end; for the best is yet to do; and here, where you are, they are coming to perform it.

Cel. Well, the beginning, that is dead and buried.

Le Beau. There comes an old man and his three sons, —

Cel. I could match this beginning with an old tale.   101

Le Beau. Three proper young men, of excellent growth and presence.

Ros. With bills on their necks, 'Be it known unto all men by these presents'.

Le Beau. The eldest of the three wrestled with Charles, the duke's wrestler; which Charles in a moment threw him and broke three of his ribs, that there is little hope of life in him: so he served the second, and so the third. Yonder they lie; the poor old man, their father, making such pitiful dole over them that all the beholders take his part with weeping.

Ros. Alas!   112

Touch. But what is the sport, monsieur, that the ladies have lost?

Le Beau. Why, this that I speak of.

Touch. Thus men may grow wiser every day: it is the first time that ever I heard breaking of ribs was sport for ladies.

Cel. Or I, I promise thee.

Ros. But is there any else longs to see this broken music in his sides? is there yet another dotes upon rib-breaking? Shall we see this wrestling, cousin?   121

Le Beau. You must, if you stay here; for here is the place appointed for the wrestling, and they are ready to perform it.

Cel. Yonder, sure, they are coming: let us now stay and see it.

Flourish. Enter DUKE FREDERICK, Lords, ORLANDO, CHARLES, *and* Attendants.

Duke F. Come on: since the youth will not be entreated, his own peril on his forwardness.

Ros. Is yonder the man?

Le Beau. Even he, madam.

Cel. Alas, he is too young! yet he looks successfully. 130

Duke F. How now, daughter and cousin! are you crept hither to see the wrestling?

Ros. Ay, my liege, so please you give us leave.

Duke F. You will take little delight in it, I can tell you;

there is such odds in the man.   In pity of the challenger's youth I would fain dissuade him, but he will not be entreated. Speak to him, ladies; see if you can move him.

Cel. Call him hither, good Monsieur Le Beau.

Duke F. Do so: I 'll not be by.

Le Beau. Monsieur the challenger, the princess' call for you.

Orl. I attend them with all respect and duty.   141

Ros. Young man, have you challenged Charles the wrestler?

Orl. No, fair princess; he is the general challenger: I come but in, as others do, to try with him the strength of my youth.

Cel. Young gentleman, your spirits are too bold for your years.   You have seen cruel proof of this man's strength: if you saw yourself with your eyes or knew yourself with your judgment, the fear of your adventure would counsel you to a more equal enterprise.   We pray you, for your own sake, to embrace your own safety and give over this attempt.

Ros. Do, young sir; your reputation shall not therefore be misprised; we will make it our suit to the duke that the wrestling might not go forward.   154

Orl. I beseech you, punish me not with your hard thoughts, wherein I confess me much guilty, to deny so fair and excellent ladies any thing.   But let your fair eyes and gentle wishes go with me to my trial: wherein if I be foiled, there is but one shamed that was never gracious; if killed, but one dead that is willing to be so: I shall do my friends no wrong, for I have none to lament me, the world no injury, for in it I have nothing; only in the world I fill up a place, which may be better supplied when I have made it empty.

Ros. The little strength that I have, I would it were with you.

Cel. And mine, to eke out hers.   165

Ros. Fare you well: pray heaven I be deceived in you!

Cel. Your heart's desires be with you!

Cha. Come, where is this young gallant that is so desirous to lie with his mother earth?

Orl. Ready, sir; but his will hath in it a more modest working.

Duke F. You shall try but one fall.

Cha. No, I warrant your grace, you shall not entreat him to a second, that have so mightily persuaded him from a first.

Orl. An you mean to mock me after, you should not have mocked me before: but come your ways. 176

Ros. Now Hercules be thy speed, young man!

Cel. I would I were invisible, to catch the strong fellow by the leg. [*Wrestle.*

Ros. O excellent young man! 180

Cel. If I had a thunderbolt in mine eye, I can tell who should down. [*Shout. Charles is thrown.*

Duke F. No more, no more.

Orl. Yes, I beseech your grace: I am not yet well breathed.

Duke F. How dost thou, Charles?

Le Beau. He cannot speak, my lord.

Duke F. Bear him away. What is thy name, young man?

Orl. Orlando, my liege; the youngest son of Sir Rowland de Boys.

Duke F. I would thou hadst been son to some man else:
The world esteemed thy father honourable, 191
But I did find him still mine enemy:
Thou shouldst have better pleased me with this deed,
Hadst thou descended from another house.
But fare thee well; thou art a gallant youth:
I would thou hadst told me of another father.
[*Exeunt Duke Fred., train, and Le Beau.*

Cel. Were I my father, coz, would I do this?

Orl. I am more proud to be Sir Rowland's son,
His youngest son,—and would not change that calling,
To be adopted heir to Frederick. 200

Ros. My father loved Sir Rowland as his soul,
And all the world was of my father's mind:
Had I before known this young man his son,

B 2 (M 7)

I should have given him tears unto entreaties,
Ere he should thus have ventured.

    Cel.   Gentle cousin,
Let us go thank him and encourage him:
My father's rough and envious disposition
Sticks me at heart.   Sir, you have well deserved:
If you do keep your promises in love
But justly, as you have exceeded all promise,   210
Your mistress shall be happy.

    Ros.   Gentleman,
                  [Giving him a chain from her neck.
Wear this for me, one out of suits with fortune,
That could give more, but that her hand lacks means.
Shall we go, coz?

    Cel.   Ay.   Fare you well, fair gentleman.

    Orl. Can I not say, I thank you?   My better parts
Are all thrown down, and that which here stands up
Is but a quintain, a mere lifeless block.

    Ros. He calls us back: my pride fell with my fortunes;
I 'll ask him what he would.   Did you call, sir?
Sir, you have wrestled well and overthrown   220
More than your enemies.

    Cel.   Will you go, coz?

    Ros. Have with you.   Fare you well.
                  [Exeunt Rosalind and Celia.

    Orl. What passion hangs these weights upon my tongue?
I cannot speak to her, yet she urged conference.
O poor Orlando, thou art overthrown!
Or Charles or something weaker masters thee.

Re-enter LE BEAU.

    Le Beau. Good sir, I do in friendship counsel you
To leave this place.   Albeit you have deserved
High commendation, true applause and love,
Yet such is now the duke's condition   230

That he misconstrues all that you have done.
The duke is humorous; what he is indeed,
More suits you to conceive than I to speak of.

Orl. I thank you, sir: and, pray you, tell me this;
Which of the two was daughter of the duke
That here was at the wrestling?

Le Beau. Neither his daughter, if we judge by manners;
But yet indeed the lesser is his daughter:
The other is daughter to the banish'd duke,
And here detain'd by her usurping uncle,   240
To keep his daughter company; whose loves
Are dearer than the natural bond of sisters.
But I can tell you that of late this duke
Hath ta'en displeasure 'gainst his gentle niece,
Grounded upon no other argument
But that the people praise her for her virtues
And pity her for her good father's sake;
And, on my life, his malice 'gainst the lady
Will suddenly break forth.   Sir, fare you well:
Hereafter, in a better world than this,   250
I shall desire more love and knowledge of you.

Orl. I rest much bounden to you: fare you well.

                              [*Exit Le Beau.*
Thus must I from the smoke into the smother;
From tyrant duke unto a tyrant brother:
But heavenly Rosalind!   [*Exit*

SCENE III.   *A room in the palace.*

Enter CELIA *and* ROSALIND.

Cel. Why, cousin! why, Rosalind!   Cupid have mercy!
not a word?

Ros. Not one to throw at a dog.

Cel. No, thy words are too precious to be cast away upon
curs; throw some of them at me; come, lame me with reasons.

Ros. Then there were two cousins laid up; when the one should be lamed with reasons and the other mad without any.

Cel. But is all this for your father?

Ros. No, some of it is for my child's father. O, how full of briars is this working-day world!   10

Cel. They are but burs, cousin, thrown upon thee in holiday foolery: if we walk not in the trodden paths, our very petti-coats will catch them.

Ros. I could shake them off my coat: these burs are in my heart.

Cel. Hem them away.

Ros. I would try, if I could cry 'hem' and have him.

Cel. Come, come, wrestle with thy affections.   18

Ros. O, they take the part of a better wrestler than myself!

Cel. O, a good wish upon you! you will try in time, in despite of a fall. But, turning these jests out of service, let us talk in good earnest: is it possible, on such a sudden, you should fall into so strong a liking with old Sir Rowland's youngest son?

Ros. The duke my father loved his father dearly.

Cel. Doth it therefore ensue that you should love his son dearly? By this kind of chase, I should hate him, for my father hated his father dearly; yet I hate not Orlando.

Ros. No, faith, hate him not, for my sake.

Cel. Why should I not? doth he not deserve well?   30

Ros. Let me love him for that, and do you love him because I do. Look, here comes the duke.

Cel. With his eyes full of anger.

Enter DUKE FREDERICK, *with* Lords.

Duke F. Mistress, dispatch you with your safest haste
And get you from our court.

Ros.   Me, uncle?

Duke F.   You, cousin:
Within these ten days if that thou be'st found

So near our public court as twenty miles,
Thou diest for it.
  Ros.   I do beseech your grace.
Let me the knowledge of my fault bear with me:
If with myself I hold intelligence   40
Or have acquaintance with mine own desires,
If that I do not dream or be not frantic,—
As I do trust I am not—then, dear uncle,
Never so much as in a thought unborn
Did I offend your highness.
  Duke F.   Thus do all traitors:
If their purgation did consist in words,
They are as innocent as grace itself:
Let it suffice thee that I trust thee not.
  Ros. Yet your mistrust cannot make me a traitor:
Tell me whereon the likelihood depends.   50
  Duke F. Thou art thy father's daughter; there's enough.
  Ros. So was I when your highness took his dukedom;
So was I when your highness banish'd him:
Treason is not inherited, my lord;
Or, if we did derive it from our friends,
What's that to me? my father was no traitor:
Then, good my liege, mistake me not so much
To think my poverty is treacherous.
  Cel. Dear sovereign, hear me speak.
  Duke F. Ay, Celia; we stay'd her for your sake, 60
Else had she with her father ranged along.
  Cel. I did not then entreat to have her stay;
It was your pleasure and your own remorse:
I was too young that time to value her;
But now I know her: if she be a traitor,
Why so am I; we still have slept together,
Rose at an instant, learn'd, play'd, eat together,
And wheresoe'er we went, like Juno's swans,
Still we went coupled and inseparable.

Duke F. She is too subtle for thee; and her smoothness,
Her very silence and her patience   71
Speak to the people, and they pity her.
Thou art a fool: she robs thee of thy name;
And thou wilt show more bright and seem more virtuous
When she is gone.   Then open not thy lips:
Firm and irrevocable is my doom
Which I have pass'd upon her; she is banish'd.

Cel. Pronounce that sentence then on me, my liege:
I cannot live out of her company.

Duke F. You are a fool. You, niece, provide yourself: 80
If you outstay the time, upon mine honour,
And in the greatness of my word, you die.

                                   [*Exeunt Duke Frederick and Lords.*

Cel. O my poor Rosalind, whither wilt thou go?
Wilt thou change fathers? I will give thee mine.
I charge thee, be not thou more grieved than I am.

Ros. I have more cause.

Cel.   Thou hast not, cousin:
Prithee, be cheerful: know'st thou not, the duke
Hath banish'd me, his daughter?

Ros.   That he hath not.

Cel. No, hath not?   Rosalind lacks then the love
Which teacheth thee that thou and I am one: 90
Shall we be sunder'd? shall we part, sweet girl?
No: let my father seek another heir.
Therefore devise with me how we may fly,
Whither to go and what to bear with us;
And do not seek to take your change upon you,
To bear your griefs yourself and leave me out;
For, by this heaven, now at our sorrows pale,
Say what thou canst, I'll go along with thee.

Ros. Why, whither shall we go?

Cel. To seek my uncle in the forest of Arden.   100

Ros. Alas, what danger will it be to us,

Maids as we are, to travel forth so far!
Beauty provoketh thieves sooner than gold.

　　Cel. I 'll put myself in poor and mean attire
And with a kind of umber smirch my face;
The like do you: so shall we pass along
And never stir assailants.

　　Ros. 　　　　　　Were it not better,
Because that I am more than common tall,
That I did suit me all points like a man?
A gallant curtle-axe upon my thigh,　　　　　　110
A boar-spear in my hand; and—in my heart
Lie there what hidden woman's fear there will—
We 'll have a swashing and a martial outside,
As many other mannish cowards have
That do outface it with their semblances.

　　Cel. What shall I call thee when thou art a man?

　　Ros. I 'll have no worse a name than Jove's own page;
And therefore look you call me Ganymede.
But what will you be call'd?

　　Cel. Something that hath a reference to my state;　　120
No longer Celia, but Aliena.

　　Ros. But, cousin, what if we assay'd to steal
The clownish fool out of your father's court?
Would he not be a comfort to our travel?

　　Cel. He 'll go along o'er the wide world with me;
Leave me alone to woo him. Let 's away,
And get our jewels and our wealth together,
Devise the fittest time and safest way
To hide us from pursuit that will be made
After my flight. Now go we in content
To liberty and not to banishment.　　　　　[*Exeunt.* 130

ACT II.

Scene I.   *The Forest of Arden.*

Enter Duke senior, Amiens, *and two or three* Lords,
like foresters.

Duke S. Now, my co-mates and brothers in exile,
Hath not old custom made this life more sweet
Than that of painted pomp? Are not these woods
More free from peril than the envious court?
Here feel we but the penalty of Adam,
The seasons' difference, as the icy fang
And churlish chiding of the winter's wind,
Which, when it bites and blows upon my body,
Even till I shrink with cold, I smile and say
'This is no flattery: these are counsellors   10
That feelingly persuade me what I am'.
Sweet are the uses of adversity,
Which, like the toad, ugly and venomous,
Wears yet a precious jewel in his head;
And this our life exempt from public haunt
Finds tongues in trees, books in the running brooks,
Sermons in stones and good in every thing.
I would not change it.
   Ami.   Happy is your grace,
That can translate the stubbornness of fortune
Into so quiet and so sweet a style.   20
   Duke S. Come, shall we go and kill us venison?
And yet it irks me the poor dappled fools,
Being native burghers of this desert city,
Should in their own confines with forked heads
Have their round haunches gored.
   First Lord.   Indeed, my lord,
The melancholy Jaques grieves at that,
And, in that kind, swears you do more usurp

Than doth your brother that hath banish'd you.
To-day my Lord of Amiens and myself
Did steal behind him as he lay along   30
Under an oak whose antique root peeps cut
Upon the brook that brawls along this wood:
To the which place a poor sequester'd stag,
That from the hunter's aim had ta'en a hurt,
Did come to languish, and indeed, my lord,
The wretched animal heaved forth such groans
That their discharge did stretch his leathern coat
Almost to bursting, and the big round tears
Coursed one another down his innocent nose
In piteous chase; and thus the hairy fool,   40
Much marked of the melancholy Jaques,
Stood on the extremest verge of the swift brook,
Augmenting it with tears.
    Duke S.   But what said Jaques?
Did he not moralize this spectacle?
    First Lord. O, yes, into a thousand similes.
First, for his weeping into the needless stream;
'Poor dear,' quoth he, 'thou makest a testament
As worldlings do, giving thy sum of more
To that which had too much': then, being there alone,
Left and abandon'd of his velvet friends,   50
''T is right': quoth he, 'thus misery doth part
The flux of company': anon a careless herd,
Full of the pasture, jumps along by him
And never stays to greet him; 'Aye', quoth Jaques,
'Sweep on, you fat and greasy citizens;
'T is just the fashion: wherefore do you look
Upon that poor and broken bankrupt there?'
Thus most invectively he pierceth through
The body of the country, city, court,
Yea, and of this our life, swearing that we   60
Are mere usurpers, tyrants and what's worse.

To fright the animals and to kill them up
In their assign'd and native dwelling-place.

Duke S. And did you leave him in this contemplation?

Sec. Lord. We did, my lord, weeping and commenting
Upon the sobbing deer.

Duke S.   Show me the place:
I love to cope him in these sullen fits,
For then he's full of matter.

First Lord. I'll bring you to him straight.   [*Exeunt.*

SCENE II.   *A room in the palace.*

Enter DUKE FREDERICK, *with* LORDS.

Duke F. Can it be possible that no man saw them?
It cannot be: some villains of my court
Are of consent and sufferance in this.

First Lord. I cannot hear of any that did see her.
The ladies, her attendants of her chamber,
Saw her a-bed, and in the morning early
They found the bed untreasured of their mistress.

Sec. Lord. My lord, the roynish clown, at whom so oft
Your grace was wont to laugh, is also missing.
Hisperia, the princess' gentlewoman,   10
Confesses that she secretly o'erheard
Your daughter and her cousin much commend
The parts and graces of the wrestler
That did but lately foil the sinewy Charles;
And she believes, wherever they are gone,
That youth is surely in their company.

Duke F. Send to his brother; fetch that gallant hither;
If he be absent, bring his brother to me;
I'll make him find him: do this suddenly,
And let not search and inquisition quail   20
To bring again these foolish runaways.   [*Exeunt.*

SCENE III. *Before* OLIVER'S *house.*

Enter ORLANDO *and* ADAM, *meeting.*

Orl. Who's there?

Adam. What, my young master?   O my gentle master!
O my sweet master!   O you memory
Of old Sir Rowland! why, what make you here?
Why are you virtuous? why do people love you?
And wherefore are you gentle, strong and valiant?
Why would you be so fond to overcome
The bonny priser of the humorous duke?
Your praise is come too swiftly home before you.
Know you not, master, to some kind of men   10
Their graces serve them but as enemies?
No more do yours: your virtues, gentle master,
Are sanctified and holy traitors to you.
O, what a world is this, when what is comely
Envenoms him that bears it!

Orl. Why, what's the matter?

Adam.   O unhappy youth!
Come not within these doors; within this roof
The enemy of all your graces lives:
Your brother—no, no brother; yet the son—
Yet not the son, I will not call him son   20
Of him I was about to call his father—
Hath heard your praises, and this night he means
To burn the lodging where you use to lie
And you within it: if he fail of that,
He will have other means to cut you off.
I overheard him and his practices.
This is no place; this house is but a butchery:
Abhor it, fear it, do not enter it.

Orl. Why, whither, Adam, wouldst thou have me go?

Adam. No matter whither, so you come not here.   30

Orl. What, wouldst thou have me go and beg my food?
Or with a base and boisterous sword enforce
A thievish living on the common road?
This I must do, or know not what to do:
Yet this I will not do, do how I can;
I rather will subject me to the malice
Of a diverted blood and bloody brother.

   Adam. But do not so.   I have five hundred crowns,
The thrifty hire I saved under your father,
Which I did store to be my foster-nurse   40
When service should in my old limbs lie lame
And unregarded age in corners thrown:
Take that, and He that doth the ravens feed,
Yea, providently caters for the sparrow,
Be comfort to my age!   Here is the gold;
All this I give you.   Let me be your servant:
Though I look old, yet I am strong and lusty;
For in my youth I never did apply
Hot and rebellious liquors in my blood,
Nor did not with unbashful forehead woo   50
The means of weakness and debility;
Therefore my age is as a lusty winter,
Frosty, but kindly: let me go with you;
I 'll do the service of a younger man
In all your business and necessities.

   Orl. O good old man, how well in thee appears
The constant service of the antique world,
When service sweat for duty, not for meed!
Thou art not for the fashion of these times,
Where none will sweat but for promotion,   60
And having that, do choke their service up
Even with the having: it is not so with thee.
But, poor old man, thou prunest a rotten tree,
That cannot so much as a blossom yield
In lieu of all thy pains and husbandry.

But come thy ways; we'll go along together,
And ere we have thy youthful wages spent,
We'll light upon some settled low content.

Adam. Master, go on, and I will follow thee,
To the last gasp, with truth and loyalty.   70
From seventeen years till now almost fourscore
Here lived I, but now live here no more.
At seventeen years many their fortunes seek;
But at fourscore it is too late a week:
Yet fortune cannot recompense me better
Than to die well and not my master's debtor.   [*Exeunt.*

SCENE IV.   *The Forest of Arden.*

Enter ROSALIND *for* GANYMEDE, CELIA *for* ALIENA,
and TOUCHSTONE.

Ros. O Jupiter, how weary are my spirits!

Touch. I care not for my spirits, if my legs were not weary.

Ros. I could find in my heart to disgrace my man's apparel and to cry like a woman; but I must comfort the weaker vessel, as doublet and hose ought to show itself courageous to petticoat: therefore courage, good Aliena!

Cel. I pray you, bear with me; I cannot go no further.

Touch. For my part, I had rather bear with you than bear you; yet I should bear no cross if I did bear you, for I think you have no money in your purse.   10

Ros. Well, this is the forest of Arden.

Touch. Ay, now am I in Arden; the more fool I; when I was at home, I was in a better place: but travellers must be content.

Ros. Ay, be so, good Touchstone.

Enter CORIN *and* SILVIUS.

Look you, who comes here; a young man and an old in solemn talk.

Cor. That is the way to make her scorn you still.

Sil. O Corin, that thou knew'st how I do love her!

Cor. I partly guess; for I have loved ere now.   20

Sil. No, Corin, being old, thou canst not guess,
Though in thy youth thou wast as true a lover
As ever sigh'd upon a midnight pillow:
But if thy love were ever like to mine—
As sure I think did never man love so—
How many actions most ridiculous
Hast thou been drawn to by thy fantasy?

Cor. Into a thousand that I have forgotten.

Sil. O, thou didst then ne'er love so heartily!
If thou remember'st not the slightest folly   30
That ever love did make thee run into,
Thou hast not loved:
Or if thou hast not sat as I do now,
Wearing thy hearer in thy mistress' praise,
Thou hast not loved:
Or if thou hast not broke from company
Abruptly, as my passion now makes me,
Thou hast not loved.
O Phebe, Phebe, Phebe!   [*Exit.*

Ros. Alas, poor shepherd! searching of thy wound,   40
I have by hard adventure found mine own.

Touch. And I mine. I remember, when I was in love I
broke my sword upon a stone and bid him take that for
coming a-night to Jane Smile; and I remember the kissing
of her batlet and the cow's dugs that her pretty chopt hands
had milked; and I remember the wooing of a peascod instead of her, from whom I took two cods and, giving her
them again, said with weeping tears 'Wear these for my
sake'. We that are true lovers run into strange capers; but
as all is mortal in nature, so is all nature in love mortal in
folly.   51

Ros. Thou speakest wiser than thou art ware of.

Touch. Nay, I shall ne'er be ware of mine own wit till I
break my shins against it.

Ros. Jove, Jove! this shepherd's passion
  Is much upon my fashion.

Touch. And mine; but it grows something stale with
 me.

Cel. I pray you, one of you question yond man
If he for gold will give us any food:
I faint almost to death.

Touch.   Holla, you clown.   60

Ros. Peace, fool: he's not thy kinsman.

Cor.   Who calls?

Touch. Your betters, sir.

Cor.   Else are they very wretched.

Ros. Peace, I say. Good even to you, friend.

Cor. And to you, gentle sir, and to you all.

Ros. I prithee, shepherd, if that love or gold
Can in this desert place buy entertainment,
Bring us where we may rest ourselves and feed:
Here's a young maid with travel much oppress'd
And faints for succour.

Cor.   Fair sir, I pity her.
And wish, for her sake more than for mine own,   70
My fortunes were more able to relieve her;
But I am shepherd to another man
And do not shear the fleeces that I graze:
My master is of churlish disposition
And little recks to find the way to heaven
By doing deeds of hospitality:
Besides, his cote, his flocks and bounds of feed
Are now on sale, and at our sheepcote now,
By reason of his absence, there is nothing
That you will feed on; but what is, come see   80
And in my voice most welcome shall you be.

Ros. What is he that shall buy his flock and pasture?

Cor. That young swain that you saw here but erewhile,
That little cares for buying any thing.

Ros. I pray thee, if it stand with honesty,
Buy thou the cottage, pasture and the flock,
And thou shalt have to pay for it of us.

Cel. And we will mend thy wages. I like this place,
And willingly could waste my time in it.

Cor. Assuredly the thing is to be sold: 90
Go with me: if you like upon report
The soil, the profit and this kind of life,
I will your very faithful feeder be
And buy it with your gold right suddenly.   [*Exeunt.*

SCENE V. *The forest.*

Enter AMIENS, JAQUES, *and* others.

SONG.

Ami.   Under the greenwood tree
               Who loves to lie with me,
               And turn his merry note
               Unto the sweet bird's throat,
          Come hither, come hither, come hither:
               Here shall he see
               No enemy
          But winter and rough weather.

Jaq. More, more, I prithee, more.

Ami. It will make you melancholy, Monsieur Jaques.   10

Jaq. I thank it. More, I prithee, more. I can suck melancholy out of a song, as a weasel sucks eggs. More, I prithee, more.

Ami. My voice is ragged: I know I cannot please you.

Jaq. I do not desire you to please me; I do desire you to sing. Come, more; another stanzo: call you 'em stanzos?

Ami. What you will, Monsieur Jaques.

Jaq. Nay, I care not for their names; they owe me nothing. Will you sing?

Ami. More at your request than to please myself.   20

Jaq. Well then, if ever I thank any man, I'll thank you; but that they call compliment is like the encounter of two dog-apes, and when a man thanks me heartily, methinks I have given him a penny and he renders me the beggarly thanks. Come, sing: and you that will not, hold your tongues.

Ami. Well, I'll end the song. Sirs, cover the while; the duke will drink under this tree. He hath been all this day to look you.   29

Jaq. And I have been all this day to avoid him. He is too disputable for my company: I think of as many matters as he, but I give heaven thanks and make no boast of them. Come, warble, come.

Song.

    Who doth ambition shun   [*All together here.*
    And loves to live i' the sun,
    Seeking the food he eats,
    And pleased with what he gets,
Come hither, come hither, come hither:
    Here shall he see
    No enemy   40
    But winter and rough weather.

Jaq. I'll give you a verse to this note that I made yesterday in despite of my invention.

Ami. And I'll sing it.

Jaq. Thus it goes:—

    If it do come to pass
    That any man turn ass,

Leaving his wealth and ease
A stubborn will to please,
Ducdame, ducdame, ducdame: 50
Here shall he see
Gross fools as he,
An if he will come to me.

Ami. What's that 'ducdame'?

Jaq. 'T is a Greek invocation, to call fools into a circle.
I'll go sleep, if I can; if I cannot, I'll rail against all the
first-born of Egypt.

Ami. And I'll go seek the duke: his banquet is prepared.
                                        [*Exeunt severally.*

SCENE VI. *The forest.*

Enter ORLANDO *and* ADAM.

Adam. Dear master, I can go no further: O, I die for
food! Here lie I down, and measure out my grave. Farewell, kind master.

Orl. Why, how now, Adam! no greater heart in thee?
Live a little; comfort a little; cheer thyself a little. If this
uncouth forest yield any thing savage, I will either be food
for it or bring it for food to thee. Thy conceit is nearer death
than thy powers. For my sake be comfortable; hold death
awhile at the arm's end: I will here be with thee presently;
and if I bring thee not something to eat, I will give thee
leave to die: but if thou diest before I come, thou art a
mocker of my labour. Well said! thou lookest cheerly, and
I'll be with thee quickly. Yet thou liest in the bleak air:
come, I will bear thee to some shelter; and thou shalt not
die for lack of a dinner, if there live any thing in this desert.
Cheerly, good Adam!   [*Exeunt.*   16

Scene VII. *The forest.*

A table set out.　Enter Duke *senior,* Amiens, *and* Lords
like outlaws.

Duke S. I think he be transform'd into a beast;
For I can no where find him like a man.

First Lord. My lord, he is but even now gone hence;
Here was he merry, hearing of a song.

Duke S. If he, compact of jars, grow musical,
We shall have shortly discord in the spheres.
Go, seek him: tell him I would speak with him.

Enter Jaques.

First Lord. He saves my labour by his own approach.

Duke S. Why, how now, monsieur! what a life is this,
That your poor friends must woo your company?　　10
What, you look merrily!

Jaq. A fool, a fool! I met a fool i' the forest,
A motley fool; a miserable world!
As I do live by food, I met a fool;
Who laid him down and bask'd him in the sun,
And rail'd on Lady Fortune in good terms,
In good set terms and yet a motley fool.
'Good-morrow, fool,' quoth I.　'No, sir,' quoth he,
'Call me not fool till heaven hath sent me fortune:'
And then he drew a dial from his poke,　　20
And, looking on it with lack-lustre eye,
Says very wisely, 'It is ten o'clock:
Thus we may see,' quoth he, 'how the world wags:
'T is but an hour ago since it was nine,
And after one hour more 't will be eleven;
And so, from hour to hour, we ripe and ripe,
And then, from hour to hour, we rot and rot;
And thereby hangs a tale.'　When I did hear
The motley fool thus moral on the time,

My lungs began to crow like chanticleer,   30
That fools should be so deep-contemplative,
And I did laugh sans intermission
An hour by his dial.   O noble fool!
A worthy fool!   Motley 's the only wear.
   Duke S. What fool is this?
   Jaq. O worthy fool!   One that hath been a courtier
And says, if ladies be but young and fair,
They have the gift to know it: and in his brain,
Which is as dry as the remainder biscuit
After a voyage, he hath strange places cramm'd   40
With observation, the which he vents
In mangled forms.   O that I were a fool!
I am ambitious for a motley coat.
   Duke S. Thou shalt have one.
   Jaq.   It is my only suit;
Provided that you weed your better judgements
Of all opinion that grows rank in them
That I am wise.   I must have liberty
Withal, as large a charter as the wind,
To blow on whom I please; for so fools have;
And they that are most galled with my folly,   50
They most must laugh.   And why, sir, must they so?
The 'why' is plain as way to parish church:
He that a fool doth very wisely hit
Doth very foolishly, although he smart,
Not to seem senseless of the bob: if not,
The wise man's folly is anatomized
Even by the squandering glances of the fool.
Invest me in my motley; give me leave
To speak my mind, and I will through and through
Cleanse the foul body of the infected world,   60
If they will patiently receive my medicine.
   Duke S. Fie on thee! I can tell what thou wouldst do.
   Jaq. What, for a counter, would I do but good?

Duke S. Most mischievous foul sin, in chiding sin:
For thou thyself hast been a libertine,
As sensual as the brutish sting itself;
And all the embossed sores and headed evils,
That thou with license of free foot hast caught,
Wouldst thou disgorge into the general world.

Jaq. Why, who cries out on pride,   70
That can therein tax any private party?
Doth it not flow as hugely as the sea,
Till that the wearer's very means do ebb?
What woman in the city do I name,
When that I say the city-woman bears
The cost of princes on unworthy shoulders?
Who can come in and say that I mean her,
When such a one as she such is her neighbour?
Or what is he of basest function
That says his bravery is not on my cost,   80
Thinking that I mean him, but therein suits
His folly to the mettle of my speech?
There then; how then? what then?   Let me see wherein
My tongue hath wrong'd him: if it do him right,
Then he hath wrong'd himself; if he be free,
Why then my taxing like a wild-goose flies,
Unclaim'd of any man.   But who comes here?

Enter ORLANDO, *with his sword drawn.*

Orl. Forbear, and eat no more.
Jaq.   Why, I have eat none yet.
Orl. Nor shalt not, till necessity be served.
Jaq. Of what kind should this cock come off?   90
Duke S. Art thou thus bolden'd, man, by thy distress,
Or else a rude despiser of good manners,
That in civility thou seem'st so empty?
Orl. You touch'd my vein at first: the thorny point
Of bare distress hath ta'en from me the show

Of smooth civility: yet am I inland bred
And know some nurture.   But forbear, I say:
He dies that touches any of this fruit
Till I and my affairs are answered.   100
   Jaq. An you will not be answered with reason, I must die.
   Duke S. What would you have?   Your gentleness shall
    force
More than your force move us to gentleness.
   Orl. I almost die for food; and let me have it.
   Duke S. Sit down and feed, and welcome to our table.
   Orl. Speak you so gently?   Pardon me, I pray you:
I thought that all things had been savage here;
And therefore put I on the countenance
Of stern commandment.   But whate'er you are
That in this desert inaccessible,   110
Under the shade of melancholy boughs,
Lose and neglect the creeping hours of time;
If ever you have look'd on better days,
If ever been where bells have knoll'd to church,
If ever sat at any good man's feast,
If ever from your eyelids wiped a tear
And know what 't is to pity and be pitied,
Let gentleness my strong enforcement be:
In the which hope I blush, and hide my sword.
   Duke S. True is it that we have seen better days,   120
And have with holy bell been knoll'd to church
And sat at good men's feasts and wiped our eyes
Of drops that sacred pity hath engender'd:
And therefore sit you down in gentleness
And take upon command what help we have
That to your wanting may be minister'd.
   Orl. Then but forbear your food a little while
Whiles, like a doe, I go to find my fawn
And give it food.   There is an old poor man,
Who after me hath many a weary step   130

Limp'd in pure love: till he be first sufficed,
Oppress'd with two weak evils, age and hunger,
I will not touch a bit.

Duke S.   Go find him out,
And we will nothing waste till you return.

Orl. I thank ye; and be blest for your good comfort!

[*Exit.*

Duke S. Thou seest we are not all alone unhappy:
This wide and universal theatre
Presents more woeful pageants than the scene
Wherein we play in.

Jaq.   All the world's a stage,
And all the men and women merely players: 140
They have their exits and their entrances;
And one man in his time plays many parts,
His acts being seven ages.   At first the infant,
Mewling and puking in the nurse's arms.
And then the whining school-boy, with his satchel
And shining morning face, creeping like snail
Unwillingly to school.   And then the lover,
Sighing like furnace, with a woeful ballad
Made to his mistress' eyebrow.   Then a soldier,
Full of strange oaths and bearded like the pard,   150
Jealous in honour, sudden and quick in quarrel,
Seeking the bubble reputation
Even in the cannon's mouth.   And then the justice,
In fair round belly with good capon lined,
With eyes severe and beard of formal cut,
Full of wise saws and modern instances;
And so he plays his part.   The sixth age shifts
Into the lean and slipper'd pantaloon,
With spectacles on nose and pouch on side,
His youthful hose, well saved, a world too wide   160
For his shrunk shank; and his big manly voice,
Turning again toward childish treble, pipes

And whistles in his sound.   Last scene of all,
That ends this strange eventful history,
Is second childishness and mere oblivion,
Sans teeth, sans eyes, sans taste, sans everything.

Re-enter ORLANDO *with* ADAM.

Duke S. Welcome.   Set down your venerable burden
And let him feed.
 Orl. I thank you most for him.
  Adam.   So had you need:
I scarce can speak to thank you for myself. 170
 Duke S. Welcome; fall to: I will not trouble you
As yet, to question you about your fortunes.
Give us some music; and, good cousin, sing.

SONG.

Ami.   Blow, blow, thou winter wind,
    Thou art not so unkind
     As man's ingratitude;
    Thy tooth is not so keen,
    Because thou art not seen,
     Although thy breath be rude.
Heigh-ho! sing, heigh-ho! unto the green holly: 180
Most friendship is feigning, most loving mere folly;
    Then, heigh-ho, the holly!
    This life is most jolly.

    Freeze, freeze, thou bitter sky,
    That dost not bite so nigh
     As benefits forgot:
    Though thou the waters warp,
    Thy sting is not so sharp
     As friend remember'd not
Heigh-ho! sing, &c. 190

Duke S. If that you were the good Sir Rowland's son,
As you have whisper'd faithfully you were,
And as mine eye doth his effigies witness
Most truly limn'd and living in your face,
Be truly welcome hither: I am the duke
That loved your father: the residue of your fortune,
Go to my cave and tell me.   Good old man,
Thou art right welcome as thy master is.
Support him by the arm.   Give me your hand,
And let me all your fortunes understand.   [*Exeunt.*   200

ACT III.

SCENE I.   *A room in the palace.*

Enter DUKE FREDERICK, Lords, *and* OLIVER.

Duke F. Not see him since?   Sir, sir, that cannot be:
But were I not the better part made mercy,
I should not seek an absent argument
Of my revenge, thou present.   But look to it:
Find out thy brother, wheresoe'er he is;
Seek him with candle; bring him dead or living
Within this twelvemonth, or turn thou no more
To seek a living in our territory.
Thy lands and all things that thou dost call thine
Worth seizure do we seize into our hands,   10
Till thou canst quit thee by thy brother's mouth
Of what we think against thee.
    Oli. O that your highness knew my heart in this!
I never loved my brother in my life.
    Duke F. More villain thou.   Well, push him out of doors;
And let my officers of such a nature
Make an extent upon his house and lands·
Do this expediently and turn him going   [*Exeunt.*
C   (M 7)

SCENE II.   *The forest.*

Enter ORLANDO, *with a paper.*

Orl. Hang there, my verse, in witness of my love:
    And thou, thrice-crowned queen of night, survey
With thy chaste eye, from thy pale sphere above,
    Thy huntress' name that my full life doth sway.
O Rosalind! these trees shall be my books
    And in their barks my thoughts I'll character;
That every eye which in this forest looks
    Shall see thy virtue witness'd everywhere.
Run, run, Orlando; carve on every tree   9
The fair, the chaste and unexpressive she.   [*Exit*

Enter CORIN *and* TOUCHSTONE.

Cor. And how like you this shepherd's life, Master Touchstone?

Touch. Truly, shepherd, in respect of itself, it is a good
life; but in respect that it is a shepherd's life, it is naught.
In respect that it is solitary, I like it very well; but in respect
that it is private, it is a very vile life.   Now, in respect it is
in the fields, it pleaseth me well; but in respect it is not in
the court, it is tedious.   As it is a spare life, look you, it fits
my humour well; but as there is no more plenty in it, it goes
much against my stomach.   Hast any philosophy in thee,
shepherd?   21

Cor. No more but that I know the more one sickens the
worse at ease he is; and that he that wants money, means
and content is without three good friends; that the property
of rain is to wet and fire to burn; that good pasture makes
fat sheep, and that a great cause of the night is lack of the
sun; that he that hath learned no wit by nature nor art may
complain of good breeding or comes of a very dull kindred.

Touch. Such a one is a natural philosopher.   Wast ever in
court, shepherd?   30

Cor. No, truly.

Touch. Then thou art damned.

Cor. Nay, I hope.

Touch. Truly, thou art damned, like an ill-roasted egg all on one side.

Cor. For not being at court? Your reason. 36

Touch. Why, if thou never wast at court, thou never sawest good manners; if thou never sawest good manners, then thy manners must be wicked; and wickedness is sin, and sin is damnation. Thou art in a parlous state, shepherd.

Cor. Not a whit, Touchstone: those that are good manners at the court are as ridiculous in the country as the behaviour of the country is most mockable at the court. You told me you salute not at the court, but you kiss your hands! that courtesy would be uncleanly, if courtiers were shepherds. 45

Touch. Instance, briefly; come, instance.

Cor. Why, we are still handling our ewes, and their fells, you know, are greasy.

Touch. Why, do not your courtier's hands sweat? and is not the grease of a mutton as wholesome as the sweat of a man? Shallow, shallow. A better instance, I say; come.

Cor. Besides, our hands are hard.

Touch. Your lips will feel them the sooner. Shallow again. A more sounder instance, come. 54

Cor. And they are often tarred over with the surgery of our sheep; and would you have us kiss tar? The courtier's hands are perfumed with civet.

Touch. Most shallow man! thou worms-meat, in respect of a good piece of flesh indeed! Learn of the wise, and perpend: civet is of a baser birth than tar, the very uncleanly flux of a cat. Mend the instance, shepherd. 61

Cor. You have too courtly a wit for me: I'll rest.

Touch. Wilt thou rest damned? God help thee, shallow man! God make incision in thee! thou art raw.

Cor. Sir, I am a true labourer: I earn that I eat, get that I wear, owe no man hate, envy no man's happiness, glad of other men's good, content with my harm, and the greatest of my pride is to see my ewes graze and my lambs suck.

Touch. That is another simple sin in you, to bring the ewes and the rams together. If thou beest not damned for this, the devil himself will have no shepherds; I cannot see else how thou shouldst 'scape.   72

Cor. Here comes young Master Ganymede, my new mistress' brother.

Enter ROSALIND, *with a paper, reading.*

Ros. From the east to western Ind,
No jewel is like Rosalind.
Her worth, being mounted on the wind,
Through all the world bears Rosalind.
All the pictures fairest lined
Are but black to Rosalind.   80
Let no fair be kept in mind
But the fair of Rosalind.

Touch. I'll rhyme you so eight years together, dinners and suppers and sleeping-hours excepted: it is the right butter-women's rank to market.

Ros. Out, fool!

Touch. For a taste:
If a hart do lack a hind,
Let him seek out Rosalind.
If the cat will after kind,   90
So be sure will Rosalind.
Winter garments must be lined,
So must slender Rosalind.
They that reap must sheaf and bind;
Then to cart with Rosalind.
Sweetest nut hath sourest rind,
Such a nut is Rosalind.
He that sweetest rose will find
Must find love's prick and Rosalind.

This is the very false gallop of verses: why do you infect
yourself with them?   101
    Ros. Peace, you dull fool! I found them on a tree.
    Touch. Truly, the tree yields bad fruit.
    Ros. I 'll graff it with you, and then I shall graff it with a
medlar: then it will be the earliest fruit i' the country; for
you 'll be rotten ere you be half ripe, and that 's the right
virtue of the medlar.
    Touch. You have said; but whether wisely or no, let the
forest judge.

                    Enter CELIA, *with a writing.*

    Ros. Peace!   110
Here comes my sister, reading: stand aside.
    Cel. [*Reads.*]

            Why should this a desert be?
                For it is unpeopled?   No;
            Tongues I 'll hang on every tree,
                That shall civil sayings show:
            Some, how brief the life of man
                Runs his erring pilgrimage,
            That the stretching of a span
                Buckles in his sum of age;
            Some, of violated vows   120
                'Twixt the souls of friend and friend:
            But upon the fairest boughs,
                Or at every sentence end,
            Will I Rosalinda write,
                Teaching all that read to know
            The quintessence of every sprite
                Heaven would in little show.
            Therefore Heaven Nature charged
                That one body should be fill'd

  With all graces wide-enlarged: 130
   Nature presently distill'd
  Helen's cheek, but not her heart,
   Cleopatra's majesty,
  Atalanta's better part,
   Sad Lucretia's modesty.
  Thus Rosalind of many parts
   By heavenly synod was devised,
  Of many faces, eyes and hearts,
   To have the touches dearest prized.
  Heaven would that she these gifts should have, 140
  And I to live and die her slave.

Ros. O most gentle pulpiter! what tedious homily of love
have you wearied your parishioners withal, and never cried
'Have patience, good people'!

Cel. How now! back, friends! Shepherd, go off a little
Go with him, sirrah.

Touch. Come, shepherd, let us make an honourable re-
treat; though not with bag and baggage, yet with scrip and
scrippage.   [*Exeunt Corin and Touchstone.*

Cel. Didst thou hear these verses?   150

Ros. O, yes, I heard them all, and more too; for some of
them had in them more feet than the verses would bear.

Cel. That's no matter: the feet might bear the verses.

Ros. Ay, but the feet were lame and could not bear themselves without the verse and therefore stood lamely in the
verse.

Cel. But didst thou hear without wondering how thy name
should be hanged and carved upon these trees?

Ros. I was seven of the nine days out of the wonder before
you came; for look here what I found on a palm-tree. I was
never so berhymed since Pythagoras' time, that I was an
Irish rat, which I can hardly remember.   162

 Cel. Trow you who hath done this?

Ros. Is it a man?

Cel. And a chain, that you once wore, about his neck. Change you colour?

Ros. I prithee, who?

Cel. O Lord, Lord! it is a hard matter for friends to meet; but mountains may be removed with earthquakes and so encounter. 170

Ros. Nay, but who is it?

Cel. Is it possible?

Ros. Nay, I prithee now with most petitionary vehemence, tell me who it is.

Cel. O wonderful, wonderful, and most wonderful wonderful! and yet again wonderful, and after that, out of all hooping! 177

Ros. Good my complexion! dost thou think, though I am caparisoned like a man, I have a doublet and hose in my disposition? One inch of delay more is a South-sea of discovery; I prithee, tell me who is it quickly, and speak apace. I would thou couldst stammer, that thou mightst pour this concealed man out of thy mouth, as wine comes out of a narrow-mouthed bottle, either too much at once, or none at all. I prithee, take the cork out of thy mouth that I may drink thy tidings. Is he of God's making? What manner of man? Is his head worth a hat, or his chin worth a beard? 188

Cel. Nay, he hath but a little beard.

Ros. Why, God will send more, if the man will be thankful: let me stay the growth of his beard, if thou delay me not the knowledge of his chin.

Cel. It is young Orlando, that tripped up the wrestler's heels and your heart both in an instant.

Ros. Nay, but the devil take mocking: speak, sad brow and true maid.

Cel. I' faith, coz, 't is he.

Ros. Orlando?

Cel. Orlando. 199

Ros. Alas the day! what shall I do with my doublet and hose? What did he when thou sawest him? What said he? How looked he? Wherein went he? What makes he here? Did he ask for me? Where remains he? How parted he with thee? and when shalt thou see him again? Answer me in one word.

Cel. You must borrow me Gargantua's mouth first: 't is a word too great for any mouth of this age's size. To say ay and no to these particulars is more than to answer in a catechism. 209

Ros. But doth he know that I am in this forest and in man's apparel? Looks he as freshly as he did the day he wrestled?

Cel. It is as easy to count atomies as to resolve the propositions of a lover; but take a taste of my finding him, and relish it with good observance. I found him under a tree, like a dropped acorn.

Ros. It may well be called Jove's tree, when it drops forth such fruit.

Cel. Give me audience, good madam.

Ros. Proceed. 220

Cel. There lay he, stretched along, like a wounded knight.

Ros. Though it be pity to see such a sight, it well becomes the ground.

Cel. Cry 'holla' to thy tongue, I prithee; it curvets unseasonably. He was furnished like a hunter.

Ros. O, ominous! he comes to kill my heart.

Cel. I would sing my song without a burden: thou bringest me out of tune.

Ros. Do you not know I am a woman? when I think, I must speak. Sweet, say on. 230

Cel. You bring me out. Soft! comes he not here?

Enter ORLANDO *and* JAQUES.

Ros. 'T is he: slink by, and note him.

Jaq. I thank you for your company; but, good faith, I had as lief have been myself alone.

Orl. And so had I; but yet, for fashion sake, I thank you too for your society.

Jaq. God be wi' you: let's meet as little as we can.

Orl. I do desire we may be better strangers.

Jaq. I pray you, mar no more trees with writing love-songs in their barks.   240

Orl. I pray you, mar no moe of my verses with reading them ill-favouredly.

Jaq. Rosalind is your love's name?

Orl. Yes, just.

Jaq. I do not like her name.

Orl. There was no thought of pleasing you when she was christened.

Jaq. What stature is she of?

Orl. Just as high as my heart.   249

Jaq. You are full of pretty answers. Have you not been acquainted with goldsmiths' wives, and conned them out of rings?

Orl. Not so; but I answer you right painted cloth, from whence you have studied your questions.

Jaq. You have a nimble wit: I think 't was made of Atalanta's heels. Will you sit down with me? and we two will rail against our mistress the world and all our misery.

Orl. I will chide no breather in the world but myself, against whom I know most faults.

Jaq. The worst fault you have is to be in love.   260

Orl. 'T is a fault I will not change for your best virtue. I am weary of you.

Jaq. By my troth, I was seeking for a fool when I found you.

C 2   (M 7)

Orl. He is drowned in the brook: look but in, and you shall see him.

Jaq. There I shall see mine own figure.

Orl. Which I take to be either a fool or a cipher.

Jaq. I 'll tarry no longer with you: farewell, good Signior Love.   270

Orl. I am glad of your departure: adieu, good Monsieur Melancholy.   [*Exit Jaques.*

Ros. [*Aside to Celia*] I will speak to him like a saucy lackey and under that habit play the knave with him. Do you hear, forester?

Orl. Very well: what would you?

Ros. I pray you, what is 't o'clock?

Orl. You should ask me what time o' day: there 's no clock in the forest.   279

Ros. Then there is no true lover in the forest; else sighing every minute and groaning every hour would detect the lazy foot of Time as well as a clock.

Orl. And why not the swift foot of Time? had not that been as proper?

Ros. By no means, sir: Time travels in divers paces with divers persons.   I 'll tell you who Time ambles withal, who Time trots withal, who Time gallops withal and who he stands still withal.

Orl. I prithee, who doth he trot withal?   289

Ros. Marry, he trots hard with a young maid between the contract of her marriage and the day it is solemnized: if the interim be but a se'nnight, Time's pace is so hard that it seems the length of seven year.

Orl. Who ambles Time withal?

Ros. With a priest that lacks Latin and a rich man that hath not the gout, for the one sleeps easily because he cannot study and the other lives merrily because he feels no pain, the one lacking the burden of lean and wasteful learning, the

other knowing no burden of heavy tedious penury; these
Time ambles withal. 300

Orl. Who doth he gallop withal?

Ros. With a thief to the gallows, for though he go as softly
as foot can fall, he thinks himself too soon there.

Orl. Who stays it still withal?

Ros. With lawyers in the vacation; for they sleep between
term and term and then they perceive not how Time moves.

Orl. Where dwell you, pretty youth?

Ros. With this shepherdess, my sister; here in the skirts
of the forest, like fringe upon a petticoat.

Orl. Are you native of this place? 310

Ros. As the cony that you see dwell where she is kindled.

Orl. Your accent is something finer than you could purchase
in so removed a dwelling.

Ros. I have been told so of many: but indeed an old
religious uncle of mine taught me to speak, who was in his
youth an inland man; one that knew courtship too well, for
there he fell in love. I have heard him read many lectures
against it, and I thank God I am not a woman, to be touched
with so many giddy offences as he hath generally taxed their
whole sex withal. 320

Orl. Can you remember any of the principal evils that he
laid to the charge of women?

Ros. There were none principal; they were all like one
another, as halfpence are, every one fault seeming monstrous
till his fellow-fault came to match it.

Orl. I prithee recount some of them.

Ros. No, I will not cast away my physic but on those that
are sick. There is a man haunts the forest, that abuses our
young plants with carving 'Rosalind' on their barks: hangs
odes upon hawthorns and elegies on brambles, all, forsooth,
deifying the name of Rosalind: if I could meet that fancy-
monger, I would give him some good counsel, for he seems
to have the quotidian of love upon him. 333

Orl. I am he that is so love-shaked: I pray you, tell me your remedy.

Ros. There is none of my uncle's marks upon you: he taught me how to know a man in love; in which cage of rushes I am sure you are not prisoner.

Orl. What were his marks?

Ros. A lean cheek, which you have not, a blue eye and sunken, which you have not, an unquestionable spirit, which you have not, a beard neglected, which you have not; but I pardon you for that, for simply your having in beard is a younger brother's revenue: then your hose should be un-gartered, your bonnet unbanded, your sleeve unbuttoned, your shoe untied and every thing about you demonstrating a care-less desolation; but you are no such man; you are rather point-device in your accoutrements as loving yourself than seeming the lover of any other.   349

Orl. Fair youth, I would I could make thee believe I love.

Ros. Me believe it! you may as soon make her that you love believe it; which, I warrant, she is apter to do than to confess she does: that is one of the points in which women still give the lie to their consciences. But, in good sooth, are you he that hangs the verses on the trees, wherein Rosalind is so admired?

Orl. I swear to thee, youth, by the white hand of Rosalind, I am that he, that unfortunate he.

Ros. But are you so much in love as your rhymes speak?

Orl. Neither rhyme nor reason can express how much. 360

Ros. Love is merely a madness, and, I tell you, deserves as well a dark house and a whip as madmen do: and the reason why they are not so punished and cured is, that the lunacy is so ordinary that the whippers are in love too. Yet I profess curing it by counsel.

Orl. Did you ever cure any so?   366

Ros. Yes, one, and in this manner. He was to imagine me his love, his mistress; and I set him every day to woo me:

at which time would I, being but a moonish youth, grieve, be effeminate, changeable, longing and liking, proud, fantastical, apish, shallow, inconstant, full of tears, full of smiles, for every passion something and for no passion truly any thing, as boys and women are for the most part cattle of this colour: would now like him, now loathe him; then entertain him, then forswear him; now weep for him, then spit at him; that I drave my suitor from his mad humour of love to a living humour of madness; which was, to forswear the full stream of the world and to live in a nook merely monastic.   And thus I cured him: and in this way will I take upon me to wash your liver as clean as a sound sheep's heart, that there shall not be one spot of love in 't.   381

Orl. I would not be cured, youth.

Ros. I would cure you, if you would but call me Rosalind and come every day to my cote and woo me.

Orl. Now, by the faith of my love, I will: tell me where it is.

Ros. Go with me to it and I 'll show it you: and by the way you shall tell me where in the forest you live.   Will you go?

Orl. With all my heart, good youth.

Ros. Nay, you must call me Rosalind.   Come, sister, will you go?   [*Exeunt.* 390

SCENE III.   *The forest.*

Enter TOUCHSTONE *and* AUDREY; JAQUES *behind.*

Touch. Come apace, good Audrey: I will fetch up your goats, Audrey.   And how, Audrey? am I the man yet? doth my simple feature content you?

Aud. Your features!   Lord warrant us! what features?

Touch. I am here with thee and thy goats, as the most capricious poet, honest Ovid, was among the Goths.

Jaq. [*Aside*] O knowledge ill-inhabited, worse than Jove in a thatched house!   8

Touch. When a man's verses cannot be understood, nor a man's good wit seconded with the forward child Understanding, it strikes a man more dead than a great reckoning in a little room. Truly, I would the gods had made thee poetical.

Aud. I do not know what 'poetical' is: is it honest in deed and word? is it a true thing?

Touch. No, truly; for the truest poetry is the most feigning; and lovers are given to poetry, and what they swear in poetry may be said as lovers they do feign.   17

Aud. Do you wish then that the gods had made me poetical?

Touch. I do truly; for thou swearest to me thou art honest; now, if thou wert a poet, I might have some hope thou didst feign.

Aud. Would you not have me honest?

Touch. No, truly, unless thou wert hard-favoured; for honesty coupled to beauty is to have honey a sauce to sugar.

Jaq. [*Aside*] A material fool!   26

Aud. Well, I am not fair; and therefore I pray the gods make me honest.

Touch. Truly, and to cast away honesty upon a foul slut were to put good meat into an unclean dish.

Aud. I am not a slut, though I thank the gods I am foul.

Touch. Well, praised be the gods for thy foulness! sluttishness may come hereafter. But be it as it may be, I will marry thee, and to that end I have been with Sir Oliver Martext, the vicar of the next village, who hath promised to meet me in this place of the forest and to couple us.

Jaq. [*Aside*] I would fain see this meeting.

Aud. Well, the gods give us joy!   38

Touch. Amen. A man may, if he were of a fearful heart, stagger in this attempt; for here we have no temple but the wood, no assembly but horn-beasts. But what though? Courage! As horns are odious, they are necessary. It is said, 'many a man knows no end of his goods': right: many a man has good horns, and knows no end of them. Well, that is the dowry of his wife; 't is none of his own getting. Horns? Even so. Poor men alone? No, no; the noblest deer hath them as huge as the rascal. Is the single man therefore blessed? No; as a walled town is more worthier than a village, so is the forehead of a married man more honourable than the bare brow of a bachelor; and by how much defence is better than no skill, by so much is a horn more precious than to want. Here comes Sir Oliver.   52

Enter SIR OLIVER MARTEXT.

Sir Oliver Martext, you are well met: will you dispatch us here under this tree, or shall we go with you to your chapel?

Sir Oli. Is there none here to give the woman?

Touch. I will not take her on gift of any man.

Sir Oli. Truly, she must be given, or the marriage is not awful.

Jaq. [*Advancing*] Proceed, proceed: I 'll give her.   60

Touch. Good even, good Master What-ye-call 't; how do you, sir? You are very well met: God 'ild you for your last company; I am very glad to see you: even a toy in hand here, sir: nay, pray be covered.

Jaq. Will you be married, motley?

Touch. As the ox has his bow, sir, the horse his curb and the falcon her bells, so man hath his desires; and as pigeons bill, so wedlock would be nibbling.   68

Jaq. And will you, being a man of your breeding, be married under a bush like a beggar? Get you to church, and have a good priest that can tell you what marriage is: this fellow will but join you together as they join wainscot; then one of you will prove a shrunk panel, and, like green timber, warp, warp.

Touch. [*Aside*] I am not in the mind but I were better to be married of him than of another: for he is not like to marry

me well; and not being well married, it will be a good excuse
for me hereafter to leave my wife.

Jaq. Go thou with me, and let me counsel thee.

Touch. Come, sweet Audrey: 80
Farewell, good Master Oliver; not,—

> O sweet Oliver,
> O brave Oliver,
> Leave me not behind thee:

but,—

> Wind away,
> Begone, I say,
> I will not to wedding with thee.

[*Exeunt Jaques, Touchstone and Audrey.*

Sir Oli. 'T is no matter: ne'er a fantastical knave of them
all shall flout me out of my calling.   [*Exit.* 90

SCENE IV.   *The forest.*

Enter ROSALIND *and* CELIA.

Ros. Never talk to me: I will weep.

Cel. Do, I prithee; but yet have the grace to consider that
tears do not become a man.

Ros. But have I not cause to weep?

Cel. As good cause as one would desire; therefore weep.

Ros. His very hair is of the dissembling colour.

Cel. Something browner than Judas's: marry, his kisses
are Judas's own children.

Ros. I' faith, his hair is of a good colour.

Cel. An excellent colour: your chestnut was ever the only
colour.   11

Ros. And his kissing is as full of sanctity as the touch of
holy bread.

Cel. He hath bought a pair of cast lips of Diana: a nun
of winter's sisterhood kisses not more religiously; the very
ice of chastity is in them.

Ros. But why did he swear he would come this morning, and comes not?

Cel. Nay, certainly, there is no truth in him.

Ros. Do you think so? 20

Cel. Yes; I think he is not a pick-purse nor a horse-stealer, but for his verity in love, I do think him as concave as a covered goblet or a worm-eaten nut.

Ros. Not true in love?

Cel. Yes, when he is in; but I think he is not in.

Ros. You have heard him swear downright he was.

Cel. 'Was' is not 'is': besides, the oath of a lover is no stronger than the word of a tapster; they are both the confirmer of false reckonings. He attends here in the forest on the duke your father. 30

Ros. I met the duke yesterday and had much question with him: he asked me of what parentage I was; I told him, of as good as he; so he laughed and let me go. But what talk we of fathers, when there is such a man as Orlando?

Cel. O, that's a brave man! he writes brave verses, speaks brave words, swears brave oaths and breaks them bravely, quite traverse, athwart the heart of his lover; as a puisny tilter, that spurs his horse but on one side, breaks his staff like a noble goose: but all's brave that youth mounts and folly guides. Who comes here? 40

Enter CORIN.

Cor. Mistress and master, you have oft inquired
After the shepherd that complain'd of love,
Who you saw sitting by me on the turf,
Praising the proud disdainful shepherdess
That was his mistress.

Cel.　　　　　Well, and what of him?

Cor. If you will see a pageant truly play'd,
Between the pale complexion of true love
And the red glow of scorn and proud disdain,

Go hence a little and I shall conduct you,
If you will mark it.
  Ros.   O, come, let us remove: 50
The sight of lovers feedeth those in love.
Bring us to this sight, and you shall say
I 'll prove a busy actor in their play.   [*Exeunt.*

Scene V. *Another part of the forest.*

Enter Silvius *and* Phebe.

 Sil. Sweet Phebe, do not scorn me; do not, Phebe;
Say that you love me not, but say not so
In bitterness. The common executioner,
Whose heart the accustom'd sight of death makes hard,
Falls not the axe upon the humbled neck
But first begs pardon; will you sterner be
Than he that dies and lives by bloody drops?

Enter Rosalind, Celia, *and* Corin, *behind.*

 Phe. I would not be thy executioner:
I fly thee, for I would not injure thee.
Thou tell'st me there is murder in mine eye: 10
'T is pretty, sure, and very probable,
That eyes, that are the frail'st and softest things,
Who shut their coward gates on atomies,
Should be call'd tyrants, butchers, murderers!
Now I do frown on thee with all my heart;
And if mine eyes can wound, now let them kill thee:
Now counterfeit to swoon; why now fall down;
Or if thou canst not, O, for shame, for shame,
Lie not, to say mine eyes are murderers!
Now show the wound mine eye hath made in thee: 20
Scratch thee but with a pin, and there remains
Some scar of it; lean upon a rush,
The cicatrice and capable impressure

Thy palm some moment keeps; but now mine eyes,
Which I have darted at thee, hurt thee not,
Nor, I am sure, there is no force in eyes
That can do hurt.

   Sil.   O dear Phebe,
If ever,—as that ever may be near,—
You meet in some fresh cheek the power of fancy,
Then shall you know the wounds invisible   30
That love's keen arrows make.

   Phe.   But till that time
Come not thou near me: and when that time comes,
Afflict me with thy mocks, pity me not;
As till that time I shall not pity thee.

   Ros. And why, I pray you? Who might be your
     mother,
That you insult, exult, and all at once,
Over the wretched? What though you have no beauty,—
As, by my faith, I see no more in you
Than without candle may go dark to bed—
Must you be therefore proud and pitiless?   40
Why, what means this? Why do you look on me?
I see no more in you than in the ordinary
Of nature's sale-work. 'Od's my little life,
I think she means to tangle my eyes too!
No, faith, proud mistress, hope not after it:
'T is not your inky brows, your black silk hair,
Your bugle eyeballs, nor your cheek of cream,
That can entame my spirits to your worship.
You foolish shepherd, wherefore do you follow her,
Like foggy south puffing with wind and rain?   50
You are a thousand times a properer man
Than she a woman: 't is such fools as you
That makes the world full of ill-favoured children:
'T is not her glass, but you, that flatters her;
And out of you she sees herself more proper

Than any of her lineaments can show her.
But mistress, know yourself: down on your knees,
And thank heaven, fasting, for a good man's love:
For I must tell you friendly in your ear,
Sell when you can: you are not for all markets: 60
Cry the man mercy; love him; take his offer:
Foul is most foul, being foul to be a scoffer.
So take her to thee, shepherd: fare you well.

Phe. Sweet youth, I pray you, chide a year together:
I had rather hear you chide than this man woo.

Ros. He 's fallen in love with your foulness, and she 'll fall
in love with my anger. If it be so, as fast as she answers
thee with frowning looks, I 'll sauce her with bitter words.
Why look you so upon me?

Phe. For no ill will I bear you.   70

Ros. I pray you, do not fall in love with me,
For I am falser than vows made in wine:
Besides, I like you not. If you will know my house,
'T is at the tuft of olives here hard by.
Will you go, sister? Shepherd, ply her hard.
Come, sister. Shepherdess, look on him better,
And be not proud: though all the world could see
None could be so abused in sight as he.
Come, to our flock.   [*Exeunt Rosalind, Celia, and Corin.*

Phe. Dead shepherd, now I find thy saw of might.   80
'Who ever loved that loved not at first sight?'

Sil. Sweet Phebe,—

Phe.   Ha, what say'st thou, Silvius?

Sil. Sweet Phebe, pity me.

Phe. Why, I am sorry for thee, gentle Silvius.

Sil. Wherever sorrow is, relief would be:
If you do sorrow at my grief in love,
By giving love your sorrow and my grief
Were both extermined.

Phe. Thou hast my love: is not that neighbourly?

Sil. I would have you.

Phe.   Why, that were covetousness.   90
Silvius, the time was that I hated thee,
And yet it is not that I bear thee love;
But since that thou canst talk of love so well,
Thy company, which erst was irksome to me,
I will endure, and I 'll employ thee too:
But do not look for further recompense
Than thine own gladness that thou art employ'd.

Sil. So holy and so perfect is my love,
And I in such a poverty of grace,
That I shall think it a most plenteous crop   100
To glean the broken ears after the man
That the main harvest reaps: loose now and then
A scatter'd smile, and that I 'll live upon.

Phe. Know'st thou the youth that spoke to me erewhile?

Sil. Not very well, but I have met him oft;
And he hath bought the cottage and the bounds
That the old carlot once was master of.

Phe. Think not I love him, though I ask for him;
'T is but a peevish boy; yet he talks well;
But what care I for words? yet words do well   110
When he that speaks them pleases those that hear.
It is a pretty youth: not very pretty:
But, sure, he 's proud, and yet his pride becomes him:
He 'll make a proper man: the best thing in him
Is his complexion; and faster than his tongue
Did make offence his eye did heal it up.
He is not very tall; yet for his years he 's tall:
His leg is but so so; and yet 't is well:
There was a pretty redness in his lip,
A little riper and more lusty red   120
Than that mix'd in his cheek; 't was just the difference
Betwixt the constant red and mingled damask.
There be some women, Silvius, had they mark'd him

In parcels as I did, would have gone near
To fall in love with him; but, for my part,
I love him not nor hate him not; and yet
I have more cause to hate him than to love him:
For what had he to do to chide at me?
He said mine eyes were black and my hair black:
And, now I am remember'd, scorn'd at me: 130
I marvel why I answer'd not again:
But that's all one: omittance is no quittance,
I'll write to him a very taunting letter,
And thou shalt bear it: wilt thou, Silvius?
   Sil. Phebe, with all my heart.
   Phe.   I'll write it straight;
The matter's in my head and in my heart:
I will be bitter with him and passing short.
Go with me, Silvius.   [*Exeunt.*

ACT IV.

Scene I.   *The forest.*

Enter Rosalind, Celia, *and* Jaques.

   Jaq. I prithee, pretty youth, let me be better acquainted
with thee.

   Ros. They say you are a melancholy fellow.

   Jaq. I am so; I do love it better than laughing.

   Ros. Those that are in extremity of either are abominable
fellows and betray themselves to every modern censure worse
than drunkards.

   Jaq. Why, 't is good to be sad and say nothing.

   Ros. Why then, 't is good to be a post.   9

   Jaq. I have neither the scholar's melancholy, which is

emulation, nor the musician's, which is fantastical, nor the courtier's, which is proud, nor the soldier's, which is ambitious, nor the lawyer's, which is politic, nor the lady's, which is nice, nor the lover's, which is all these: but it is a melancholy of mine own, compounded of many simples, extracted from many objects, and indeed the sundry contemplation of my travels, in which my often rumination wraps me in a most humorous sadness.   18

Ros. A traveller! By my faith, you have great reason to be sad: I fear you have sold your own lands to see other men's; then, to have seen much and to have nothing, is to have rich eyes and poor hands.

Jaq. Yes, I have gained my experience.

Ros. And your experience makes you sad: I had rather have a fool to make me merry than experience to make me sad; and to travel for it too!

Enter ORLANDO.

Orl. Good day and happiness, dear Rosalind!

Jaq. Nay, then, God be wi' you, an you talk in blank verse.   [*Exit.* 29

Ros. Farewell, Monsieur Traveller: look you lisp and wear strange suits, disable all the benefits of your own country, be out of love with your nativity and almost chide God for making you that countenance you are, or I will scarce think you have swam in a gondola. Why, how now, Orlando! where have you been all this while? You a lover! An you serve me such another trick, never come in my sight more.

Orl. My fair Rosalind, I come within an hour of my promise.   38

Ros. Break an hour's promise in love! He that will divide a minute into a thousand parts and break but a part of the thousandth part of a minute in the affairs of love, it may be said of him that Cupid hath clapped him o' the shoulder, but I 'll warrant him heart-whole.

Orl. Pardon me, dear Rosalind.

Ros. Nay, an you be so tardy, come no more in my sight:
I had as lief be wooed of a snail.

Orl. Of a snail?   47

Ros. Ay, of a snail; for though he comes slowly, he carries
his house on his head; a better jointure, I think, than you
make a woman: besides, he brings his destiny with him.

Orl. What's that?

Ros. Why, horns, which such as you are fain to be beholding to your wives for: but he comes armed in his fortune and
prevents the slander of his wife.

Orl. Virtue is no horn-maker: and my Rosalind is virtuous.

Ros. And I am your Rosalind.

Cel. It pleases him to call you so; but he hath a Rosalind
of a better leer than you.   58

Ros. Come, woo me, woo me, for now I am in a holiday
humour and like enough to consent. What would you say
to me now, an I were your very very Rosalind?

Orl. I would kiss before I spoke.

Ros. Nay, you were better speak first, and when you were
gravelled for lack of matter, you might take occasion to kiss.
Very good orators, when they are out, they will spit; and for
lovers lacking—God warn us!—matter, the cleanliest shift is
to kiss.

Orl. How if the kiss be denied?

Ros. Then she puts you to entreaty, and there begins new
matter.   70

Orl. Who could be out, being before his beloved mistress?

Ros. Marry, that should you, if I were your mistress, or I
should think my honesty ranker than my wit.

Orl. What, of my suit?

Ros. Not out of your apparel, and yet out of your suit. Am
not I your Rosalind?

Orl. I take some joy to say you are, because I would be
talking of her.

Ros. Well in her person I say I will not have you.

Orl. Then in mine own person I die.   80

Ros. No, faith, die by attorney. The poor world is almost six thousand years old, and in all this time there was not any man died in his own person, videlicet, in a love-cause. Troilus had his brains dashed out with a Grecian club; yet he did what he could to die before, and he is one of the patterns of love. Leander, he would have lived many a fair year, though Hero had turned nun, if it had not been for a hot midsummer night; for, good youth, he went but forth to wash him in the Hellespont and being taken with the cramp was drowned: and the foolish chroniclers of that age found it was 'Hero of Sestos'. But these are all lies: men have died from time to time and worms have eaten them, but not for love.   93

Orl. I would not have my right Rosalind of this mind, for, I protest her frown might kill me.

Ros. By this hand, it will not kill a fly. But come, now I will be your Rosalind in a more coming-on disposition, and ask me what you will, I will grant it.

Orl. Then love me, Rosalind.

Ros. Yes, faith, will I, Fridays and Saturdays and all.   100

Orl. And wilt thou have me?

Ros. Ay, and twenty such.

Orl. What sayest thou?

Ros. Are you not good?

Orl. I hope so.

Ros. Why, then, can one desire too much of a good thing? Come, sister, you shall be the priest and marry us. Give me your hand, Orlando. What do you say, sister?

Orl. Pray thee, marry us.

Cel. I cannot say the words.   110

Ros. You must begin, 'Will you, Orlando—'

Cel. Go to. Will you, Orlando, have to wife this Rosalind?

Orl. I will.

Ros. Ay, but when?

Orl. Why now; as fast as she can marry us.

Ros. Then you must say 'I take thee, Rosalind, for wife'.

Orl. I take thee, Rosalind, for wife.

Ros. I might ask you for your commission; but I do take thee, Orlando, for my husband: there's a girl goes before the priest; and certainly a woman's thought runs before her actions.   122

Orl. So do all thoughts; they are winged.

Ros. Now tell me how long you would have her after you have possessed her.

Orl. For ever and a day.

Ros. Say 'a day', without the 'ever'.   No, no, Orlando; men are April when they woo, December when they wed: maids are May when they are maids, but the sky changes when they are wives.   I will be more jealous of thee than a Barbary cock-pigeon over his hen, more clamorous than a parrot against rain, more new-fangled than an ape, more giddy in my desires than a monkey: I will weep for nothing, like Diana in the fountain, and I will do that when you are disposed to be merry; I will laugh like a hyen, and that when thou art inclined to sleep.   136

Orl. But will my Rosalind do so?

Ros. By my life, she will do as I do.

Orl. O, but she is wise.

Ros. Or else she could not have the wit to do this: the wiser, the waywarder: make the doors upon a woman's wit and it will out at the casement; shut that and 't will out at the key-hole; stop that, 't will fly with the smoke out at the chimney.

Orl. A man that had a wife with such a wit, he might say 'Wit, whither wilt?'   146

Ros. Nay, you might keep that check for it till you met your wife's wit going to your neighbour's bed.

Orl. And what wit could wit have to excuse that?

Ros. Marry, to say she came to seek you there. You shall never take her without her answer, unless you take her without her tongue. O, that woman that cannot make her fault her husband's occasion, let her never nurse her child herself, for she will breed it like a fool!

Orl. For these two hours, Rosalind, I will leave thee.

Ros. Alas! dear love, I cannot lack thee two hours.   156

Orl. I must attend the duke at dinner: by two o'clock I will be with thee again.

Ros. Ay, go your ways, go your ways; I knew what you would prove: my friends told me as much, and I thought no less: that flattering tongue of yours won me: 'tis but one cast away, and so, come, death! Two o'clock is your hour?

Orl. Ay, sweet Rosalind.   163

Ros. By my troth, and in good earnest, and so God mend me, and by all pretty oaths that are not dangerous, if you break one jot of your promise or come one minute behind your hour, I will think you the most pathetical break-promise and the most hollow lover and the most unworthy of her you call Rosalind that may be chosen out of the gross band of the unfaithful: therefore beware my censure and keep your promise.   171

Orl. With no less religion than if thou wert indeed my Rosalind: so adieu.

Ros. Well, Time is the old justice that examines all such offenders, and let Time try: adieu.   [*Exit Orlando.*

Cel. You have simply misused our sex in your love-prate: we must have your doublet and hose plucked over your head, and show the world what the bird hath done to her own nest.

Ros. O coz, coz, coz, my pretty little coz, that thou didst know how many fathom deep I am in love! But it cannot be sounded: my affection hath an unknown bottom, like the bay of Portugal.   183

Cel. Or rather, bottomless, that as fast as you pour affection in, it runs out.

Ros. No, that same wicked bastard of Venus that was begot of thought, conceived of spleen and born of madness, that blind rascally boy that abuses every one's eyes because his own are out, let him be judge how deep I am in love. I 'll tell thee, Aliena, I cannot be out of the sight of Orlando: I 'll go find a shadow and sigh till he come.

Cel. And I 'll sleep. ⌈*Exeunt.*

SCENE II. *The forest.*

Enter JAQUES, Lords, *and* Foresters.

Jaq. Which is he that killed the deer?

A Lord. Sir, it was I.

Jaq. Let 's present him to the duke, like a Roman conqueror; and it would do well to set the deer's horns upon his head, for a branch of victory. Have you no song, forester, for this purpose?

For. Yes, sir.

Jaq. Sing it: 't is no matter how it be in tune, so it make noise enough.

SONG.

For.   What shall he have that kill'd the deer?   10
      His leather skin and horns to wear.
           Then sing him home;
              [*The rest shall bear this burden.*
      Take thou no scorn to wear the horn;
      It was a crest ere thou was born:
           Thy father's father wore it,
           And thy father bore it:
      The horn, the horn, the lusty horn
      Is not a thing to laugh to scorn.   ⌈*Exeunt.*

SCENE III.   *The forest.*

Enter ROSALIND *and* CELIA.

Ros. How say you now? Is it not past two o'clock? and here much Orlando!

Cel. I warrant you, with pure love and troubled brain, he hath ta'en his bow and arrows and is gone forth—to sleep. Look, who comes here.

Enter SILVIUS.

Sil. My errand is to you, fair youth;
My gentle Phebe bid me give you this:
I know not the contents; but, as I guess
By the stern brow and waspish action
Which she did use as she was writing of it,   10
It bears an angry tenour: pardon me;
I am but as a guiltless messenger.

Ros. Patience herself would startle at this letter
And play the swaggerer; bear this, bear all:
She says I am not fair, that I lack manners;
She calls me proud, and that she could not love me,
Were man as rare as phœnix.   'Od 's my will!
Her love is not the hare that I do hunt:
Why writes she so to me? Well, shepherd, well,
This is a letter of your own device.   20

Sil. No, I protest, I know not the contents:
Phebe did write it.

Ros.   Come, come, you are a fool
And turn'd into the extremity of love.
I saw her hand: she has a leathern hand,
A freestone-colour'd hand; I verily did think
That her old gloves were on, but 't was her hands:
She has a huswife's hand; but that 's no matter:
I say she never did invent this letter;
This is a man's invention and his hand.

Sil. Sure, it is hers.   30
Ros. Why, 't is a boisterous and a cruel style,
A style for challengers; why, she defies me,
Like Turk to Christian: women's gentle brain
Could not drop forth such giant-rude invention,
Such Ethiope words, blacker in their effect
Than in their countenance.   Will you hear the letter?
Sil. So please you, for I never heard it yet;
Yet heard too much of Phebe's cruelty.
Ros. She Phebes me: mark how the tyrant writes. [*Reads.*

> Art thou god to shepherd turn'd,   40
> That a maiden's heart hath burn'd?

Can a woman rail thus?
Sil. Call you this railing?
Ros. [*Reads*]

> Why, thy godhead laid apart,
> Warr'st thou with a woman's heart?

Did you ever hear such railing?

> Whiles the eye of man did woo me,
> That could do no vengeance to me.

Meaning me a beast.

> If the scorn of your bright eyne   50
> Have power to raise such love in mine,
> Alack, in me what strange effect
> Would they work in mild aspect!
> Whiles you chid me, I did love;
> How then might your prayers move!
> He that brings this love to thee
> Little knows this love in me:
> And by him seal up thy mind;
> Whether that thy youth and kind
> Will the faithful offer take   60
> Of me and all that I can make;

> Or else by him my love deny,
> And then I 'll study how to die.

Sil. Call you this chiding?

Cel. Alas, poor shepherd!

Ros. Do you pity him? no, he deserves no pity. Wilt thou
love such a woman? What, to make thee an instrument and
play false strains upon thee! not to be endured! Well, go
your way to her, for I see love hath made thee a tame snake,
and say this to her; that if she love me, I charge her to love
thee; if she will not, I will never have her unless thou entreat
for her. If you be a true lover, hence, and not a word; for
here comes more company. [*Exit Silvius.* 73

Enter OLIVER.

Oli. Good-morrow, fair ones: pray you, if you know,
Where in the purlieus of this forest stands
A sheep-cote fenced about with olive trees?

Cel. West of this place, down in the neighbour bottom:
The rank of osiers by the murmuring stream
Left on your right hand brings you to the place.
But at this hour the house doth keep itself;   80
There 's none within.

Oli. If that an eye may profit by a tongue,
Then should I know you by description;
Such garments and such years: 'The boy is fair,
Of female favour, and bestows himself
Like a ripe sister: the woman low
And browner than her brother'. Are not you
The owner of the house I did enquire for?

Cel. It is no boast, being ask'd, to say we are.

Oli. Orlando doth commend him to you both,   90
And to that youth he calls his Rosalind
He sends this bloody napkin. Are you he?

Ros. I am: what must we understand by this?

Oli. Some of my shame; if you will know of me
What man I am, and how, and why, and where
This handkercher was stain'd.

   Cel.   I pray you, tell it.

   Oli. When last the young Orlando parted from you
He left a promise to return again
Within an hour, and pacing through the forest,
Chewing the food of sweet and bitter fancy,   100
Lo, what befel! he threw his eye aside,
And mark what object did present itself:
Under an oak, whose bows were moss'd with age
And high top bald with dry antiquity,
A wretched ragged man, o'ergrown with hair,
Lay sleeping on his back: about his neck
A green and gilded snake had wreathed itself,
Who with her head nimble in threats approach'd
The opening of his mouth; but suddenly,
Seeing Orlando, it unlink'd itself,   110
And with indented glides did slip away
Into a bush: under which bush's shade
A lioness, with udders all drawn dry,
Lay couching, head on ground, with catlike watch,
When that the sleeping man should stir; for 't is
The royal disposition of that beast
To prey on nothing that doth seem as dead:
This seen, Orlando did approach the man
And found it was his brother, his elder brother.

   Cel. O, I have heard him speak of that same brother; 120
And he did render him the most unnatural
That lived amongst men.

   Oli.   And well he might so do,
For well I know he was unnatural.

   Ros. But, to Orlando: did he leave him there,
Food to the suck'd and hungry lioness?

   Oli. Twice did he turn his back and purposed so;

But kindness, nobler ever than revenge,
And nature, stronger than his just occasion,
Made him give battle to the lioness,
Who quickly fell before him; in which hurtling　　130
From miserable slumber I awaked.

  Cel. Are you his brother?

  Ros.　　　　　　　　Was 't you he rescued?

  Cel. Was 't you that did so oft contrive to kill him?

  Oli. 'T was I; but 't is not I: I do not shame
To tell you what I was, since my conversion
So sweetly tastes, being the thing I am.

  Ros. But, for the bloody napkin?

  Oli.　　　　　　　　By and by.
When from the first to last betwixt us two
Tears our recountments had most kindly bathed,
As how I came into that desert place:—　　140
In brief, he led me to the gentle duke,
Who gave me fresh array and entertainment,
Committing me unto my brother's love;
Who led me instantly unto his cave,
There stripp'd himself, and here upon his arm
The lioness had torn some flesh away,
Which all this while had bled; and now he fainted
And cried, in fainting, upon Rosalind.
Brief, I recover'd him, bound up his wound;
And, after some small space, being strong at heart,　　150
He sent me hither, stranger as I am,
To tell this story, that you might excuse
His broken promise, and to give this napkin
Dyed in his blood unto the shepherd youth
That he in sport doth call his Rosalind. [*Rosalind swoons*

  Cel. Why, how now, Ganymede! sweet Ganymede!

  Oli. Many will swoon when they do look on blood.

  Cel. There is more in it. Cousin Ganymede!

  Oli. Look, he recovers.

D　　　　　　　　　　　　　　　　(M 7)

Ros. I would I were at home.

Cel.   We 'll lead you thither.   160
I pray you, will you take him by the arm?

Oli. Be of good cheer, youth: you a man! you lack a
man's heart.

Ros. I do so, I confess it.   Ah, sirrah, a body would think
this was well counterfeited!   I pray you, tell your brother
how well I counterfeited.   Heigh-ho!

Oli. This was not counterfeit: there is too great testimony
in your complexion that it was a passion of earnest.

Ros. Counterfeit, I assure you.   169

Oli. Well, then, take a good heart and counterfeit to be a
man.

Ros. So I do: but, i' faith, I should have been a woman
by right.

Cel. Come, you look paler and paler: pray you, draw
homewards.   Good sir, go with us.

Oli. That will I, for I must bear answer back
Hcw you excuse my brother, Rosalind.

Ros. I shall devise something: but, I pray you, commend
my counterfeiting to him.   Will you go?   [*Exeunt.*   179

ACT V.

Scene I.   *The forest.*

Enter Touchstone *and* Audrey.

Touch. We shall find a time, Audrey; patience, gentle
Audrey.

Aud. Faith, the priest was good enough, for all the old
gentleman's saying.

Touch. A most wicked Sir Oliver, Audrey, a most vile
Martext.   But, Audrey, there is a youth here in the forest
lays claim to you.

Aud. Ay, I know who 't is; he hath no interest in me in the world: here comes the man you mean.

Touch. It is meat and drink to me to see a clown: by my troth, we that have good wits have much to answer for; we shall be flouting; we cannot hold.   12

Enter WILLIAM.

Will. Good even, Audrey.

Aud. God ye good even, William.

Will. And good even to you, sir.

Touch. Good even, gentle friend.   Cover thy head, cover thy head; nay, prithee, be covered.   How old are you, friend?   18

Will. Five and twenty, sir.

Touch. A ripe age.   Is thy name William?

Will. William, sir.

Touch. A fair name.   Wast born i' the forest here?

Will. Ay, sir, I thank God.

Touch. 'Thank God'; a good answer.   Art rich?

Will. Faith, sir, so so.

Touch. 'So so' is good, very good, very excellent good, and yet it is not; it is but so so.   Art thou wise?

Will. Ay, sir, I have a pretty wit.   28

Touch. Why, thou sayest well.   I do now remember a saying, 'The fool doth think he is wise, but the wise man knows himself to be a fool'.   The heathen philosopher, when he had a desire to eat a grape, would open his lips when he put it into his mouth; meaning thereby that grapes were made to eat and lips to open.   You do love this maid?

Will. I do, sir.

Touch. Give me your hand.   Art thou learned?

Will. No, sir.   37

Touch. Then learn this of me: to have, is to have; for it is a figure in rhetoric that drink, being poured out of a cup into a glass, by filling the one doth empty the other; for all your writers do consent that ipse is he: now, you are not ipse, for I am he.

Will. Which he, sir?   43

Touch. He, sir, that must marry this woman. Therefore, you clown, abandon, — which is in the vulgar leave, — the society,—which in the boorish is company,—of this female,— which in the common is woman; which together is, abandon the society of this female, or, clown, thou perishest; or, to thy better understanding, diest; or, to wit, I kill thee, make thee away, translate thy life into death, thy liberty into bondage: I will deal in poison with thee, or in bastinado, or in steel; I will bandy with thee in faction; I will o'er-run thee with policy; I will kill thee a hundred and fifty ways: therefore tremble, and depart.   54

Aud. Do, good William.

Will. God rest you merry, sir.   [*Exit.*

Enter CORIN.

Cor. Our master and mistress seeks you; come, away, away!

Touch. Trip, Audrey! trip, Audrey! I attend, I attend.

[*Exeunt.*

SCENE II.   *The forest.*

Enter ORLANDO *and* OLIVER.

Orl. Is't possible that on so little acquaintance you should like her? that but seeing you should love her? and loving woo? and, wooing, she should grant? and will you persever to enjoy her?

Oli. Neither call the giddiness of it in question, the poverty of her, the small acquaintance, my sudden wooing, nor her sudden consenting; but say with me, I love Aliena; say with her that she loves me; consent with both that we may enjoy each other: it shall be to your good; for my father's house

and all the revenue that was old Sir Rowland's will I estate
upon you, and here live and die a shepherd.   11

Orl. You have my consent.   Let your wedding be to-
morrow: thither will I invite the duke and all 's contented
followers.   Go you and prepare Aliena; for look you, here
comes my Rosalind.

Enter ROSALIND.

Ros. God save you, brother.

Oli. And you, fair sister.   ´   [*Exit.*

Ros. O, my dear Orlando, how it grieves me to see thee
wear thy heart in a scarf!

Orl. It is my arm.   20

Ros. I thought thy heart had been wounded with the claws
of a lion.

Orl. Wounded it is, but with the eyes of a lady.

Ros. Did your brother tell you how I counterfeited to
swoon when he showed me your handkercher?

Orl. Ay, and greater wonders than that.   26

Ros. O, I know where you are: nay, 't is true: there was
never any thing so sudden but the fight of two rams and
Cæsar's thrasonical brag of 'I came, saw, and overcame':
for your brother and my sister no sooner met but they
looked, no sooner looked but they loved, no sooner loved
but they sighed, no sooner sighed but they asked one another
the reason, no sooner knew the reason but they sought the
remedy; and in these degrees have they made a pair of
stairs to marriage which they will climb incontinent: they
are in the very wrath of love and they will together; clubs
cannot part them.   37

Orl. They shall be married to-morrow, and I will bid the
duke to the nuptial.   But, O, how bitter a thing it is to look
into happiness through another man's eyes!   By so much
the more shall I to-morrow be at the height of heart-

heaviness, by how much I shall think my brother happy in having what he wishes for.

Ros. Why then, to-morrow I cannot serve your turn for Rosalind?

Orl. I can live no longer for thinking.   46

Ros. I will weary you then no longer with idle talking. Know of me then, for now I speak to some purpose, that I know you are a gentleman of good conceit: I speak not this that you should bear a good opinion of my knowledge, insomuch I say I know you are; neither do I labour for a greater esteem than may in some little measure draw a belief from you, to do yourself good and not to grace me. Believe then, if you please, that I can do strange things: I have, since I was three year old, conversed with a magician, most profound in his art and yet not damnable. If you do love Rosalind so near the heart as your gesture cries it out, when your brother marries Aliena, shall you marry her: I know into what straits of fortune she is driven; and it is not impossible to me, if it appear not inconvenient to you, to set her before your eyes to-morrow human as she is and without any danger.

Orl. Speakest thou in sober meanings?   62

Ros. By my life, I do; which I tender dearly, though I say I am a magician. Therefore, put you in your best array; bid your friends; for if you will be married to-morrow, you shall, and to Rosalind, if you will.

Enter Silvius *and* Phebe.

Look, here comes a lover of mine and a lover of hers.

Phe. Youth, you have done me much ungentleness,
To show the letter that I writ to you.

Ros. I care not if I have: it is my study   70
To seem despiteful and ungentle to you:
You are there followed by a faithful shepherd;
Look upon him, love him; he worships you.

Phe. Good shepherd, tell this youth what 't is to love.

Sil. It is to be all made of sighs and tears;
And so am I for Phebe.

Phe. And I for Ganymede.

Orl. And I for Rosalind.

Ros. And I for no woman.

Sil. It is to be all made of faith and service   80
And so am I for Phebe.

Phe. And I for Ganymede.

Orl. And I for Rosalind.

Ros. And I for no woman.

Sil. It is to be all made of fantasy,
All made of passion and all made of wishes,
All adoration, duty, and observance,
All humbleness, all patience and impatience,
All purity, all trial, all † observance;
And so am I for Phebe.   90

Phe. And so am I for Ganymede.

Orl. And so am I for Rosalind.

Ros. And so am I for no woman.

Phe. If this be so, why blame you me to love you?

Sil. If this be so, why blame you me to love you?

Orl. If this be so, why blame you me to love you?

Ros. Why do you speak too, 'Why blame you me to love you'?

Orl. To her that is not here, nor doth not hear.   99

Ros. Pray you, no more of this; 't is like the howling of Irish wolves against the moon.—[*To Sil.*] I will help you, if I can:—[*To Phe.*] I would love you, if I could.—To-morrow meet me all together.—[*To Phe.*] I will marry you, if ever I marry woman, and I 'll be married to-morrow:—[*To Orl.*] I will satisfy you, if ever I satisfied man, and you shall be married to-morrow:—[*To Sil.*] I will content you, if what pleases you contents you, and you shall be married to-morrow.—[*To Orl.*] As you love Rosalind, meet!—[*To Sil.*] as you love

Phebe, meet! and as I love no woman, I 'll meet.—So fare
you well: I have left you commands.   110

Sil. I 'll not fail, if I live.

Phe. Nor I.

Orl. Nor I.   *Exeunt.*

SCENE III.   *The forest.*

Enter TOUCHSTONE *and* AUDREY.

Touch. To-morrow is the joyful day, Audrey; to-morrow
will we be married.

Aud. I do desire it with all my heart; and I hope it is no
dishonest desire to desire to be a woman of the world.   Here
come two of the banished duke's pages.

Enter two Pages.

First Page. Well met, honest gentleman.

Touch. By my troth, well met.   Come, sit, sit, and a song.

Second Page. We are for you: sit i' the middle.

First Page. Shall we clap into 't roundly, without hawking
or spitting or saying we are hoarse, which are the only prologues to a bad voice?   11

Second Page. I' faith, i' faith; and both in a tune, like two
gipsies on a horse.

SONG.

It was a lover and his lass,
    With a hey, and a ho, and a hey nonino,
That o'er the green corn-field did pass
    In the spring time, the only pretty ring time,
When birds do sing, hey ding a ding, ding:
Sweet lovers love the spring.

Between the acres of the rye,   20
    With a hey, and a ho, and a hey nonino,
These pretty country folks would lie,
    In spring time, &c.

This carol they began that hour,
   With a hey, and a ho, and a hey nonino,
How that a life was but a flower
   In spring time, &c.

And therefore take the present time,
   With a hey, and a ho, and a hey nonino;
For love is crowned with the prime   30
   In spring time, &c.

Touch. Truly, young gentlemen, though there was no great
matter in the ditty, yet the note was very untuneable

First Page. You are deceived, sir: we kept time, we lost
not our time.

Touch. By my troth, yes; I count it but time lost to hear
such a foolish song. God be wi' you; and God mend your
voices! Come, Audrey.   [*Exeunt.*

SCENE IV. *The forest.*

Enter DUKE senior, AMIENS, JAQUES, ORLANDO, OLIVER
and CELIA.

Duke S. Dost thou believe, Orlando, that the boy
Can do all this that he hath promised?

Orl. I sometimes do believe, and sometimes do not;
As those that fear they hope, and know they fear.

Enter ROSALIND, SILVIUS, *and* PHEBE.

Ros. Patience once more, whiles our compact is urged.
You say, if I bring in your Rosalind,
You will bestow her on Orlando here?

Duke S. That would I, had I kingdoms to give with her.

Ros. And you say, you will have her, when I bring her?

Orl. That would I, were I of all kingdoms king.   10

Ros. You say, you 'll marry me, if I be willing?

D 2   (M 7)

Phe. That will I, should I die the hour after.

Ros. But if you do refuse to marry me,
You'll give yourself to this most faithful shepherd?

Phe. So is the bargain.

Ros. You say, that you'll have Phebe, if she will?

Sil. Though to have her and death were both one thing.

Ros. I have promised to make all this matter even.
Keep you your word, O duke, to give your daughter;
You yours, Orlando, to receive his daughter: 20
Keep your word, Phebe, that you'll marry me,
Or else refusing me, to wed this shepherd:
Keep your word, Silvius, that you'll marry her,
If she refuse me: and from hence I go,
To make these doubts all even. [*Exeunt Rosalind and Celia.*

Duke S. I do remember in this shepherd boy
Some lively touches of my daughter's favour.

Orl. My lord, the first time that I ever saw him
Methought he was a brother to your daughter:
But, my good lord, this boy is forest-born,   30
And hath been tutored in the rudiments
Of many desperate studies by his uncle,
Whom he reports to be a great magician,
Obscured in the circle of this forest.

Enter TOUCHSTONE *and* AUDREY.

Jaq. There is, sure, another flood toward, and these couples
are coming to the ark. Here comes a pair of very strange
beasts, which in all tongues are called fools.

Touch. Salutation and greeting to you all!

Jaq. Good my lord, bid him welcome: this is the motley-
minded gentleman that I have so often met in the forest: he
hath been a courtier, he swears.   41

Touch. If any man doubt that, let him put me to my purgation. I have trod a measure; I have flattered a lady; I have

been politic with my friend, smooth with mine enemy; I have undone three tailors; I have had four quarrels, and like to have fought one.

Jaq. And how was that ta'en up?

Touch. Faith, we met, and found the quarrel was upon the seventh cause.

Jaq. How seventh cause? Good my lord, like this fellow.

Duke S. I like him very well.   51

Touch. God 'ild you, sir; I desire you of the like. I press in here, sir, amongst the rest of the country copulatives, to swear and to forswear; according as marriage binds and blood breaks: a poor virgin, sir, an ill-favoured thing, sir, but mine own; a poor humour of mine, sir, to take that that no man else will: rich honesty dwells like a miser, sir, in a poor house; as your pearl in your foul oyster.

Duke S. By my faith, he is very swift and sententious.

Touch. According to the fool's bolt, sir, and such dulcet diseases.   61

Jaq. But, for the seventh cause; how did you find the quarrel on the seventh cause?

Touch. Upon a lie seven times removed:—bear your body more seeming, Audrey:—as thus, sir. I did dislike the cut of a certain courtier's beard: he sent me word, if I said his beard was not cut well, he was in the mind it was: this is called the Retort Courteous. If I sent him word again 'it was not well cut', he would send me word, he cut it to please himself: this is called the Quip Modest. If again 'it was not well cut', he disabled my judgment: this is called the Reply Churlish. If again 'it was not well cut', he would answer, I spake not true: this is called the Reproof Valiant. If again 'it was not well cut', he would say I lied: this is called the Countercheck Quarrelsome: and so to the Lie Circumstantial and the Lie Direct.   76

Jaq. And how often did you say his beard was not well cut?

Touch. I durst go no further than the Lie Circumstantial

nor he durst not give me the Lie Direct; and so we measured
swords and parted.   80

Jaq. Can you nominate in order now the degrees of the lie?

Touch. O, sir, we quarrel in print, by the book; as you
have books for good manners: I will name you the degrees.
The first, the Retort Courteous; the second, the Quip Modest;
the third, the Reply Churlish; the fourth, the Reproof Valiant;
the fifth, the Countercheck Quarrelsome; the sixth, the Lie
with Circumstance; the seventh, the Lie Direct.   All these
you may avoid but the Lie Direct; and you may avoid that
too, with an If.   I knew when seven justices could not take
up a quarrel, but when the parties were met themselves, one
of them thought but of an If, as, 'If you said so, then I said
so'; and they shook hands and swore brothers.   Your If is
the only peace-maker; much virtue in If.   93

Jaq. Is not this a rare fellow, my lord? he's as good at
any thing and yet a fool.

Duke S. He uses his folly like a stalking-horse and under
the presentation of that he shoots his wit.

Enter HYMEN, ROSALIND, *and* CELIA.
Still Music.

Hym. Then is there mirth in heaven,
        When earthly things made even
                Atone together.   100
        Good duke, receive thy daughter:
        Hymen from heaven brought her,
                Yea, brought her hither,
        That thou mightst join her hand with his
        Whose heart within her bosom is.

Ros. [*To Duke*] To you I give myself, for I am yours.
[*To Orl.*] To you I give myself, for I am yours.

Duke S. If there be truth in sight, you are my daughter.

Orl. If there be truth in sight, you are my Rosalind.

Phe. If sight and shape be true,　　　　　　　　110
Why then, my love adieu!

Ros. I 'll have no father, if you be not he:
I 'll have no husband, if you be not he:
Nor ne'er wed woman, if you be not she.

Hym. Peace, ho! I bar confusion:
　　　'T is I must make conclusion
　　　　　Of these most strange events:
　　　Here 's eight that must take hands
　　　To join in Hymen's bands,
　　　　　If truth holds true contents.　　　120
　　　You and you no cross shall part:
　　　You and you are heart in heart:
　　　You to his love must accord,
　　　Or have a woman to your lord:
　　　You and you are sure together,
　　　As the winter to foul weather.
　　　Whiles a wedlock hymn we sing,
　　　Feed yourselves with questioning;
　　　That reason wonder may diminish,
　　　How thus we met, and these things finish.　　　130

SONG.

　　　Wedding is great Juno's crown:
　　　　　O blessed bond of board and bed!
　　　'T is Hymen peoples every town;
　　　　　High wedlock then be honoured:
　　　Honour, high honour and renown,
　　　To Hymen, god of every town!

Duke S. O my dear niece, welcome thou art to me!
Even daughter, welcome in no less degree.

Phe. I will not eat my word, now thou art mine;
Thy faith my fancy to thee doth combine.　　　140

Enter JAQUES DE BOYS.

Jaq. de B. Let me have audience for a word or two:

I am the second son of old Sir Rowland,
That bring these tidings to this fair assembly.
Duke Frederick, hearing how that every day
Men of great worth resorted to this forest,
Address'd a mighty power; which were on foot,
In his own conduct, purposely to take
His brother here and put him to the sword:
And to the skirts of this wild wood he came:
Where meeting with an old religious man,   150
After some question with him, was converted
Both from his enterprise and from the world,
His crown bequeathing to his banish'd brother,
And all their lands restored to them again
That were with him exiled.   This to be true,
I do engage my life.
   Duke S.   Welcome, young man;
Thou offer'st fairly to thy brothers' wedding,
To one his lands withheld, and to the other
A land itself at large, a potent dukedom.
First, in this forest let us do those ends   160
That here were well begun and well begot:
And after, every of this happy number
That have endured shrewd days and nights with us
Shall share the good of our returned fortune,
According to the measure of their states.
Meantime, forget this new-fall'n dignity
And fall into our rustic revelry.
Play, music.   And you, brides and bridegrooms all,
With measure heap'd in joy, to the measures fall.
   Jaq. Sir, by your patience.   If I heard you rightly,   170
The duke hath put on a religious life
And thrown into neglect the pompous court.
   Jaq. de B. He hath
   Jaq. To him will I: out of these convertites
There is much matter to be heard and learn'd.

[*To Duke*] You to your former honour I bequeath:
Your patience and your virtue well deserves it:
[*To Orl.*] You to a love that your true faith doth merit:
[*To Oli.*] You to your land and love and great allies:
[*To Sil.*] You to a long and well-deserved bed: 180
[*To Touch.*] And you to wrangling; for thy loving voyage
Is but for two months victuall'd. So, to your pleasures:
I am for other than for dancing measures.
   Duke S. Stay, Jaques, stay.
   Jaq. To see no pastime I: what you would have
I 'll stay to know at your abandon'd cave.   [*Exit.*
   Duke S. Proceed, proceed: we will begin these rites,
As we do trust they 'll end, in true delights.   [*A dance.*

Epilogue.

   Ros. It is not the fashion to see the lady the epilogue; but
it is no more unhandsome than to see the lord the prologue.
If it be true that good wine needs no bush, 't is true that a
good play needs no epilogue; yet to good wine they do use
good bushes, and good plays prove the better by the help of
good epilogues. What a case am I in then, that am neither
a good epilogue nor cannot insinuate with you in the behalf
of a good play! I am not furnished like a beggar, therefore
to beg will not become me: my way is to conjure you; and
I 'll begin with the women. I charge you, O women, for the
love you bear to men, to like as much of this play as please
you: and I charge you, O men, for the love you bear to
women—as I perceive by your simpering, none of you hates
them—that between you and the women the play may please.
If I were a woman I would kiss as many of you as had beards
that pleased me, complexions that liked me and breaths that
I defied not; and, I am sure, as many as have good beards
or good faces or sweet breaths will, for my kind offer, when
I make curtsy, bid me farewell.   [*Exeunt.* 19

NOTES.

[In the notes, Abb. refers to Dr. Abbott's *Shakespearian Grammar*: Kellner to L. Kellner's *Historical Outlines of English Syntax*: Mätzner to Eduard Mätzner's *Englische Grammatik*. Abbott and Kellner are referred to by sections, Mätzner by pages. O.E. = Old English: M.E. = Middle English: E.E. = Elizabethan English: Md. E. = Modern English: F 1 = First Folio: F 2 = Second Folio: Ff. = Folios.]

The Title. The name *As You Like It* was doubtless suggested by a phrase in Lodge's preface, "If you like it, so; and yet I will be yours in duty, if you be mine in favour". Its significance is sufficiently plain from the epilogue: "I charge you, O women, for the love you bear to men, to like as much of this play as please you: and I charge you, O men, for the love you bear to women...that between you and the women the play may please". It is merely a playful challenge to the audience.

Dramatis Personæ. *Jaques.* Is 'Jaques' a monosyllable or a disyllable? The answer depends upon another question, 'Is the name French or English?' As an English name it was common in Shakespeare's native county of Warwick, and was pronounced and even written 'Jakes'. But in the only two places in this play where the metre is a guide we require a disyllable. These are ii. 1. 26—"The melancholy Ja-ques grieves at that", and v. 4. 200, "Stay, Ja-ques, stay". Now, if the name is French, Shakespeare would sound the final *es*, as he does in Parollés. And there can be no reasonable objection to a French name in a play which already includes Amiens, Dennis, and Le Beau.

The names *Oliver* and *Orlando* are from the legends of Charlemagne, and their use may have been suggested by Lodge's reference to the "twelve peers" of France. Orlando is an Italian form of Rowland. *Silvius* and *Phebe*, the idyllic characters, have conventional Latin names; *William* and *Audrey*, the comic rustics, are plain English. *Corin* stands half-way between them, and his name is a homely form of Virgil's Corydon. *Touchstone* explains itself.

Rosalind (Spanish = 'rose-sweet') is a favourite name in the literature of the period. Shakespeare has taken it, in this instance, from Lodge; but he has a Rosaline in *Love's Labour's Lost*, and another in *Romeo and Juliet*; and the name occurs also in Spenser, and in Marston.

112

Act I.—Scene I.

It is the first care of every story-teller to let us know where we are. The novelist can do this directly, by means of description and narration; but such a course is not open to the dramatist within the limits of his own art. He may indeed use a Prologue, like Quince in *A Midsummer-Night's Dream*:

> "This man is Pyramus, if you would know;
> This beauteous lady Thisby is certain".

But the Prologue is obviously no part of the play; and Shakespeare generally discards it, and gives the required information by properly dramatic means.

The dramatist's next care is to get his action under way. Shakespeare was sometimes content to secure these objects one at a time; then the explanatory scene is merely a veiled, or represented, prologue. But as a rule he tries to combine both functions. In *As You Like It* Orlando's opening speech is of the nature of a represented prologue; yet so far starts the action, as it leaves him warm for the quarrel that follows. The action thus fairly started, the further explanations necessary are given incidentally in the course of the scene.

For Orlando and Oliver the situation is created by the terms of their father's will. Here Shakespeare might have followed Lodge, and put before us the old knight's deathbed and his testamentary depositions. But such a scene would be too remote in time, and of too little interest in itself. By making Orlando pour out his wrongs to Adam he secures another advantage. We see not only how things stand between the brothers, but also—and this is equally important—the temper in which Orlando takes his situation.

We are now enlightened about the hero. The entry of Charles gives Shakespeare the chance of showing a little more of his canvas, and disclosing the outward circumstances of the heroine. Oliver greets the wrestler, and in a series of casual questions (for his mind is full of his recent discomfiture) asks the news at court. By this means we learn that the old duke has been banished by his brother, and now lives an exile in Arden; while his daughter Rosalind stays on at court with her dear cousin. Oliver and Charles then concert their plot, and prepare us for the wrestling scene.

1-4. If the text is sound we must take "it was bequeathed" and "(It was) charged" impersonally = 'a thousand crowns were bequeathed to me', and 'my brother was charged'. But "it was charged my brother" is very harsh for 'my brother was charged'; and there is nothing to which we can refer "his blessing". The best and easiest emendation is "it was upon this fashion; he bequeathed, &c.". *He* may easily have been overlooked before *be*. It is impossible to understand a subject to *bequeathed*; v. 4. **151** is not a real parallel, for there a subject has been expressed two lines before.

2. **but poor a thousand crowns.** On the analogy of *so*+adj. +article, we sometimes find *a* placed between the adjective and the noun, even when the former is qualified by other adverbs than *so*, *e.g.* by *but* in this case. (Kellner, § 462.) Cf. "With more tame a tongue", *Measure for Measure*, ii. 2. 46. This condition is most important for understanding Oliver's character. See Introduction III.

3. **on his blessing,** on pain of losing his blessing.

5. **school:** in Shakespeare=any place of instruction: here, a university. We still speak of a 'school of medicine'.

11. **riders dearly hired:** supply 'are'.

15. **his countenance,** his deportment towards me. Walker thinks that the word is here used for 'allowance', 'maintenance'. But this sense of *countenance* is confined to legal writers. See Glossary.

16. **bars me the place,** debars me from the position. The preposition is often omitted after verbs of 'ablation'.

17. **mines my gentility,** undermines my gentle birth. It is characteristic of Orlando, that what he feels most is the neglect of his education.

25. **what make you here?** Oliver simply means 'what are you doing here?' Orlando plays on the word in the sense of 'produce'.

28. **Marry** keeps up the punning. As an expletive it means 'By (the Virgin) Mary'.

30. **be naught awhile.** This form of words was common, as a petty malediction, like 'and be hanged to you'. But Oliver also plays on the literal meaning—'Better be nothing than be marring yourself'.

32. **What prodigal portion have I spent,** what portion have I spent like a prodigal. The word which should qualify the action is transferred by anticipation to the object. This proleptic use of the adjective, as it is called [Gk. πρόληψις = anticipation], is common in Shakespeare. The reference is to the parable of the Prodigal Son, *Luke* xv. [Schmidt thinks *prodigal* simply = 'ample'. But the obvious reference to the parable makes this unlikely.]

37. **him I am before.** *Him* for *he* is fairly common after *than* and *as*. Here it may be due to attraction to *whom* understood.

38-64. Throughout this dialogue, observe that Orlando is insisting not so much on his claims as a brother as on his rights as a gentleman.

38. **I know you are my eldest brother.** Both words are emphatic. 'Remember that though younger I am still your brother'.

38. **in the gentle condition of blood,** as becomes well-born brothers. *Gentle*, as often, connotes good birth: for *blood* in the sense of relationship, see ii. 3. 37.

39. The courtesy of nations, the usage of the civilized world, *jus gentium*: *viz.* the law of primogeniture.

41. tradition, customary usage.

43. nearer to his reverence: the fact that you are my elder gives you more claim to the respect due to him.

45, 46. With the words "What, boy!" Oliver strikes at Orlando, who, stung by the taunt and the blow, seizes him by the throat. The meaning of "you are too young in this" is clear from the passage in Lodge by which it was suggested: "though I am the eldest by birth", says Saladin, "I am the youngest (*i.e.* least experienced) to perform any martial exploits".

47. villain. Oliver uses the word in its modern sense; literally it means a low-born person, a serf; and so it suits Orlando to take it. See Glossary.

48. Orlando feels that the insult to himself is an insult to his father. Filial piety is a trait which he shares with Rosalind.

48. With this fierce punning cf. Gaunt's bitter play on his own name, *Richard II.*, ii. 1. 73: Shakespeare often makes intense feeling express itself in biting jests.

54. for your father's remembrance, for the sake of your father's memory.

59. obscuring and hiding from me. These two words, one Latin and the other English, may mean exactly the same thing (Bilingualism), like "acknowledge and confess" in the Prayer Book; "left and abandoned" (ii. 1. 50); "search and inquisition" (ii. 2. 20); "sanctified and holy" (ii. 3. 13). This kind of tautology dates from M.E., when French and English existed side by side, and the English term was needed to paraphrase the French. Or the meaning may be 'obscuring (in me) and hiding from me'.

63. allottery, share. See Glossary.

65-69. Observe the use of *thou* and *you* in this speech and throughout the whole scene. *Thou* (like *Du* in German) was the pronoun of familiarity, and of the contempt it is said to breed: *you* (like German *Sie*) of more ceremonious intercourse. But when a person is addressed with the formal *sir*, even in contempt, the pronoun is regularly *you*. (Abb. §§ 231, 232.)

70. At Orlando's little attempt at peacemaking Oliver turns and vents his spleen on Adam, whose fault is to have witnessed his discomfiture.

74. grow upon me, encroach upon me, 'put out your horns', as we might say. The metaphor is continued in **rankness,** *i.e.* luxuriant growth, insolence. In Oliver's defence it should be noted that to give up the thousand crowns would be to confess himself in the wrong. His motive is not mere greed.

75. no...neither: in early English two or more negatives may be used, simply to strengthen the negation.

82. Again it should be noted in extenuation that Oliver acts in a passion. The chance of revenge flashes upon him, and, in Shakespeare's own words, "the sight of means to do ill deeds makes ill deeds done". In Lodge, the brothers continue some time in amity, and the plot is concerted in cold blood.

83. to-morrow. This is the first of those "short-time notes" which are scattered through the play. See Introduction III.

85. Good Monsieur Charles is itself a greeting, and there is no need to read (with Walker) "Good morrow, Monsieur Charles".

87. Nor need we either make Oliver ask "what's the news", or Charles answer "there's no new news". Indeed, "there's no new news but the old news" is absurd.

89. In this speech of the wrestler's, Shakespeare can hardly be said to conceal his art. Oliver already knows that there is a new court. After this, however, his inquiries about Rosalind follow naturally enough.

94. the duke's daughter. Charles, as a court servant, calls the new duke simply "the duke". Perhaps he means to correct Oliver; at any rate Oliver in his next question speaks of the "old duke".

95. By making the two Dukes brothers (as in the *Tempest*) Shakespeare has refined on Lodge. He has reduplicated the motif of fraternal enmity: and he has given the friendship of Rosalind and Celia a natural ground in their blood-relationship—nature's protest, as it were, against the feud between their fathers.

96. died to stay, died from staying. Cf. v. 2. 94, "Why blame you me to love you", *i.e.* for loving you. Such infinitives are different cases of the gerund (=*manendo, ob amandum*), with which *to* was originally used, in its locative sense; cf. Ger. *zu*=at, and our 'to-day'.

99. Where will the old duke live? The use of the future, and Charles's 'already', show that the Duke's flight is recent.

100. Arden. The real forest of Ardennes lies partly in the French department of that name, but chiefly in Namur, Liège, and Luxemburg. But Shakespeare's forest is in fairyland—an English fairyland with glimpses of the classical Arcadia. The name 'Arden' also belonged to the wooded part of Warwickshire, and this may have been in Shakespeare's mind as well.

101. a many merry men. We still say 'a few men'. In older English the indefinite article was prefixed to other adjectives of number as well. Some think that *many* is a noun here=a many (*i.e. menie*=company) of merry men.

104. **fleet the time**, make the time flit. *Fleet* is elsewhere intransitive. Cf. iii. 5, 5, "falls not the axe"=does not let fall; and note there.

105. **the golden world**, the Golden Age, *i.e.* the state of innocence from which, as the ancients thought, man had gradually degenerated. For *world*=state of things, cf. i. 2. 250, "hereafter in a better world than this". This is in accordance with the etymology—O.E. *wer-eld*, age of men.

108. **a matter**, a certain matter.

112. **shall acquit him**, will have to acquit himself. *Shall* originally means 'to owe', and here retains the notion of compulsion (Abb. § 315).

115. **withal**: an emphatic 'with', generally used at the end of a sentence. Here it means 'with it'.

118. This is a theme which Shakespeare has often handled—*e.g. King John*, iii. 3, (John and Hubert plot Arthur's death); *Tempest*, ii. 1, (Antonio and Sebastian plot Alonzo's death). Here there are no indirect suggestions and dark hints, but plain lying and an appeal to fear. The wrestler is an innocent accomplice. In Lodge, he is bribed "with rich rewards".

122. **it is**: used of persons; here in a tone of contempt.

123. **emulator**: properly, a rival: here in bad sense. See Glossary.

124. **contriver**, plotter. **natural brother**, *i.e.* brother by birth, with no idea of illegitimacy.

125. **I had as lief**, I would as soon. For *lief* see Glossary.

126. **thou wert best**: properly "(to) thee (it) were best". The impersonal construction has yielded to the personal. Cf. 'if it please you' and 'if you please'; 'it likes me' and 'I like it' (Kellner, § 338).

128. **grace himself on thee**, distinguish himself at your expense.

133. **brotherly**, with the reserve natural to a brother.

133. **anatomize him as he is**, expose his real nature.

137. **I'll give him his payment**, I'll pay him out, punish him.

141. **gamester**, lively fellow. See Glossary.

142. **he**, for *him*. The brevity of the expression disguises the bad grammar.

143. **noble device**, lofty aspirations.

144. **enchantingly**, as if it were the effect of an enchantment. Cf. "If the rascal have not given me medicines to make me love him, I'll be hanged", *1 Henry IV.*, ii. 2. 19.

145. in the heart of, beloved by.

148. kindle, incite.

148. Of this soliloquy Coleridge said in 1810, "This has always seemed to me one of the most un-Shakespearian speeches in all the genuine works of our poet". But in 1818 he wrote, "I dare not say that this seeming unnaturalness is not in the nature of an abused wilfulness, when united with a strong intellect". "An abused wilfulness" is the key to Oliver's character.

Scene 2.

This scene falls naturally into two parts, (1) the conversation of the ladies with each other, with Touchstone, and with Le Beau: (2) the wrestling match, and love at first sight. The first part is entirely of Shakespeare's invention. In Lodge, Rosalind's first appearance is among the ladies who are watching the wrestling. But Shakespeare leaves Oliver's plot to work itself out, and carries us on to make the acquaintance of the heroine, that we may watch the wrestling by her side and see Orlando through her eyes.

Rosalind's circumstances we already know; we are now to see how she bears them. She is not rebellious, like Orlando, but there is a cloud upon her spirits, due partly to her father's banishment, partly to the shadow cast by coming events. Celia's superior cheerfulness gives her the lead at first. Rosalind takes only a half-hearted share in bantering Touchstone. But when she learns that the successful wrestler is the son of her father's old friend her heart is touched, and Celia begins to slip into her natural place of the amused and interested ally.

1. sweet my coz, a common inversion in addresses. *Coz* is short for 'cousin'. See Glossary.

3. would you yet I. *I* is not in the Ff. It was added in Rowe's 2nd edition.

4. learn, teach. For the origin of this common confusion, see Glossary.

7. that I love thee. Shakespeare often omits the second preposition, when it can be easily supplied.

8. so, provided that. In full, "were (subj.) it so that".

10. if the truth...so righteously tempered. The expression is a trifle tautologous: 'if the composition of your love were really as perfect'. To *temper* is in Shakespeare to bring into condition, by mixing (of drink), by melting (of wax), or by hardening (of metal). We still say 'to temper mortar' as well as 'to temper steel'.

11. so...as, for *as...as*, is common in Shakespeare, and still in vulgar language—'So merry as a grig' (Q.).

14. but I. When *but* and *save* are followed by the nominative they should be regarded as conjunctions, rather than prepositions, with some verb omitted (Kellner, § 207). Cf. i. 1. 142.

21. Note the dramatic irony of the proposed 'sport'. Before the scene is over she is in love in earnest. Cf. Lodge:—"She accounted love a toy...that as it was taken in with a gaze, might be shaken off with a wink". But Shakespeare's Rosalind would not talk so after she had seen Orlando.

24. with safety of a pure blush. 'With preservation of your modesty' is an abstract equivalent: but Shakespeare thinks in images.

27. the good housewife Fortune. "Good housewife" here only = good dame. In *Antony*, iv. 15, 44, "that the false housewife Fortune break her wheel", it means 'hussy', which is merely a short form of the word. Fortune has a wheel, to signify, as Fluellen explains (*Henry V.*, iii. 6. 35), "that she is turning, and inconstant, and mutability, and variation". Celia means to drive her into constancy with wit.

30. blind woman. Walker thinks that we should print *blind-woman*, *wiseman*, &c., as single words, with the accent on the first syllable. Cf. 'blindman's buff', and Bunyan's 'Mr. Worldly Wiseman'. In O.E. the adjective was more strongly accented than the noun after it.

33. honest, chaste. See Glossary.

34. ill-favouredly. The adverb here expresses, not manner or degree, but state or condition, *i.e.* it has the force of an adjective.

35. Shakespeare is fond (as Moberly points out) of thus contrasting Nature with the other powers which operate in life; with Fortune as here: with Law and Custom as in i. 1. 40: with the Supernatural as in *Tempest*, v. 243, "more than nature Was even conduct of"; and with Art, as in *Winter's Tale*, iv. 4. 90, "over that art Which you say adds to nature, is an art That nature makes".

38. Celia retorts 'Though Fortune cannot make our natural gifts, she can mar them'.

Enter TOUCHSTONE. The Ff. have "enter Clowne", and his speeches throughout this scene are marked *Clo*. The change was made by Theobald in his 2nd edition. Wright thinks that the early description of Touchstone as "the clownish fool" and "the roynish clown" hardly prepares us for the motley-minded gentleman of the later acts: and Furness goes so far as to suggest that the Clown of this scene is not Touchstone at all. But see Appendix B.

43. natural, an idiot. The word has still this sense in Scotch. Touchstone is of course no 'natural', but it suits Rosalind's punning wit to call him so. If she speaks of his 'dulness' here, she calls him a "dull fool" in iii. 2. 112, even when he has turned squire of dames.

45. **perceiving.** F 1, *perceiveth*. We must either correct as in the text, with F 2, or read 'and hath'.

48. An allusion to the saying "Wit, whither wilt?" Cf. iv. 1. 146.

49. **Mistress**: improperly used by Touchstone in addressing princesses. Costard makes the same blunder (*Love's Labour's Lost*, iv. 1. 49).

71. In F 1 this speech is given to Rosalind. See Appendix B.

71. **honour him enough**: so F 1, and this makes good sense, 'My father's love is enough to put him beyond your satire'. Many edd. read "honour him: enough!" (Hanmer).

72. **taxation**, satire; cf. ii. 7. 86, and see Glossary.

77. Mr. Fleay sees in this a reference to the burning of satirical books by public authority, 1st June, 1599.

80. Cf. *Love's Labour's Lost*, v. 2. 315, where Biron says of Boyet: "This fellow pecks up wit as pigeons pease, and utters it again when God doth please".

As Rosaline in *Love's Labour's Lost* is in a way a pale sketch of Rosalind, so Le Beau reminds us of Boyet; and we may have here an unconscious reminiscence of the earlier play. "I always liked Le Beau," says Lady Martin; and, though the ladies make fun of the formal courtier, his advice to Orlando at the end of the scene shows sense and good feeling.

83. **Bon jour.** Such touches (cf. i. 1. 85) remind us that the scene is in France.

85-7. Celia outdoes Le Beau in his own style. 'Colour' is 'kind', as in iii. 2. 383 "cattle of this colour", and in *Twelfth Night*, ii. 3. 182, "a horse of that colour". Le Beau might have understood the word in such a connection, but Celia's use of it puzzles him. Collier thought that Le Beau pronounces 'sport' affectedly 'spot'; hence Celia's retort. But the above explanation is satisfactory.

89. **laid on with a trowel**, clumsily done, dabbed on.

91. Rosalind's puns must not be judged by modern standards of taste.

92. **amaze**, bewilder. The word (*a*, intensive; *maze*) means originally to stun, to stupefy. In E.E. it is used of any confusing emotion. We have confined it to the emotion of strong surprise.

96. **is to do**, is to be done. In O.E. the infinitive is indifferent with regard to voice, and is regularly used in the active when there is action without a subject. In Shakespeare this use of the active infinitive is especially common in this phrase; cf. "What's to do?" *Twelfth Night*, iii. 3. 38; and our "This house to let" (Kellner §§ 364, 5).

100. There comes. When the verb comes first, and the subject is as yet undetermined, the singular is the rule; especially with 'There is' (Abb. § 335).

104. As it stands the only point of Rosalind's speech is a poor pun on 'presence' and 'presents'. To better this, Farmer proposed to give the words "with bills on their necks" to Le Beau. 'Bills' will then mean forest-bills; cf. Lodge, "Rosader came pacing towards them with his forest-bill on his neck". This would give us two puns instead of one. "Be it known unto all men, &c." is a translation of *Noverint univers. per præsentes*, the usual preamble of bills. Nash (1589) speaks of those (? Shakespeare) "who had left the trade of *noverint*, whereto they were born, for handfuls of tragical speeches". Cf. iii. 1. 17, and note there.

106. By describing the wrestling instead of representing it, Shakespeare saves up our interest for the final bout; and perhaps, though he has no objection to plenty of blood in his tragedies, he felt that the scene would be too harrowing for the occasion. The rib-breaking reminds us of Gamelyn—

"And kast him on the left syde, that three ribbes to-brake,
And therto his oon arm, that yaf a gret crake". (245–6.)

Lodge's wrestler kills his men outright. See Appendix A.

107. which Charles. *Which* being originally an adj. (E. E. *hwilc* = who-like) is used with the repeated antecedent, for greater exactness (Abb. § 269).

112. So far Rosalind has been the wit. The woman now begins to come out.

119. is there any else longs. *Any* = anybody. This construction, explained by Abb. (§ 244) as omission of the relative, is really a relic of an earlier construction out of which the relative clause grew. This is the so-called ἀπὸ κοινοῦ construction of one subject with two predicates. (Kellner, §§ 111, 274.)

119. see…this music. *See* is used of perception in general. Cf. 'When ye see the south wind blow'.

119. broken music is part music, arranged for different instruments > < consort-music, for sets of the same instrument. Cf. Bacon, *Sylva*, § 278, "In that music which we call broken-music or consort-music, some consorts of instruments are sweeter than others". Shakespeare has the same pun again in *Henry V.*, v. 2. 263, and in *Troilus*, iii. 1. 52.

127. 'Let him take the risk of his obstinacy.' For **entreated**, see Glossary. The Duke's first words, and his contemptuous 'crept', mark the choleric tyrant.

130. successfully: see i. 2. 34.

131. are you crept. In O.E. *be* was used with intransitive, *have* with transitive verbs. Shakespeare commonly uses *be* with intransitive verbs of motion; so do we still with 'come' and 'go'.

135. such odds in the man. In Shakespeare *odds* means superiority quite as often as inequality. There is no need, therefore, to read *men*.

140. princess' call (so Dyce). Ff. *princesse cals*; but Orlando says "I attend them", and though it was Celia who gave the order, it is Rosalind who asks the question. Most edd. read *princesses call*, with Theobald. It is allowed that *s* may be omitted after sibilants in the possessive sing.; König (p. 17) gives sixteen instances of plurals in which, though printed (in the folios), it is not pronounced: and (p. 16) three in which it is not printed. These are *Antipholus* (*Comedy of Errors*, v. 1. 357): *mistress'* (*Taming of the Shrew*, i. 2. 277); and *princess* (*Tempest*, i. 2. 173). Add *mistress* (pl.) in *Lover's Complaint*, 142. This is a relic of M.E. usage. Cf. also Abb. § 471.

148. The emphasis is on *saw* and *knew*: 'If you used your senses, you would see'. There is no need to read *our eyes...our judgment*.

152. therefore, on that account.

154. might: more respectful than *may*. So we say 'we wished to ask', when we mean 'we wish', putting it as if our hearer's mind were already made up.

156. wherein. The natural antecedent would be 'thoughts': but, after 'guilty', *in* is always used of the crime; we must therefore supply 'therein', as antecedent. **to deny=**in denying. So the sentence means 'Punish me not for what I own I am guilty of, viz. of denying, &c.'. I have punctuated accordingly.

156. much. The use of *much* as adv. with adj. probably comes from its use with participles, where it represents the instrumental case (Herford).

162. only goes with **fill** and would now be placed next to it. Shakespeare transposes advs. freely (for emphasis), especially advs. of limitation, such as *only*, *but*. (Abb. § 420.) The whole of this dialogue between Orlando and the ladies is of Shakespeare's own invention. It helps to engage their interest (and ours) in the hero, and to show the real spirit—far from that of the 'gamester'—in which he has entered the lists. We never sympathize with him more than at this last confession of quiet hopelessness.

168. These lines accentuate the difference between Orlando's modesty and the "haughty heart" that "goeth before a fall".

175. An suggested by Theobald. The printer, say Clark and Wright, may have mistaken *Orl. And* for *Orland*. For the spelling *and* see Glossary.

176. ways: not the plural but genitive singular in locative sense.

Cf. German *weges*. The genitive of space is much less common in O.E. than the genitive of time.

177. Hercules, the god of strength in classical mythology.

179. *Wrestle*: **182.** *Shout*: the imperative form of these stage-directions seems to show that the play was printed from an acting copy. See Appendix B.

186. In Lodge the wrestler is killed outright.

189. "When they knew him to be the youngest son of Sir John of Bordeaux, the King rose from his seat and embraced him" (Lodge). This slight change is a great gain (1) *in dramatic point*—Orlando has not yet reached the nadir of his fortunes; (2) *in dramatic propriety*—it affords a reason for Orlando's sudden retirement from the court, and furnishes a double bond between him and Rosalind, the bond of sympathy and the bond of hereditary friendship; (3) *in characterization*—it gives a new colour to the action of the Duke in banishing Oliver (see further on iii. 1), and stirs his smouldering temper into the blaze which results in the banishment of Rosalind.

Note how the Duke recurs in the last line of his speech to the thought of the first.

192. still, always.

193. shouldst. Shakespeare uses *should* even in the conclusion of a condition, with no notion of duty.

199. His youngest son—, Orlando breaks off. **calling,** title; not elsewhere used in this sense.

208. sticks me at heart. The two meanings of *stick*, (1) stab, (2) cleave, are not far apart in Shakespeare. The question here is rather one of construction—'stabs me (acc.) to the heart'; or 'cleaves to my heart', in which case *me* is dative. But for this Shakespeare would probably have said 'sticks in my heart'.

210. Abb. scans

'But just' | ly as' | you have' | exceed" | all pro' | mise'.

His instances, however, do not support such a slurring of *-ed* after *-d*, and I prefer to scan (with König),

'But just' | ly as' | you've ex' | ceed'ed | all pro' | mise'.

See Prosody, 4 *a β*.

211. shall be, will certainly be. Cf. i. 1. 119.

Dr. Johnson complains that the ladies give away their hearts too easily. Three times in this single play Shakespeare has treated the theme of love at first sight, handling it each time in a way that gives some notion of his infinite variety. In Rosalind's case generous sympathy leads up to love. Note her shy, ambiguous confession and lingering withdrawal. Orlando, like the ideal lover he is, is simply tongue-tied. His prototype in the novel shows much more self-possession: he steps into a tent and acknowledges his devotion in a sonnet.

212. out of suits with fortune, out of fortune's suite, *i.e.* service. Schmidt compares the feudal term 'suit and service'.

213. could give, could find it in her heart to give.

217. quintain. The quintain in its simplest form was a post with revolving arms. At this the tilter ran, his object being to strike one arm and dodge the swing of the other. Later it was made in the form of a Turk or Saracen, with a shield on his left arm and a sword in his right hand. This is the form Orlando has in mind. 'I stand like a stock, a man of wood.' For derivation, see Glossary.

221. Celia slily repeats Rosalind's "Shall we go, coz?" of half a dozen lines before.

222. Have with you, come along. This use of *have* in such phrases as 'have with', 'have at', 'have after', &c., has not been explained. It dates from M.E., where it is used as a colloquialism (Mätzner, i. 386). From Lodge's expression, "I will have amongst you with my sword", we should infer an ellipse of 'I will'. But this full form is not found in M.E.

228. Le Beau is formal, even in doing a kindness.

230. condition, state of mind, disposition.

232. humorous. In ancient physiology, the 'humours' are the four essential fluids of the body: bile, blood, black-bile, and phlegm; corresponding to the four elements: fire, air, earth, and water. The mixture of these humours produced the temperament (κρᾶσις, mixture) of a man, which was choleric, sanguine, melancholy, or phlegmatic according to the 'humour' which predominated. A humorous man is one who is at the mercy of his moods, whatever they may be. In the Duke's case, choler seems to be the predominant humour, but Le Beau is intentionally vague. See also iii. 2. 386.

233. than I to speak of. In Shakespeare (as in M.E.) we sometimes find the nominative and infinitive where we should expect the accusative, after substantives, adjectives, and impersonal verbs. Cf. *Comedy of Errors*, i. 1. 33, "A heavier task could not have been imposed Than I to speak my griefs unspeakable"='than that I should speak'. So here, "than I to speak of"='than that I should speak of it'. (Kellner § 406.)

238. lesser: so Spedding. Ff. *taller*. See App. B.

243-249. There was no hint of this in what Charles told Oliver; but Le Beau belongs to the inner circle at the court. This explanation is thrown forward here to prepare us for the Duke's outburst in the next scene. Doubtless Le Beau gives the true reason for his conduct. Lodge's Torismond is a far more politic tyrant. He fears that one of the peers may marry Rosalind and aspire to the crown.

253. from the smoke into the smother, out of the frying-pan into the fire. See Glossary.

Scene 3.

This scene falls into three part; (1) the prose dialogue between the ladies, ll. 1–33; (2) the sentence of banishment, ll. 34–82; (3) the preparations for flight, ll. 83 to end.

The first part is all Shakespeare's own. His object (as in i. 2) is to let us see the mind of the heroine, and to show how far the bud of love which peeped out in the wrestling scene is on its way to flower. Le Beau's information (i. 2. 243–248) throws a tinge of dramatic irony over this light talk. We know the fate that hangs over Rosalind, but she (as her amazed "Me, uncle?" shows) has no suspicion of it. Her sighs are all for Orlando now, as in i. 2 they were for her father. (This is the real reason for preferring the old reading in line 9.)

Observe that Rosalind and Celia talk prose when alone. Lines 83 to end are the exception which proves the rule. With the entrance of the Duke the feeling rises to the pitch of verse: when he has left, Rosalind and Celia continue to use verse because the excitement of Rosalind's doom is still upon them.

1. Cupid. The god of love in classical mythology. Observe the number of these classical allusions throughout the play, and especially in the conversation of the ladies. Hercules (i. 2. 177), Cupid and Juno in this scene, Jupiter (ii. 4. 1), Pythagoras (iii. 2. 171), Troilus, Hero and Leander (iv. 1. 86–91), &c.—all in speeches by Rosalind or Celia. Some of this is no doubt due to Lodge; but in the main it betokens the immense influence of Ovid. Note that Celia, who is fancy-free, still does most of the talking.

5. reasons, talk. Rosalind plays on the word.

9. my child's father: changed by Rowe (and Coleridge) to *my father's child.* But see introductory note, and the warning on i. 2. 91.

10. working-day world, every-day state of things; also 'work-a-day'.

14. coat, petticoat. Shakespeare does not use it elsewhere in this sense; but it is common enough in ballad-poetry.

17. cry 'hem' and have him. A proverb? or a game? The pun is bettered by pronouncing *ha'him*: cf. *Taming of the Shrew,* v. 2. 181, where "ha't" rhymes to "Kate".

22. on such a sudden. Shakespeare has "on a sudden" else-where, but not "on such a sudden". For adjs. used as nouns cf. Abb. § 5.

27. by this kind of chase, by this way of following the argument. The word 'dear' may (intentionally or unintentionally) have sug-

gested the metaphor. Cf. the pun in *Merry Wives*, v. 5. 122, "I
will always count you for my deer".

28. dearly, excessively. Cf. "my dearest foe", *Hamlet*, i. 2. 182.
The word is used in E.E. "of anything that touches us nearly, in
love or hate, joy or sorrow" (Wright); and, in fact, of anything
excessive in its kind: cf. "your dearest speed", *I Henry IV.*,
v. 5. 36.

30. We must not analyse these negatives too curiously. "Why
should I not?"—hate him or not hate him. "Doth he not deserve
well?" to be hated, as the son of my father's enemy, or (absolutely)
"are not his deserts high?" Rosalind takes as many of the negatives
as suit her.

33. Cf. Lodge: "the figure of wrath portrayed in his brow".

34. Mistress: "used with some unkindness or contempt of or
to women, from whom the affections of the speaker have been
estranged". (Schmidt.) Cf. iii. 5. 45. **with your safest haste:**
the sooner the better for you.

36. Cf. Lodge (Torismond to Saladin): "See thy departure be
within ten days".

36. if that. *That* is added to *if, though, since,* &c. on the analogy
of 'who that', 'when that', &c. In the latter case it was added to
give a relative sense to words originally interrogative. The full
form is found in Chaucer, *Pardoner's Tale*, 375, "If so were that I
might": which shows that after these conjunctions an ellipsis must
be supplied. Cf. i. 3. 108, "because that"; ii. 7. 75, "when that"
(Abb. § 287).

45. The Duke makes no specific charge, because he has none to
make, nothing but general mistrust, bred of his own "rough and
envious disposition".

46. purgation, exculpation, a quasi-legal use of a legal term.
Cf. v. 4. 42; and note on iii. 1. 17.

52. At the implied insult to her father, Rosalind is up in arms at
once. This is the first hint of that high spirit which carries her
through all her trials and lies behind her buoyant wit. If she is a
woman she is a princess too.

55. friends, relatives. Herford attributes this sense (still a common one) to Scandinavian influence; O.N. *frœndi* always = kinsmen.

57-8. so much to think: *as* omitted, says Abb. § 281. But
perhaps this is a relic of the gerundial infinitive; 'to think' = in
thinking.

63. remorse, compassion, as generally in Shakespeare. Less
often = compunction.

64. Note the lapse of time implied, and see Introd. III. With this
speech compare the picture of girl-friendship, less tender but still

charming, between Helena and Hermia—*A Midsummer-Night's Dream*, iii. 2. 203, &c.—

> "We, Hermia, like two artificial gods,
> Have with our needles created both one flower,
> Both on one sampler, on one cushion sitting,
> Both warbling of one song, both in one key.
>   ...So we grew together
> Like to a double cherry, seeming parted,
> But yet an union in partition".

Beatrice and Hero, in *Much Ado*, are a very different pair. In spite of Beatrice's chivalrous warmth in her cousin's cause, their natures are too unlike for such perfect intimacy.

68. Juno's swans. See App. B. Ovid (*Met.* x. 708) speaks of the *junctis cygnis*, 'coupled swans', of Venus's car. Shakespeare must have known the passage well, for it comes after the story of Atalanta (see iii. 2. 144) and before that of the death of Adonis. The words may be a misprint after all, *Iuno's* for *Venus'*.

73. Thou art a fool: cf. 80, "You are a fool". The Duke has a trick of repeating himself, like George III. (Cf. i. 2. 190 with i. 2. 196, and note there.) Here the change of pronouns shows that he has left argument for authority. He treats Celia like a child. Lodge's usurper, afraid of endangering his crown, banishes his daughter when she tries to defend her cousin—an act as unnatural as it is unnecessary.

90. Johnson's defence of the text is sufficient. "Where," he asks, "would be the absurdity of saying, 'You know not the law which teaches you to do right'?" Here, too, the use of the indicative ("Which teacheth", not "Which would teach") subtly implies that the love is really there, and gives the sentence a rhetorical turn.

90. am for *are*. In E.E., as in Latin, the verb may go with the nearest subject.

91. For a moment the greatness of her love gives Celia the lead. But as soon as Rosalind has recovered from the shock of her sentence she appropriates Celia's proposal and improves upon it. She is eminently 'efficient', like most of Shakespeare's women. Note that the suggestion of male disguise comes from her, as well as the proposal to steal the fool. From this point onward there is no doubt as to the relative positions of the cousins.

95. change, change of fortune. F 2, *charge*, *i.e.* burden; but *charge* (= burden entrusted or accepted) would hardly apply to Rosalind's sentence.

97. Note the 'pathetic fallacy' common in all poetry, which sees in Nature the reflex of our moods. Cf. Milton, *Paradise Lost*, ix 101—

> "Sky loured, and, muttering thunder, some sad drops
>   Wept at completing of the mortal Sin
>   Original".

107. Cf. Lodge: "I, thou seest, am of a tall stature, and would very well become the person and apparel of a page; thou shalt be my mistress, and I will play the man so properly that, trust me, in what company soever I come, I will not be discovered. I will buy me a suit, and have my rapier very handsomely at my side, and if any knave offer wrong, your page will show him the point of his weapon."

Shakespeare makes Rosalind play the brother, a more proper escort for an errant lady, and better suited for the prominent part she is to take in the forest scenes. Rosalind has no occasion to display her valour, but Shakespeare has used the hint again in *Twelfth Night* (iii. 4), in Viola's duel with Sir Andrew Aguecheek.

109. **all points.** The preposition is often omitted in adverbial expressions of time, manner, &c. Cf. iii. 1. 2.

114. **mannish** is to 'masculine' as 'womanish' to 'feminine': *ish* is contemptuous.

115. **outface it.** *It* is used indefinitely as the object of a verb when the action is (so to speak) its own object. (Abb. § 226; Kellner, § 283). Cf. the colloquialisms 'rough it', 'go it', &c. **outface.** Vbs. compounded with *out* mean (1) to excel in, or (2) to carry to an end, the action of the verb; (1) is the commoner meaning in E.E., *e.g. outbrag, outswear, outherod. Outface* has both : (1) to face down, to cow; (2) to face out, to brazen a thing out. Cf. *Merchant of Venice,* iv. 2. 17, "we'll outface them and outswear them too."

118. **Ganymede,** a beautiful boy, beloved by Jupiter, who (in the form of an eagle) carried him off and made him his cup-bearer. (Ovid, *Met.* x. 155-161.)

121. Scan 'No lónger Céliá but Áliéna'. **Celia** is a trisyllable as in line 60. **Aliéna** (Lat.)=stranger. These names are taken from Lodge.

130, 131. With Rosalind's banishment a natural pause in the action is reached, and the First Act closes. It closes upon the word 'content', the word which strikes the key-note of the Second Act. 'Content' is the last word that Orlando utters as he turns his back upon his brother's house. 'Content' is the burden of the exiled Duke's first speech. The lovers once safe together in Act Third, a livelier sentiment begins to prevail.

Act II.   Scene I.

Leaving Rosalind meditating flight, we are carried on to see the place in which the rest of her fortunes are to be transacted. This scene contributes nothing to the action of the play. It has two closely allied functions: (1) to describe the natural background, the free forest life in which the lovers are to meet: (2) to describe the moral background, in the persons of the Duke and Jaques. Moreover, coming where they do, these forest scenes supply a broad bar of neutral colour between the somewhat gloomy hues of Act i. and the radiant mirth and tenderness of Act iii.

1. **co-mates**: a fine redundancy, only here.

2. **old custom**: 6. **The seasons' difference.** We are meant to feel that years have been passed in exile. (See Introduction III.)

3. Note the abundant alliteration throughout this scene, especially on the labials *p, f, b*, and the liquids *l* and *m*, which English verse loves. There is little of this in the plain narrative of Act i: its use now marks a more elaborate and brooding style.

5. **Here feel we but the penalty of Adam.** Ff. *not,* Theobald *but.* Theobald's correction seems absolutely necessary. The penalty of Adam is the difference of the seasons. Shakespeare follows the Classical, not the Biblical account. Ovid (*Met.* i. 107) describes the Golden Age as a perpetual spring. Cf. also Virgil, *Georgics*, ii. 336; and Milton, *Paradise Lost*, x. 678—

> " else had the spring
> Perpetual smiled on earth with vernant flowers ".

Those who defend the Folios explain the penalty of Adam as the curse of labour (*Genesis* iii. 17; " cursed is the ground for thy sake ") and mark a long parenthesis between "the seasons' difference" and "these are counsellors".

6. Here begins the description of the natural background, which is deftly continued in the First Lord's speech. The winter's wind, the antique oak, the deer, the brawling brook, these taken together form a picture sufficiently complete, of which Amiens gives the lyrical rendering.

6. **as**, such as: often introduces all the instances, and so comes to be = namely.

8. **Which**, as to which. Owing to the interposed clauses, the form of the sentence is changed (anacoluthon).

11. **feelingly**, by making themselves felt.

13. **venomous.** This popular belief, like so many others, has some truth in it. The pustules of the toad's skin really contain an irritant poison.

14. This wide-spread superstition is probably an instance of popular etymology. The Batrachites or toad-stone of the ancients was so called because it was like the toad in colour; but popular derivation took the termination *-ites* to represent—as it often does—the natural product of the animal.

18. So Upton, much to the improvement of the sense. The Ff. give the whole line to Amiens.

E

(M 7)

19, 20. "This is one of the interesting passages in which a great writer reflects upon his own expressions with pleasure or surprise" (Moberly). Shakespeare thus reflects once or twice upon songs; cf. especially *Twelfth Night*, ii. 4. 44, "Mark it, Cesario, it is old and plain, &c.".

21. us, for ourselves; the so-called *dativus commodi* (Kellner, § 190).

22. it irks me, it vexes me.

22. fools: in E.E. often a term of endearment or pity. Cf. line 40 below. Compare 'silly' = (1) blessed (*selig*), (2) innocent (often in E.E.), (3) weak-minded. And contrast 'fond'.

23. native burghers. Lodge twice has the same 'conceit': "To fat thy sheep, the citizens of field"; "Around her wondering stood The citizens of wood".

24. Forked heads were distinguished from barbed heads by having the points turned the other way. But here the expression seems to be used loosely for arrowheads in general.

26. Jaques, the most important of the 'background characters', is now elaborately introduced. Such an introduction is needed to interest us beforehand in a person who contributes nothing to the action. By using narrative (as in i. 1) Shakespeare is able to present him in a characteristic attitude, which could not have been put on the stage. Note that he is at once dubbed with his proper epithet, and contrasted with the Duke. Both are moralists in grain; but while the Duke sees good in everything, to Jaques the incidents of the forest are but a repetition of the selfishness and 'inane distress' of the world he has left behind.

31. Observe the rare and beautiful vowel-alliteration. Cf. Milton *Paradise Lost*, viii. 1, "The angel ended, and in Adam's ear". On this line Coleridge remarks, "Shakespeare never gives a description of rustic scenery merely for its own sake, or to show how well he can paint natural objects; he is never tedious or elaborate, but... usually only touches upon the larger features and broader characteristics, leaving the fillings up to the imagination...Other and inferior writers would have dwelt on this description, and worked it out with all pettiness and impertinence of detail. In Shakespeare the 'antique root' furnishes the whole picture". This is too indiscriminate. Nothing could be less true of the youthful Shakespeare. It was only after a long apprenticeship that he learned the art of suggestion, leaving details "unseen save to the eye of mind".

32. brawls: a fine poetic word, appealing at once to eye and ear.

38. These lines show Shakespeare's sympathy with animals. It was a current opinion that the deer shed tears when dying. The metaphor in line 39 is suggested by the hunt, and is appropriate in the mouth of the First Lord.

41. marked of. In O.E. the agent after passives is regularly introduced by *from*: in M.E. *of* is the rule, *with* is not uncommon, *by* is the exception: in the 16th century *by* becomes general, but *of* is still frequent in Shakespeare. (Kellner, §§ 433–435.)

44. moralize, draw a moral lesson from.

45. This incontinence of the comparing faculty Jaques shares with Shakespeare's Richard II. "The curious intellect of Jaques gives him his distinction" (Dowden). What in Richard is only the æsthetic indulgence of an unbridled fancy, is in Jaques always tagged with a sour moral—the poet making bricks for the philosopher.

46. weeping: one syllable. See Prosody, 4 *b* ε 2.

46. needless. The adj., like the verb, is either transitive or intransitive, active or passive. In E.E. many adjs. (especially those in *-ful*, *-less*, *-ble*, and *-ive*) are indifferent with regard to voice. Cf. ii. 6. 8, "comfortable", and iii. 2. 10, "unexpressive" (Kellner, §§ 249, 250).

57. Moberly thinks that Shakespeare had his father's bankruptcy in mind. But those material troubles were long past; the draft of a grant of coat-arms to Shakespeare's father is in existence, dated Oct. 1596.

61. and what's worse, *et si quid pejus.* The expression is now used parenthetically.

62. up. Added to verbs, *up* shows that the action is completed, and in this intensive sense is very common in Shakespeare.

65. Jaques, says Dowden, came to life again as Lawrence Sterne. "In Arden he wept and moralized over the wounded deer, and at Namport his tears and sentiment gushed forth for the dead donkey."

67. cope, encounter: used transitively in E.E.; but also intransitive—'cope with', as now.

68. matter, *i.e.* matter of discourse.

Scene 2.

This short scene prepares us for iii. 1, the banishment of Oliver. It throws more light on the suspicious and wayward character of the Duke (see ii. 3 and 21). The implied threat in line 19, "I'll make him find him", thus thrown forward before the final revelation of Oliver's treachery, gives a hint of the retribution he is bringing on himself.

3. consent and sufferance: a metaphor from law. The term is "applied to a landlord who takes no steps to eject a tenant whose time is expired" (Moberly).

5. her attendants of her chamber. Two nouns joined by *of* are sometimes treated as a compound noun; hence the repetition of the possessive adjective (Abb. § 423).

7. untreasured, a bold coinage of Shakespeare's own: only used here; and 'treasure' as a verb, only in Sonnet vi. 3.

10. There is a Hesperië in Ovid, *Met.* xi. 769.

13. wrestler: three syllables. See Prosody, 4 *b* ε 1.

15, 16. A very gentlewomanly conclusion!

17. that gallant, *i.e.* Orlando.

19. suddenly, at once, without any notion of unexpectedness.

21. Observe the plural. Celia (i. 3. 130) only anticipated pursuit after *her* flight; but the 'humorous Duke' has already swallowed his wrath against Rosalind, or forgotten it in his anxiety for his daughter. Note, too, the word 'foolish', by which the choleric usurper puts on others the blame for his own ill-temper.

Scene 3.

This scene takes the place of a long and boisterous episode in the novel. (See Introduction III.) It is essential that the wrong should be all on Oliver's side. Orlando must remain as gentle as he is strong and valiant; and here is a new testimony to the charm of his character, in the love and loyalty which it evokes.

3. memory, memorial. The use of abstract nouns in a concrete sense is very common in E.E.

4. The thought of his old master is always present to the mind of the old servant.

8. bonny, big, stalwart—a rare but not unexampled meaning. Scott (*Fortunes of Nigel*, c. 1) calls grim Richie Moniplies "the bonny Scot". For a contemporary parallel, cf. Hooker, *Sermon VII.*: "Issachar, though bonny and strong enough, &c." (1600 A.D.). There is therefore no need to read 'bony', which, as Wright points out, would mean skeleton-like rather than big-boned.

8. priser, one who contends for a prize, a champion. See Glossary.

9. Yet Orlando left the court at once.

10. some kind of men. Cf. *Lear*, ii. 2. 107, "These kind of knaves". These expressions admit a historical explanation. In O.E. they said not 'all kinds of men' but '*alles cunnes weras*', 'men of every kind'. But (1) as the sense of inflection decayed, the construction was forgotten—we find 'alles kynnes'; (2) the French phrase 'all manner of' came into use. Hence we find such hybrid constructions as this on the one hand, and "what manner musicke" (Spenser, *Faerie Queene*, ii. 12. 70) on the other. (Kellner, §§ 167–172.)

11. them: redundant object (Abbott, § 214).

12. No more do yours, yours are not more serviceable to you.

14, 15. Shakespeare may have been thinking of the shirt of Nessus, which 'envenomed' Hercules (Ovid, *Met.* ix. 152–175). He refers to it again in *Antony and Cleopatra*, iv. 12. 43. Without some such reference the expression is curious.

23. use, are wont. We still employ the past in this sense.

27. no place, no dwelling-place; *i.e.* no home, but a shambles. For **butchery,** see Glossary.

32, 33. 'Or turn highwayman.' Orlando's indignation enforces this with four vigorous adjectives.

37. diverted blood, blood diverted from the course of nature.

39. thrifty hire, hire saved by thrift. Cf. i. 1. 32; and line 67 below.

42. It is better to repeat *lie* from line 41 than to supply *be* with Abb. § 403.

43–4. Cf. *Luke* xii. 6 and 24: "Are not five sparrows sold for two farthings, and not one of them is forgotten before God?" "Consider the ravens; for they neither sow nor reap;...and God feedeth them."

48–54. This is one of the most didactic passages in Shakespeare. The praise of temperance and chastity is appropriate in the mouth of Adam; but it is difficult to believe that it has merely a dramatic significance.

49. in may depend on 'rebellious'; but it seems to go well with the verb. The 'liquors' are applied in, not directly to, the blood.

53. kindly, seasonable. See Glossary.

56–62. For poetic purposes, at least, Shakespeare adopts the fiction of 'the good old times'. In the *Sonnets* he again speaks of the "old age" as a time of primitive simplicity and truth:— "In him those holy antique hours are seen, Without all ornament, itself and true" (Sonnet 68): "In the old age black was not counted fair" (Sonnet 127). In reality he probably believed that history repeated itself. (See note on ii. 7. 139, the doctrine of cycles.) He has certainly no conception of continual progress.

58. sweat: past tense. The *ed* may be simply dropped after *t* for euphony; cf. 'quit' for 'quitted', 'waft' for 'wafted', &c. (Abb. § 241); or *sweat* may represent a strong form *swat*; *swet* occurs in M.E.

61–2. 'Service is killed off by the very promotion it gains.'

62-3-5. The rhymes here are probably accidental.

65. in lieu of, in return for, as always in Shakespeare. Properly = in place of.

67. thy youthful wages, the wages of thy youth. The adjective is often used where we should expect a genitive. The influence of

Latin may have something to do with the frequency of this idiom in
E.E. (Kellner, § 252).

71. seventeen: so Rowe; Ff. *seauentie* or *seventy*.

74. too late a week, too late by a week, *i.e.* by a good deal—a
proverbial expression. Wright, however, thinks *a* = in the, as in
'a-night' (ii. 4. 44).

Scene 4.

This scene is a good example of the way in which Shakespeare
transmutes his material. The prose parts are his own, in the rest
he follows the novel. But the presence of the clown, with his burlesque comments, makes all the difference between the sentimental
and the comic. As minor changes we note (1) that in Lodge Ganymede and Aliena learn Montanus's love from poems hung on trees.
Shakespeare uses this hint later in iii. 2. (2) That the conversation
overheard between Corin and Silvius takes the place of a long
eclogue in the novel. (3) That Montanus stays on to the end of
the scene, and escorts the ladies to their cottage.

1. weary: so Theobald, Ff. *merry*. Furness, who defends *merry*,
says that this is make-believe, and that Rosalind's second speech is
an aside. But Touchstone's joke requires *weary*.

2. The fool brings us down at once to the level of the commonplace.

4. the weaker vessel: cf. *1 Peter*, iii. 7, "giving honour unto
the wife as unto the weaker vessel". Shakespeare seems to have
found the expression comic: cf. *2 Henry IV.*, ii. 4. 66: "you are
the weaker vessel, as they say, the emptier vessel".

9. cross. The ancient penny had a double cross marked on it.
(Hence the expression, "crossing the palm".) For the pun, cf.
Matthew x. 38: "he that taketh not his cross", &c.

12. Arden: perhaps a pun—'a den'.

25. As introduces a statement "qualifying or even contradicting
what goes before". (Ingleby.) This use seems to have escaped
Schmidt. Cf. iii. 5. 38.

27. fantasy, here = love, or rather love-thoughts, a common meaning of the shorter form 'fancy' in E.E. See Glossary.

32-35-38. These short lines, repeated at regular intervals, give a
dithyrambic effect, proper to the expression of intense feeling.

34. Wearing, fatiguing. So F 1. The later folios (and the
Globe) have *wearying*.

39. Silvius's sudden exit is very effective. He has said enough
to prepare for the pastoral sub-plot. Perhaps, too, Shakespeare
purposely avoids an encounter between him and Touchstone.

40. searching of. The verbal retains so much of the noun that it takes 'of' after it = 'a searching of'. (Abb. § 178.) The metaphor is from surgery; search = probe.

44. the kissing of. "The substantival use of the verbal, with 'the' before and 'of' after it, seems to have been regarded as colloquial". (Abb. § 93.) It is Touchstone that is speaking.

45. batlet: F 2; F 1, *batler.* See Glossary.

45. chopt. *Chop* is another form of *chap.*

46. peascod. A country lass, when she finds a pod with nine peas, will still place it above the door, and the first man who enters is to be her husband. In Shakespeare's time it was a favourite love-token. The peascod must mean here the whole plant, which Touchstone mistakes for his sweetheart, as he mistakes a stone for his rival. Hence *whom* and *her* (line 47) refer to the plant, as *him* in line 43 to the stone. *Cods* (line 47) are pods.

48. weeping tears. This is usually taken to be a hit at Lodge, who uses the expression seriously. But it is common in E.E., and is only an instance of the use of the verbal in a passive sense (Kellner, § 420).

50. mortal in folly, excessively foolish. See Glossary.

52. ware of. In two senses, 'aware of' and 'beware of'.

60. clown. Touchstone means 'bumpkin', and Rosalind plays on the word.

62. betters, superiors. Again Corin takes the word to mean those who are better off.

68. We may assume an ellipsis of 'who is' after 'maid' or of 'she' before 'faints'. But probably this is only a form of the ἀπὸ κοινοῦ construction referred to on i. 2. 119.

69. faints for succour, for want of succour. Cf. "die for food", ii. 6. 1. Schmidt classes these among the cases where a negative is "borne in mind though not expressed". Cf. also iii. 2. 28. This detail is added by Shakespeare, to make the cases of the fugitives alike—cf. scene 6. In the novel Aliena and Ganymede "pulled forth such victuals as they had".

81. in my voice, as far as I have a voice in the matter. In *Measure for Measure,* i. 2. 185, "in my voice" = 'in my name': *Hamlet,* v. 2. 367, "dying voice" = 'dying vote'.

82. What is he. Abb. (§ 254) suggests that in Shakespeare's time the first question about any one might naturally be, "What is his rank?" If so the difference is one of thought, not of grammar.

82. shall, is going to. The restriction of *shall* to the first person is modern.

85. stand with honesty, be consistent with fair-dealing, *i.e.* toward Sylvius.

93. feeder, shepherd.   The word is used for 'servant' in *Antony and Cleopatra*, iii. 13. 109, but with a contemptuous sense (Schmidt renders 'parasite') which is out of place here.

Scene 5.

This scene is entirely Shakespeare's. It is interposed here between Rosalind's arrival in the forest (scene 4) and Orlando's (scene 6). The sentiment of the songs is intended to recall that of the elder duke's first speech. Jaques is at last introduced in person — the discord in this woodland harmony.

1. Greenwood songs have been popular in England since the days of Robin Hood—"In summer when the shaws be green".   This song may have been in Bunyan's mind when he wrote "Who would true valour see" (*Pilgrim's Progress*, part ii).

3. turn his merry note unto, adapt it to. The phrase is on the analogy of 'turn a tune', which is still common in dialect. Cf. Hall, *Sat.* vi. 1, "While thread-bare Martial turns his merry note".

14. ragged, rough, broken. Common in E.E. for anything with a rough edge, where we should say 'rugged'.

15. Jaques is still in the sullen fit, but his melancholy has passed from the pathetic to the brusque. Brusquerie is as much part of his pose as pathos.

16. call you 'em stanzos? Cotgrave confirms this spelling. Shakespeare thought the word new-fangled and affected—he has a good deal of the British contempt for foreign things—and puts it into the mouth of the pedant Holofernes in *Love's Labour's Lost*, iv. 2. 107: "Let me hear a staff, a stanze, a verse".

18. names, in the legal sense of the Lat. *nomina, i.e.* names of debts owed.

22. that. The relative is omitted—probably because identical in form with the demonstrative (Abb. § 244).

23. dog-apes, probably dog-faced baboons.

24. beggarly thanks, thanks like a mendicant's. The adj. represents a genitive; see on ii. 3. 67.

27. cover, lay the cloth. The Duke is going to 'drink', *i.e.* take dessert, under the tree. See 'banquet', line 58, below.

27. the while. *While* is originally a noun, = time: so *the while* = (in) the (mean) time (Abb. § 137).

29. look. The prep. *for* is often omitted with this verb, which thus becomes transitive (Abb. § 200).

31. **disputable**: in active sense = disputatious. Cf. ii. 1. 46. This from Jaques!

32. Cf. *Much Ado*, iii. 3. 19, "Give God thanks, and make no boast of it".

34. Note the form of the stage direction, and cf. i. 2. 197, 201, 247.

43. **in despite of my invention**, to spite my barren imagination. *Invention* is here the poetic faculty.

46. Shakespeare is an excellent parodist—witness his caricatures of Euphuism and his burlesque of the Cambyses' vein in Pistol—and never better than when he is parodying himself. Cf. iii. 2. 88.

50. **Ducdáme**: a meaningless refrain, metrically parallel to Amiens' "Come hither". Halliwell quotes a similar refrain, "Dusadam-me-me", from a MS. of *Piers Plowman*, where the printed copies have "How trolly-lolly".

A world of ingenuity has been wasted on this word, to prove it Latin, Welsh, Gaelic, &c. It was corrected by Hanmer to *duc ad me*, bring him to me. If any change is necessary the best is Mr. Ainger's *Ducdóme*, which makes a rhyme (with "come tó me") where at present there is only an assonance.

57. **all the first-born of Egypt**, all who are worth satirizing. The phrase is from *Exodus*, xi. 5.

64. **banquet**, dessert. See note on line 27.

Scene 6.

This scene is adapted from the novel, except that there it is Rosader who gives way to despair, while Adam cheers him and offers to open his own veins to relieve him. By such slight changes does Shakespeare gain tenderness and truth. Orlando remains the type of manly gentleness.

1. **I die for food**: cf. ii. 4. 69.

5. **comfort**: here used reflexively. There has always been a tendency in English to drop the reflexive pronoun (Kellner, § 345).

6. For **uncouth** and **savage** see Glossary.

7. 'You are not so near death as you imagine.' **conceit** = imagination; see Glossary.

8. **comfortable**: usually explained as passive: but the word is always active elsewhere in Shakespeare, and so here = cheerful.

9. **presently**: in E.E. = at once: now = soon but not at once.

12. **well said**, well done. Shakespeare uses the phrase even when no words are actually uttered.

Scene 7.

This somewhat complex scene falls naturally into two parts, (1) dialogue between the Duke and Jaques before Orlando's entrance and during his absence; (2) Orlando's demand and reappearance with Adam. (1) is all Shakespeare's own: (2) is adapted from Lodge. But Rosader, as usual, is more of a swashbuckler than Orlando. He offers to support his demand by fighting any one of the company: only famine and the thought that all things were savage there make Orlando for a moment forget his natural courtesy. The encounter with the fool, narrated by Jaques, shows that all the chief characters are now in the forest—they are not all brought together till the last scene—and serves (dramatically) to fill up the time between Orlando's exit in scene 6 and his entrance in scene 7.

1. I think he be. *Be* (in O.E. generally future, then exclusively subjunctive) gives a tinge of doubt (*a*) in questions: (*b*) after verbs of thinking. The *locus classicus* is *Othello*, iii. 3. 384, "I think my wife be honest, and think she is not". (Abb. §§ 295, 299).

5. compact of jars, composed of discords.

6. discord in the spheres. The Ptolemaic system was still the common one in Shakespeare's day: it was held even by Bacon; and adopted for poetic purposes by Milton. According to the Platonic version of the theory (*Republic*, x. 616, 617), the earth is the centre of a system of eight concentric spheres, in which are fixed the Sun, the Moon, the five planets, and the fixed stars. These spheres revolve round the Earth, each carrying its orb with it, and each as it turns utters a note, the eight notes yielding a harmony. This musical fancy (attributed to Pythagoras) is a favourite both with Shakespeare and with Milton. Cf. *Merchant of Venice*, v. 1. 60—

> "There's not the smallest orb which thou behold'st
> But in his motion like an angel sings,
> Still quiring to the young-eyed cherubins".

12. Jaques enters in an entirely new, but quite consistent mood. He had grown somewhat bored with the company in the forest when in scene 5 he went off to sleep. He returns in an ecstasy over his new acquaintance, in whom he sees a privileged philosopher.

13. a miserable world. Even at the height of his mirth Jaques remembers to interject a groan.

17. motley. A parti-coloured dress was the regular costume of the professional jester, and survives in the clown of the pantomime.

19. Alluding to the proverb, *Fortuna favet fatuis*, Fortune favours fools.

20. dial, a watch, or perhaps a pocket-dial. The word is used in E.E. for anything to measure time, on which the hours are marked.

20. poke. A large pouch was part of the jester's outfit.

23. In spite of this mock-philosophy, there is nothing in life which really impresses Shakespeare so much as Time and Change.

28. And thereby hangs a tale: an expression implying vast reserves, like Mr. Kipling's "But that's another story". It is used by characters like Mrs. Quickly (*Merry Wives*, i. 4. 159), and the clown in *Othello* (iii. 1. 8).

29. moral, moralize. (But Schmidt thinks it an adj.)

34. the only wear, the only thing worth wearing.

36. O worthy fool! Jaques has not yet had his laugh out.

39. In Shakespeare's physiology a dry brain is slow but retentive.

40. places, may be a translation of Lat. *loci*, itself a translation of Gr. τόποι, "commonplaces", a rhetorical term for heads of argument. But the ordinary sense is sufficient.

44. suit: with a pun.

45. better: proleptic adj. 'weed your judgments and so make them better'. Cf. i. 1. 38.

55. Not to, added by Theobald, is required by the sense, the metre and the obvious antithesis between "doth very wisely" and "doth very foolishly". Jaques is explaining why those whom he galls most must laugh most: for, he says, if a fool hits you cleverly your only sensible course is to pretend not to feel it; if you wince, you expose yourself.

56. anatomized. Shakespeare's use (and for the matter of that his spelling) of Greek words seems to show that he did not feel the etymology. *Anatomize* (which he spells 'anathomize') is hardly the right word here or in i. 1. 133.

57. even. This particle (says Prof. Herford) "is often introduced in recurring to an obvious fact (previously referred to, or forming a part of the dramatic situation), which explains a bold or figurative thought just expressed".

57. squandering glances, random shots. See Glossary.

58–69. The medical metaphor is kept up. Jaques thinks that his satire will be a purge: the Duke that it will be a poison.

63. counter, a metal disc used in counting.

64–87. These lines amount to an attack on, and defence of, satire. But the defence does not meet the attack. Your satire, says the Duke, will display an acquaintance with vice that will corrupt your hearers (a truth that might be illustrated *ad nauseam* from Latin literature). Jaques replies that it need offend no one: it is general, and the man who takes offence only shows that the cap fits.

65–69. This glimpse into Jaques' past is in Shakespeare's 'epic' manner. He likes, as far as the conditions of his art allow, to show not only what his characters are, but how they have come to be what they are. But Jaques' profligacy is thrown back in time, not to form too harsh a contrast to the prevailing tone of the play.

66. the brutish sting, animal passion.

67. embossed sores and headed evils. The redundancy gives emphasis. *Embossed* (see Glossary) is 'protuberant': *headed evils* are boils grown to a head, *evil* being concrete, as in 'king's evil'.

73. wearer's: so Singer: F1 *wearie.* Singer's emendation is convincing: Jaques is speaking of the pride of dress.

75, 76. The extravagance of the City dames in their attempts to ape the court ladies is frequently referred to in the Elizabethan Drama, and is the subject of Massinger's *City Madam.*

79. function, office, occupation.

84. do him right, do him justice.

85. if he be free, if he have a clear conscience.

93. civility, has in E.E. a somewhat higher sense than now. Cf. "civil sayings", iii. 2. 115.

97. inland bred, bred in inland (*i.e.* civilized) parts. *Inland* in this sense is opposed not to the coast, but to upland or outlandish parts. I have heard the word so used in Scotch—"a mair inland look", *i.e.* a more cultivated aspect.

102. Note the arrangement—gentleness: force: force: gentleness.

109. commandment, command, as constantly in E.E.

110 et seq. These lines have the high classic note above any others in the play. The versification here—a string of single lines in "linked sweetness"—reminds us of his earlier manner.

118. Orlando returns to the antithesis between force and gentleness.

120. The Duke repeats Orlando's words with fine variations.

125. upon command, for the asking.

127. Observe again the alliteration on the labial *f*; and Orlando's characteristic simile "like a doe".

132. weak, causing weakness. Cf. ii. 1. 46. This is prolepsis in the full sense, when the attribute of an effect is transferred by anticipation to the cause.

137. Shakespeare, though not proud of his calling, naturally abounds in theatrical metaphors.

139. wherein we play in. The prep. is often repeated (cf. line 90 above), though rarely after so short an interval. But it is hardly felt in *wherein.*

139-166. The metaphor suggested by the Duke is seized on by

Jaques, and elaborated with his usual fulness of fancy. As to this famous speech, observe (1) that it serves dramatically to fill up the interval of Orlando's absence: (2) that it is characteristic of Jaques' *ab extra* view of life: (3) that all the parts are presented in absurd or sordid lights—the infant mewling, the school-boy whining, the lover sighing, the soldier swearing, &c. The thought is that of the Ecclesiast, "The thing that hath been, it is that which shall be . . . and there is no new thing under the sun" (*Ecclesiastes*, i. 9). In Sonnet 123, Shakespeare recurs to the thought, so common in Greek philosophy, that the history of the world repeats itself in periods or cycles.

139. This comparison may have been suggested by the motto of the Globe Theatre, then newly erected, *Totus mundus agit histrionem*, 'all the world plays the actor'. But the thought is very old; it is worked out by Lucian.

140. merely, simply, absolutely, like Lat. *merus*. Contrast note on line 56.

143. In describing the Seven Ages of Man Shakespeare may have had some picture in his mind, such as one still sees sometimes, with the Ages arranged on steps, ascending to the prime of life, and descending to the grave.

148. ballad: before last century = song of any sort.

148-157. Observe the amount of local colour in the parts of the lover, the soldier, and the justice. (1) In the end of the 16th century there was an outburst of sonneteering unparalleled till our own day. (2) The soldier may have learned his oaths in Flanders, where many an Englishman (Ben Jonson and Chapman among them) 'trailed a pike'. Deighton aptly compares Bobadil, the braggart captain in *Every Man in his Humour*, who swears by Pharaoh's foot, by the body of Cæsar. (3) It was common to curry favour with magistrates by making them presents in kind, which often took the form of capons.

150-156. The cut of the beard showed the profession of the wearer.

155. lined: in E.E. of contents generally, as still in colloquial language.

157. modern, commonplace, as always in Shakespeare. **instances**, anything cited in proof—Lat. *instantiae*.

163. his, its. In O.E. and M.E. *his* is both masculine and neuter. *Its* dates from Tudor English: it is not found in Spenser nor in the Bible of 1611, and seldom in Shakespeare or Bacon. In fact it is not general before the Restoration. Alexander Gil, the grammarian (1619), does not recognize it. (Mätzner, p. 287.)

175. unkind: see Glossary, under *kind*.

178. 'Because you do not add insult to injury by braving us with your presence.'

180. "Songs of the holly were current long before the time of Shakespeare. It was the emblem of mirth." (Halliwell.)

187. warp, distort. For the derivation see Glossary. But the derivation is not always a safe guide to Shakespeare's meaning. It is more important to see what picture he had in his mind. The image here is of the wrinkling surface of a pool on which ice is forming, not of its ruffling by the wind, for 'thou' in this stanza is the 'bitter sky'.

189. As friend remember'd not. This is probably an instance of the use of the past participle in active sense, for which see note on iii. 3. 7. Shakespeare frequently has "to be remembered" in the sense of (1) to recollect, cf. iii. 5. 130: (2) to consider: "O be remembered, no outrageous thing From vassal actors can be wiped away"; *Lucrece*, 607.

191. At this point in the novel Rosader informs Gerismond of Rosalind's banishment. See Introduction III.

191. If that you were implies no doubt, but merely alludes to the fact that Sir Rowland is dead.

193. effígies, likeness. Straight from Latin, hence the accent.

200. Here Adam disappears from the scene. There are so many threads in the action that Shakespeare has his hands full without him.

ACT III. Scene I.

This is the climax of the anteplot. It would come somewhat earlier in the prosaic order of events, perhaps after ii. 3; but Shakespeare disregards the natural sequence for the sake of the dramatic contrast. With the next scene the complication is complete and the denouement begins.

1. Not see him since implies 'I did not see him since' on Oliver's part. Modern usage would require the perfect.

2. the better part, more than half. Cf. i. 3. 109.

4. thou present: nom. absol., a construction helped by the participial form of the adjective.

6. Cf. *Luke*, xv. 8, the parable of the pieces of silver.

11. quit, acquit. **by thy brother's mouth**, on his evidence.

15. More villain thou. This is one of the great dramatic moments in the play, when the tyrant Duke crushes the tyrant brother, and in so doing condemns himself out of his own mouth.

16. **of such a nature**, whose duty it is. In Md. E. *nature* and *kind* have partly exchanged meanings.

17. **extent**, seizure in execution of a writ of extent (*extendi facias*), *i.e.* a writ to recover debts of record due to the Crown, under which the body, lands, and goods of the debtor might be seized at once. This passage is quoted by Lord Campbell as an instance of Shakespeare's technical knowledge of the law. It seems correct in so far as a writ of extent applies to "house and lands"; but here there is no question of debt, nor is Oliver's person seized. (For derivation see Glossary.)

18. **expediently**, promptly. See Glossary.

Scene 2.

This great scene, the longest and most important in the play, seems to consist of a number of detached dialogues, connected merely by happening in one place. But a Shakespearian scene has generally an internal unity, and leads up to a definite culmination, which constitutes a fresh step towards the denouement. So everything here leads up to the meeting of Orlando and Rosalind, and the proposed wooing in masquerade. (1) Orlando has not said a word about love since i. 2 : his introductory lines are needed to prepare us for the poems found by Rosalind and Celia. (2) The dialogue between Corin and Touchstone connects the scene with the pastoral life of the forest, as (3) that between Orlando and Jaques connects it with the sylvan. These interludes, as well as the conversation in which Rosalind learns that Orlando is near, are of Shakespeare's own invention: the idea of the poems hung on trees, and that of the mock wooing, are suggested by Lodge (see ii. 4), but only suggested.

2. **thrice-crowned queen of night.** The same goddess was worshipped as Luna (the moon) in the heavens, Diana on earth, and Proserpine in the under-world.

3. **pale sphere.** See note on ii. 7. 5. Observe that the *sphere* of a planet is properly neither the orb nor the orbit, but the hollow shell in which it is fixed, and which carries it round. Shakespeare, however, seems to use it inaccurately for the planet itself.

4. Diana, the goddess of the chase, is also the goddess of chastity (cf. iii. 4. 14); and Rosalind is spoken of as one of her attendant nymphs. Cf. Lodge: "I pray thee, tell me, Forester, what is this Rosalind for whom thou pinest away in such passion? Is she some nymph that waits upon Diana's train, whose chastity thou has deciphered in such epithets?"

5. To carve names on trees is a common device in pastoral poetry. Cf. Virgil, *Eclogue* x. 53, "tenerisque meos incidere amores Arboribus"—'to carve my tale of love on tender trees'.

10. **unexpressive**, inexpressible. See note on ii. 1. 46.

10. she: used by Shakespeare as a noun = woman. Cf. *he*, line 368 below.

11–74. Since Touchstone last appeared in ii. 4, his wit has suffered a wood-change. The moralizings reported by Jaques (ii. 7) give a hint of this transformation. To Corin he poses as a man of the world, but on Rosalind's appearance he relapses into the buffoon.

13. On this judicial summing up of the contrast latent in all pastoralism, Hazlitt exclaims in ecstasy, "Zimmerman's celebrated work on Solitude discovers only half the sense of this passage".

20. hast: 29. wast. The marked inflection of the 2nd person singular allows the pronoun to be omitted.

35. all on one side qualifies **ill-roasted**, not **damned.** Shakespeare's similes, says Malone, rarely run on four feet. Similes seldom do, and Shakespeare sometimes exhibits the inadequacy of an image by the vividness with which he sees it.

37. With this string of fallacies, wherewith Touchstone tries to bewilder Corin, compare the rhetoric with which he bamboozles William (v. 1); and the "argals" of the First Gravedigger in *Hamlet.* The fallacy here turns on the ambiguity of "good" and "manners". "Manners", like Lat. *mores* = morals, as well as deportment. Cf. "evil communications corrupt good manners". Shakespeare does not use "morals".

40. parlous, a vulgar form of *perilous.*

44. you salute not...but you kiss, you never salute without kissing.

47. fells, the skin with the hair (or wool) on.

49. your: used indefinitely of what is well-known. Cf. in this play v. 1. 40; v. 4. 58; v. 4. 92—all in speeches by Touchstone. It is also a favourite idiom with Bottom.

50. mutton, sheep; see Glossary.

54. more sounder. The rise of double comparatives in M.E. was perhaps due to a struggle between the French and English modes of comparison. (Kellner, § 254.) In E.E. they serve to give emphasis.

58. in respect of, in comparison with.

59. perpend, reflect. (Lat. *per: pendere,* to weigh.) A pedantic word, put into the mouth of Polonius, Pistol, and the clown in *Twelfth Night.*

64. God make incision in thee: refers to blood-letting.

64. raw: not literally raw, but inexperienced.

65. Corin is driven to defend himself seriously, in spite of his declaration "I'll rest"; but his defence only gives another opening to Touchstone's inexhaustible wit.

67. **harm,** ill-fortune. This fine speech contains the gist of all real "praises of the country"; but Touchstone is bent on finding fault with everything.

75. **east** (adj.) belongs to **Ind,** which is pronounced to rhyme with *mind.* It is spelt *Inde* in F 1.

79. **lined,** drawn.

80. **black to,** black compared to.

81. **fair,** so Walker. Ff. *face. Fair* is a substantive here = beauty. This use of the adjective for an abstract substantive, though rare in the preceding century, becomes very common again in E.E., probably owing to the influence of Latin (Kellner, § 248).

83. **I'll rhyme you.** *You* is the so-called *dativus ethicus.*

85. **the right butter-women's rank,** the regular jog-trot of butter-women going to market in a row. *Rank* = row: cf. iv. 3. 78, "The rank of osiers". Wright plausibly conjectures *rack*, which, as appears from Holme, is a pace between a trot and an amble.

90. **cat will after kind:** a proverb. See Glossary, under *kind.*

92. **Winter garments.** Ff. 1, 2, have *wintred*, which Schmidt defends as an adjective, from the noun 'winter', and compares "bribed buck" = buck given as a bribe, *Merry Wives,* v. 5. 27. See note on iii. 3. 10.

100. **false gallop.** The phrase is still used in horsemanship of a galloping horse which lifts the wrong foot first. The metaphor of line 85 is kept up.

100. **infect.** Shakespeare uses *infection* and *contagion* for 'pollution', whether moral or physical.

105. This passage might be cited to prove that Shakespeare was not a gardener, for the medlar is a late fruit, and besides the season of the graft makes no difference to that of the stock. But of course it is all banter, and in a sense a fruit which is "rotten before it is ripe" may be called early. The medlar is not really eaten rotten; for the pun on *meddler* cf. *Timon,* iv. 3. 307-9.

106. **right:** with *a* = real, down-right ("a right maid", *Midsummer-Night's Dream,* iii. 2. 302): with *the* = proper, true. Cf. 85 above.

108. Touchstone owns himself worsted: Rosalind has carried the war into his own territory.

113. **For.** Shakespeare uses *for* to introduce a reason (1) (as at present) by a co-ordinate sentence; (2) by a subordinate clause, as here = because. In the latter sense he also has the full form, *for that.*

115. **civil sayings,** maxims of civilized life. Cf. ii. 7. 96.

117. erring, wandering, in the literal sense of Lat. *errare.*

123. sentence end. For the omission of the *'s* see note on i. 2. 140. It is common in dissyllables ending in a sibilant. (Abb. § 217.)

126. quintessence. Over and above the four elements (fire, air, earth, and water), the mediæval alchemists figured a fifth essence, *quinta essentia,* or ether, purer even than fire. This quintessence is to the world as the spirit to the body. Hence it is used loosely for the concentrated essence of anything, perhaps with a confused idea that the name means "essence five times distilled". For the accent cf. Ben Jonson's dictum, "all nouns, both dissyllabic (if they be 'simple') and trisyllabic, are accented on the first". See Prosody, 4 *a β.*

127. in little. From the number of astrological allusions in these verses ('quintessence', 'distilled', 'heavenly synod') it is probable that there is a reference here to the view of man as a microcosm or epitome of the great world. Cf. *Richard II.,* v. 5. 9, "this little world "—of his own mind.

130. wide-enlarged, spread through the world, till they are concentrated in Rosalind. *Enlarge* in Shakespeare is, regularly, not to make large, but to set at large, to spread abroad.

131. With this eulogy cf. *Romeo and Juliet,* ii. 4. 41; "Laura to his lady was but a kitchen wench...Dido a dowdy; Cleopatra a gipsy; Helen and Hero hildings and harlots".

132. Helen, the wife of Menelaus, and the most beautiful woman of Greece. She was carried off by Paris and so caused the Trojan War. Shakespeare introduces her in *Troilus and Cressida.*

133. Cleopatra, queen of Egypt in Julius Caesar's time. Her beauty bewitched Antony, and nearly broke up the Roman Empire. She is the heroine of Shakespeare's *Antony and Cleopatra.*

134. Atalanta, according to Greek legend, challenged her suitors to race with her. The prize was her hand; the penalty death. Hippomenes outstripped her by dropping golden apples in her way. (Ovid, *Met.* x. 562, &c.) What is her "better part"? Not her beauty, for Rosalind already has "Helen's cheek"; nor her chastity, for she has "Lucretia's modesty". It is her speed for which she is always celebrated in classical literature (cf. line 260 below), and speed, or grace of motion, is a fitting attribute for one of Diana's huntresses (cf. line 4 above).

135. Lucretia, a Roman lady, dishonoured by Tarquin. She is the heroine of Shakespeare's *Rape of Lucrece.* For *sad* and *modesty* see Glossary.

141. And I to live. Abb. (§ 416) includes this among the instances of "construction changed for clearness". But the construction can be explained historically. In M.E. the infinitive was used in absolute constructions to supply the place of the missing future participle—*rege morituro*, "the king to die"—and so used freely to alternate with any principal clause. Cf. Bacon (*Advt. of Learning*, 284), " But on this condition, that she should follow him, and he not to follow her ". (Kellner, § 400.)

142. pulpiter: so Spedding. Ff. *Jupiter.* Spedding's emendation is irresistible, though the Folio text does not absolutely call for emendation. Rosalind swears by Jupiter, ii. 4. 1, and by Jove, ii. 4. 55. But "most gentle Jupiter" is very odd. For the form *pulpiter* cf. " moraler ", *Othello*, ii. 3. 301; " justicer ", *Lear*, iii. 6. 23. Shakespeare manufactures names of agents by simply adding *-er* to other nouns: in the last example this *-er* = French *-eur*.

148. scrip, a shepherd's or pilgrim's wallet. Cf. *Samuel*, xvii. 40, " and put them in a shepherd's bag...even in a scrip ". *Scrip-page* is coined by Touchstone on the analogy of *baggage.*

150-231. This delightful dialogue is of Shakespeare's own invention. In Lodge, the two ladies are together when they discover Rosader and his sonnet simultaneously. Shakespeare leads gradually up to this climax. First Rosalind finds verses: then comes Celia with more. But Rosalind calmly dissembles curiosity till Celia (175) drops a very broad hint that the author is Orlando. Then she can restrain herself no longer; she besieges Celia with demands for his name, and gives her playful cousin a fine opening for that admiring banter in which she excels. After forty lines (203) Celia yields up the name—Orlando, and is immediately overwhelmed with another torrent of questions. As she is getting breath to reply, Orlando enters in person.

155. without, outside.

157. how thy name should be hanged. Abb. (§ 328) gives this as an instance of the use of *should* in reported speech = was said to be. This use, though not uncommon in E.E. (cf. Ger. *sollen*), and still found in dialect, is not in place here. The clause depends on *wondering*, and 'should be' = came to be. This periphrastic use of *should* is common after 'amaze', 'wonder', 'strange', &c. Cf. *Henry V.*, i. 1. 53, "which is a wonder how his grace should glean it ".

159. A wonder is proverbially supposed to last nine days.

160. a palm-tree. The flora and fauna of Arden must not be judged by prosaic rules. Cf. the lioness in iv. 3. 113; and the " tuft of olives " iii. 5. 74. Shakespeare was not afraid of inconsistencies and anachronisms when they suited his dramatic purpose. (Some edd. explain the palm here as the goat-willow, the catkins of which are still called ' palms' in Scotland.)

161. since Pythagoras' time. Pythagoras, an ancient Greek philosopher, is credited with the doctrine of the transmigration of souls (Ovid, *Met.* xv.). Shakespeare alludes to it again in *Merchant*

of Venice, iv. 1. 131: and *Twelfth Night*, iv. 2. 54–62. that =
when (Abb. § 284).

162. **an Irish rat.** It was a current belief in Shakespeare's day
that Irish enchanters could rhyme rats to death.

163. Celia is still trying to provoke Rosalind's curiosity. "Is it
a man?" asks Rosalind coolly. But Celia has her revenge when
she mentions the chain. Cf. i. 2. 211.

165. **And a chain,** with a chain. This use of 'and' in answers
implies "Yes", and adds something more.

168–170. "Friends may meet, but mountains never greet." Ray's
Proverbs.

169. **with earthquakes.** In O.E. *mid* (with) represents the
instrumental case; in M.E. it frequently introduces the agent (see
note on ii. 1. 41); and in E.E. it is often used with agent or cause,
where we now use 'by'.

176. **out of all hooping,** beyond all exclamations of surprise. Cf.
Henry V., ii. 2. 108, "That admiration did not hoop at them".

178. **Good my complexion!** Rosalind adjures her blushes not
to betray her. Cf. Celia's "Change you colour?" (line 176). For
the order of the words, cf. i. 2. 1.

179. **caparisoned:** properly of horses: here used in comic exag-
geration.

180. **One inch...South-sea of discovery,** delay another minute
and I'll overwhelm you with an ocean of questions.

186. **Is he of God's making?** or his tailor's? (Wright.)

191. **stay,** wait for, as often in Shakespeare.

195. **speak, sad brow and true maid,** speak seriously, as you
are a true maid. Without the comma, *brow* and *maid* are accusative.
Cf. line 263 below, "I answer you right painted cloth". With the
comma they are rather to be taken as vocatives.

200. Rosalind naturally thinks first of her dress. But only for a
moment. The thought that her lover is near, and that Celia has
seen him, expels everything but a desire to hear about him. Only
she wants to know "Did he ask for me?" forgetting in her excitement that Orlando would not recognize Celia in her disguise.

202. **Wherein went he?** how was he dressed? She thinks
about Orlando's clothes too. This use of "go in" is common in
Shakespeare.

203. **parted...with,** parted from. *With* is used, by a sort of
inversion, of separation from things or persons with which one has
been connected. We still 'part with' things: in E.E. with persons
as well.

206. Gargantua's mouth. Gargantua is the giant in Rabelais who swallows five pilgrims in a salad. There was as yet no transla-tion of Rabelais in English, but a chap-book history of Gargantua was very popular in the 16th century.

209. catechism, catechising.

213. atomies, motes, the Shakespearian form of *atoms.*

215. observance, attention.

217. Jove's tree. The oak was sacred to Jupiter (perhaps from the oak groves at his shrine of Dodona), as the poplar to Hercules, &c.

221. Celia enters into the spirit of the situation with her mock heroics.

223. ground: perhaps=background. But the natural meaning is satisfactory, unless Rosalind intends a pun.

224. For **holla** (=woa!) see Glossary.

226. heart, a pun on *hart.* Rosalind's irrepressible excitement vents itself in fanciful word-play. "There is a natural, an almost irresistible, tendency in the mind, when immersed in one strong feeling, to connect that feeling with every sight and object around it" (Coleridge). Rosalind sees every point in Celia's description as it rises, and interprets it by her own heart.

227. would is often used conditionally = 'I should wish' (if you would let me), not 'I did wish'.

227. burden, refrain. See Glossary.

227. bringest, puttest. Celia is getting a little impatient at these continual interruptions, and Rosalind at once drops into tender-ness—"Sweet, say on".

232-272. This interlude, besides contrasting Orlando and Jaques, gives Rosalind time to recover herself. Eager as she was for news of her lover, her first instinct, when he actually appears, is to "slink by". She is rewarded by hearing him proclaim his love and dis-comfit the scoffer.

232. Jaques has attached himself to Orlando, as the most recent addition to society in the Forest. But he can make nothing of him, and tells him so rather rudely. Jaques has been accustomed to have his brusque ways humoured by the foresters, and is beaten with his own weapons when Orlando retorts. It must be owned that Orlando's repartees only amount to saying "You're another" with variations: but they serve their purpose.

234. myself alone, alone by myself. In the nominative, *myself, himself,* &c., are short for prepositional phrases, *by, of, for myself,* &c. (Abb. § 20).

235. for fashion sake. The *'s* of the possessive is here omitted for euphony. Cf. note on i. 2. 140.

237. God be wi' you: Ff. *God buy you*: Md. E. 'Good-bye'. But Jaques does not go yet. He tries a parting shot, and, failing to get the last word, returns to the fray.

239. On more and **moe** see Glossary.

252. rings: referring to the mottoes or 'posies' engraved on rings. Cf. *Merchant of Venice*, v. 1. 147, "a paltry ring...whose posy was —'Love me and leave me not'."

253. I answer you right painted cloth. For the construction cf. *Othello*, ii. 3. 281, "speak parrot", and Horace's *saltare Cyclopa*, to dance the Cyclops. Hangings of painted canvas were used as a substitute for tapestry. The subjects were generally scriptural, and ornamented with moral sayings.

255. Jaques' compliment is meant for a flag of truce. He wants some one to talk to. But Orlando doesn't want him; and their repartees come down to plain "Fool".

256. Again compare Jaques with *Richard II.* (iii. 2. 155)—

> "For God's sake, let us sit upon the ground
> And tell sad stories of the death of kings".

And note the difference between the pathetic indulgence of the one sentimentalist and the satirical indulgence of the other.

258. breather, living being. For the formation cf. line 152 above. This manly and characteristic utterance effectively marks the contrast between Orlando and Jaques.

267. Jaques falls rather too easily into this obvious "booby-trap".

273–end. This is the proper climax of the scene and of the play. From this point Rosalind is almost transformed. It is only the presence of Orlando which can evoke from her this dazzling play of wit and fancy.

275. Orlando is naturally not in the best of tempers after his encounter with Jaques. At Rosalind's saucy "Do you hear?" he turns and answers somewhat drily—as man to boy—"Very well".

279. Cf. Lodge: "for the sun and our stomachs are shepherds' dials".

280. Rosalind at once starts the subject of love, eager to make Orlando disclose to herself the passion he was not ashamed to own to Jaques; but he takes up her epigram by the other end.

281. Cf. *Richard II.*, v. 5. 51..."My thoughts are minutes...the sound that tells what hour it is Are clamorous groans".

286. who...withal. *Who* for *whom* is common when the governing word succeeds; not so common when it precedes.

290. There seems to be some inconsistency here, though perhaps it is prosaic to expect consistency in metaphors. To the bride, Time's hard trot makes a week seem long: to the condemned thief, his gallop makes the trip to the gallows seem all too short. (1) We may suppose (with Wright) that a hard trot means not a fast but an uneasy pace, which makes the journey seem long. But all the other terms refer to speed. Or (2) that the antithesis is between the trot and the amble, and that when we come to the gallop the point of view is changed. The bride, full of hopes and fears, seems to have lived seven years in a week: the easy-going priest hardly feels himself older. Here we are looking back, and it is a psychological fact that periods which seem short in passing seem long in retrospect, and *vice versa.* The condemned thief, looking forward, sees the gallows approaching at lightning speed. (Cf. Ward's article Psychology (p. 65) in the *Encyc. Brit.*)

292. a se'nnight, a week; cf. 'a fortnight'='a fourteen-night'.

293. seven year. This use of the singular for the plural is common in Shakespeare after numerals, especially in the language of vulgar persons. In O.E. certain neuter substantives, *e.g.* 'year', 'night', &c., had the same form in both numbers.

298. Learning has always been held to be emaciating. Chaucer says of his clerk of Oxenford, "And he was not right fat, I undertake". Cf. also *Julius Caesar*, i. 2. 194, "Yond Cassius has a lean and hungry look. He thinks too much".

307. Orlando has quite forgotten his ill-humour, and grown interested in the sprightly boy before him.

309. like fringe upon a petticoat. The simile, suggested by *skirts*, is thoroughly feminine. Shakespeare's women talk like women. So Imogen says (*Cymbeline*, i. 1. 167): "I would they were in Afric both together; Myself by with a needle, that I might prick The goer-back".

310. native: always an adj. in Shakespeare when used of persons.

313. removed, sequestered.

315. religious: probably = belonging to a religious order. Cf. v. 4. 166.

316. courtship: in both senses, of courtly manners, and of courting. Rosalind is resolved to bring the conversation back to the subject of love. This time she gets as far as women.

323. like one another as half-pence are. See Introduction II. The simile is apt, for there was much less uniformity in the rest of the coinage.

326. Orlando would like to hear her descant on the faults of women as she has descanted on the paces of Time. But Rosalind is not to be put off.

331. fancy-monger, dealer in love. Compounds with *-monger* have generally a contemptuous sense when used metaphorically.

333. quotidian, a fever or ague recurring daily, and supposed to be a symptom of love. For the formation (Lat. *cotidiana* [*febris*], daily [fever], from *cotidie*, every day) cf. 'quartan ague', an ague recurring every fourth day.

334. love-shaked. This word shows that the "quotidian of love" is thought of as a cold ague rather than as a fever. In the p. part. Shakespeare has the weak form *shaked*, as well as *shaken*, and *shook*. *Shaked* is found as early as Skelton and as late as the 18th century.

336. Orlando has said it: but Rosalind, eager to hear more, pretends to doubt that he is in love, or that love is such a serious thing at all. She calls it a cage of rushes, to indicate the flimsy nature of its bonds.

340. Rosalind throws herself with renewed zest into the description of the disconsolate lover. Her inventory gives her an excuse for noting Orlando's appearance, and answering to herself some of the questions she poured out on Celia—"How looked he? Wherein went he?"

340. a blue eye, *i.e.* blue round the lids.

341. unquestionable, averse to talk. *Question* often = conversation in E.E. Cf. iii. 4. 31; v. 4. 151. For the termination *-able* cf. 'disputable' (ii. 5. 31), and note on ii. 1. 46.

343. simply, without qualification. **having**, possession, as often in Shakespeare.

345. your bonnet unbanded. *Bonnet* in E.E. is synonymous with hat. Hatbands were worn in various colours. With the whole passage Malone compares Heywood's *Fair Maid of the Exchange* (1637): "Shall I defy hatbands, and tread garters and shoe-strings under my feet? &c."—a passage probably inspired by the present.

348. point-device, precise. See Glossary.

350. Orlando is serious now. The "Fair youth" of this line, as compared with the "pretty youth" of line 317, shows his gradual change of demeanour towards Rosalind. In v. 4. 28 he says to the Duke—

"My lord, the first time that I ever saw him
Methought he was a brother to your daughter".

And though he certainly has no suspicion here as to who she really is—a clumsy ingenuity of Gervinus's—the resemblance and the femininity of her charm win on him unawares.

352. This is the first of those *double entendres* in which so much of the humour of the situation consists. But it is more than humorous. It helps to relieve her own heart, and to encourage Orlando.

353-360. As Rosalind gets serious, Orlando gets jocular. But he says the words she wants to hear before she recovers the tone of disbelief.

362. This was the usual treatment of lunatics till not very long ago.

365. In this off-hand way does Rosalind introduce her plan for getting Orlando to come and court her. In Lodge, the suggestion is not made till their second meeting.

369. moonish, variable like the moon.

374, 375. entertain...forswear, receive his addresses at one time, at another refuse to have anything to do with him.

376. living, real, not affected. ' From being madly in love, I made him mad in earnest.' Walker would read *loving*; but *living* is like enough in sound for the jingle, and gives point to the antithesis. **Humour** is used with a slight variation of sense: ' mad humour '=silly whim: ' living humour '=actual vein (of madness). Cf. note on i. 2. 232. This looser sense of *humour*, which marks the transition to its common modern meaning, seems to have been coming into vogue at this date. Ben Jonson (Induction to *Every Man in his Humour*) after defining the true sense adds:

> " Now if an ideot
> Have but an apish or fantastic strain,
> It is his humour ".

And the cant use of it by Nym on every occasion is clearly a hit at some current form of slang.

380. This metaphor is in Rosalind's assumed character of Shepherd-boy. The liver was supposed, as in Greek and Latin poetry, to be the seat of the passions, especially of love, jealousy, and courage. " Liver, brain, and heart " sum up the human faculties (*Twelfth Night*, i. 1. 37).

389. Come, sister. All this while Celia has said nothing. Her humour blooms for Rosalind, as Rosalind's for Orlando.

Scene 3.

An entirely Shakespearian interlude. The climax of the main plot having been reached, Shakespeare proceeds, in this and the next two scenes, to work in his comic and pastoral sub-plots.

1. Audrey, short for Ethelreda. Hence *tawdry*, from the gew-gaws sold at St. Audrey's fair.

2. goats. Audrey's goats mark a more pronounced rusticity than that of the shepherd characters. In Greek Pastoral, ' goat-herd ' is a term of contempt (Theocritus, i. 85; vi. 7): in Christian Pastoral the goatherd is the wicked character—in allusion to the Scriptural metaphor, " the sheep on his right hand and the goats on his left "— as Spenser explains in his notes to his 7th Aeglogue: " by Gotes, in scrypture, be represented the wicked and reprobate, whose pastour also must needes be such".

3. feature, appearance in general (see Glossary). Audrey does not understand the Latin word, any more than she understands "poetical" (line 12 below). If there is any more recondite joke it is hopelessly lost.

4. warrant: see Glossary.

6. capricious (Lat. *capra*, she-goat) keeps up the pun on *goats* and *Goths.* Ovid was banished by Augustus to Tomi on the Euxine, in the country of the Getae, or Goths, as Shakespeare calls them.

7. ill-inhabited, having a bad habitation. Shakespeare's bold formations in *-ed* have a twofold origin. The suffix is (1) adjectival, (2) participial. (1) *-ed* added to substantives connotes the possession of that substantive: *e.g.* 'charmed power', 'furred moss', &c. But when there is no corresponding substantive (*e.g.* 'becomed love' = becoming love), the form must be (2) participial, an instance of the p. part. in active sense. This is a relic of the time when the part. was indifferent as to voice (cf. Lat. *cenatus*, having supped), and is proved for Shakespeare by the existence of forms in *-en* (*e.g.* 'for-gotten'=forgetful) which cannot be adjectives, though used adjecti-vally. The frequence of active forms in *-ed* as compared to those in *-en* is due to the ambiguous nature of that suffix. (The adjectival *-ed* is probably in the last resort participial; cf. Lat. *auritus*, eared and Greek adjectives in *-τος* formed directly from nouns.)

7. Having failed to make anything of Orlando, Jaques has attached himself to Touchstone, for whose sapient folly he has the critical relish of the intellectual epicure.

8. Jove in a thatched house. Jupiter and Mercury, wander-ing about in human figure, were hospitably received by Baucis and Philemon, an old couple in Phrygia (Ovid, *Met.* viii. 630). The story is told in English by Swift.

11. a great reckoning in a little room, a long bill in a poor inn.

15. the truest poetry is ever the most feigning. Shake-speare's criticisms on his own art are interesting, even when made in jest. Cf. *Midsummer-Night's Dream*, v. 1. 14—

> "And as imagination bodies forth
> The forms of things unknown, the poet's pen
> Turns them to shapes and gives to airy nothing
> A local habitation and a name".

Bacon, too, calls poetry "feigned history", and Sidney's view of it is the same.

17. Two constructions are confused (1) 'may be said to be feigned'; (2) 'it may be said they do feign'.

18. Audrey's reiterated allusions to the gods are in the conventional pastoral manner.

24. **hard-favoured,** harsh-featured. See Glossary under *favour*. For the sentiment, cf. the Scotch proverb, "Butter to butter's nae kitchen" (*i.e.* no relish).

26. **material,** full of matter, in the sense of ii. 1. 68.

29. **foul.** Touchstone means 'dirty', Audrey means 'plain'.

34. **Sir:** properly applied to knights, baronets, and B.A.'s. In the last sense, it is said to represent the Dominus still preserved in Cambridge Tripos lists; but the title was allowed by the Pope to priests who had no degree ("pope's knights" they were called). Cf. Sir Nathaniel in *Love's Labour's Lost*; Sir Hugh Evans in *Merry Wives*; and Sir Topas in *Twelfth Night*. From what Jaques says below (line 72) Sir Oliver would seem to be but a hedge-parson. Cf. the use of Dan and Dom, both abbreviations of *dominus*, and applied to clerics.

40. **stagger,** hesitate.

41. **what though?** what though it be so? This ellipsis is common after *if; e.g.* 'or if' (it be so); 'which if' (it be so).

42. **necessary,** unavoidable. See Glossary.

46. **Horns?...alone?** F 1, *hornes, even so poor men alone.* The punctuation is Theobald's.

47. **rascal,** a deer out of season. (See Glossary.) As applied to persons, the word has now lost some of its colour. In E.E. it still means 'good for nothing'.

51. **defence,** the art of self-defence.

52. **to want,** to be without: 'a horn is better than nothing'.

53. **dispatch us,** settle our business.

62. **God 'ild you,** God yield you, *i.e.* reward you. See Glossary. The occasion referred to must be the meeting related by Jaques in ii. 7.

64. **pray be covered,** please put on your hat. As an old courtier himself, Touchstone is on his manners at the sight of a gentleman, and apologizes for his present company; but his patronizing tone extends itself to Jaques, an unconscious retort on Jaques' own air towards him.

66. **bow:** not the yoke, but the flexible collar to which it was attached.

67. **the falcon her bells.** In older English, the falcon is the female, the tercel the male goshawk.

75. The quality of Touchstone's love may be judged from this aside. He regards marriage as a second-best course. **I am not in the mind but,** I am not sure that I had not.

82. This is a scrap of a ballad. In 1584, Richard Jones entered the ballad, " Oh sweet Oliver, Leave me not behind thee ". The names of Roland and Oliver, Charlemagne's peers, were popular in ballad poetry.

86. wind, turn and go. See Glossary.

88. The marriage is deferred in order that Touchstone and Audrey may form a fourth couple at the wedding in the last scene.

Scene 4.

This scene seems to be laid on the morning after iii. 2. Rosalind is really, anxiously, in love, and fretful at Orlando's non-appearance. Celia assents with alacrity to all her reproaches till she drives Rosalind into defending him, exaggerates her defence till Rosalind comes back to reproaches, and protests her disbelief till the entrance of Corin creates a diversion. The prose part is Shakespeare's own.

6. According to the physiognomy of that day the colour of the hair was thought to denote the disposition; red hair inclining to black was the index of a deceitful and malicious nature.

7. In old tapestries Judas was represented with a red beard. So in Matthew Arnold's *Saint Brandan*: " Of hair that red and tufted fell".

13. holy bread: probably sacramental bread, though Barron Field says it was "merely one of the ceremonies which Henry VIII.'s Articles of Religion pronounced good and lawful ".

14. cast, left-off. If one may buy a pair of lips, one may buy them at second-hand. The ludicrous expression is intentional. Ff. 2, 3, 4 read *chast* (*i.e.* chaste), an obvious correction by the editor.

15. Celia invents a new Order of nuns, to symbolize cold chastity.

23. a covered goblet. " A goblet with its cover on is a better emblem of hollowness than with it off" (Deighton).

30. Perhaps Celia introduces this reference to the old Duke intentionally, to turn the conversation from Orlando. Rosalind and she had come to seek the Duke, but to reveal themselves as yet would spoil everything. Rosalind's excuse is also Shakespeare's apology for this little breach of faith. Cf. note on v. 2. 27.

37. traverse, across. The tilter tried to carry his lance fair upon his adversary's shield, so that if broken it split lengthways. To break it across implied awkwardness.

37. lover: in E.E. of either sex. We still speak of a "pair of lovers ".

41–end. In these lines Shakespeare has simply versified Lodge. The incident now introduced comes considerably later in the novel, after the arrival of Saladin and the rescue of Celia from the robbers. (See Introduction III.) Shakespeare starts both the comic and the pastoral sub-plot in this third Act; if left to the end of the fourth they would delay the action when it should be hastening to its close.

42. **that:** 43. **who.** As *that* introduces an essential characteristic it generally comes nearer to the antecedent than *who* or *which*. (Abb. § 260.)

47. **pale complexion.** Sighing was believed to drain the blood from the heart.

52. For the monosyllabic first foot, cf. ii. 4. 63, and Prosody, 3 *a β*.

Scene 5.

Shakespeare still follows the novel pretty closely. The rest of this episode he treats with a freer hand. (See iv. 3.) In *Twelfth Night* he returns to the theme—of one woman falling in love with another—and touches it to finer issues. Cf. especially *Twelfth Night*, i. 5, and iii. 1. Olivia differs from Phebe as high-born dame from humble shepherdess. She does not disclose her passion so abruptly and naively, nor sue to Viola as a superior being: but finally throws away the pride of birth and rank, and offers herself with equal abandon.

5. **falls,** lets fall. In O.E. transitive verbs could be formed from intransitives by addition of *-ja* to the past stem, and change of the root vowel. The existence of verbs in which the two forms were identical facilitated the use of intransitive verbs as transitive without change of form—a license very common in E.E. (Kellner, §§ 360–364.)

6. **but first begs pardon,** without first begging pardon. For the practice referred to, cf. Webster, *Vittoria Corombona* (v. 2)—

> "Thou hast too good a face to be a hangman.
> If thou be, do thy office in right form;
> Fall down upon thy knees and ask forgiveness".

7. **dies and lives,** makes his living from the cradle to the grave. Mr. Arrowsmith has shown that this inversion ("die and live" for "live and die") is by no means uncommon. But his examples do not explain the meaning here, where *live* = subsist. It is a violent zeugma; *i.e. by bloody drops* is joined to both verbs, when it properly goes only with *lives*. Shakespeare probably meant to end the sentence differently, and was led astray by the double meaning of *lives*.

8. Phebe meets Silvius' protestations with contemptuous common-sense. They have no meaning to her as yet.

12–13. **that...who:** see on iii. 4. 42. *Who* personifies.

17. **swoon.** The Folios spell *swound* here, *swoon* in iv. 3. 157, and *sound* in v. 2. 25. The pronunciation was in a state of transition.

22. F 2 reads *lean but upon*, to mend the metre. But a syllable is sometimes omitted in this place. See Prosody, 3 *a β*.

23. capable impressure, impression that can be perceived. *Capable* is here passive = sensible: as in *Hamlet*, iii. 4. 126, "His form...preaching to stones, Would make them capable", it is active = sentient. See Glossary.

24. some moment. With singular nouns of time, *some* = 'about a', is not uncommon; *e.g.* 'some hour hence', 'some minute'.

26. nor...no. The double negative is especially common in this form.

32. Disbelieving in a passion she has never felt, Phebe challenges her fate; and deserves it.

35. Rosalind has come meaning "to prove a busy actor in their play", and her energetic performance shows her strong character in a new light. In every line we feel the woman speaking, and speaking to an inferior. No boy could scold a woman so. The plain-directness of these home-thrusts is in marked contrast to her airy manner with Orlando.

36. and all at once, and that too all in a breath.

37. have no beauty. This is the sting of Rosalind's scolding: do you think your plainness an excuse for pride?' She repeats the charge of ugliness again and again. Lines 46, 47 are not meant for praise: Phebe certainly does not take them as a compliment (see lines 129, 130). The text is sound.

38, 39. "That is, without exciting any particular desire for light to see it by" (Moberly).

43. sale-work, ready-made goods, as Wright says.

43. 'Od's my little life. *'Od's* is for 'God's'. Rosalind is fond of these "pretty oaths".

46, 47. These are meant for very rustic charms. Brunettes were not the fashion in Shakespeare's day at the court of a fair-haired Queen. Cf. Sonnet 127, "In the old age, black was not counted fair", and for the "cheek of cream", the scornful description of Rosaline in *Love's Labour's Lost*, iii. 198, as

"A whitely wanton with a velvet brow,
        With two pitch-balls stuck in her face for eyes".

47. bugle, a black glass bead. Here an adjective.

48. entame. *En-*, originally locative (cf. 'enclose'), is used in E.E. of bringing into any state. Cf. 'enfree', to set free; 'engross', to make fat.

50. The south is the rainy wind.

52. Still addressed to Silvius. ' But for fools like you, who think them pretty, ugly women would not get married and fill the world with ugly children.'

53. That makes. The relative, perhaps from its want of inflection, often takes a singular verb though the antecedent is plural, and 3rd person, though the antecedent is 1st or 2nd (Abb. § 247).

55. out of you: as her mirror; 'in the reflection of your flattery'. *Out of*, as often in E.E., indicates the source: cf. *King John*, ii. 100, "These eyes, these brows, were moulded out of his".

61. cry the man mercy, beg his pardon.

62. 'Ugliness is ugliest in a scornful person.'

69. Why look you so upon me? Shakespeare believes that love is "engender'd in the eyes, with gazing fed". Cf. *Twelfth Night*, ii. 2. 20 (Viola of Olivia)—

> "She made good view of me; indeed, so much,
> That sure methought her eyes had lost her tongue,
> For she did speak in starts distractedly"—

with Phebe's short and abrupt answers here. The fruit of her gazing is given below, in her description of Rosalind.

74. Why does Rosalind tell Phebe where to find her? (The remark is clearly addressed to Phebe, for Silvius knows her home already— cf. lines 106, 107). Perhaps, with a mischievous sense of justice, she wants to keep up the 'play' a little longer.

77. And be not proud. Phebe is more harshly drawn by Shakespeare than by Lodge. Lodge's Phœbe rejects Montanus "not in pride but in disdain", not because she scorns him, but because she hates love. Shakespeare has made this change to justify the severity of her punishment.

77, 78. Rosalind clinches her advice with a rhyming couplet. See Prosody, 3 *d*.

80. shepherd: for poet, in the conventional pastoral manner. This convention is in regular use as early as Bion. So in Spenser's *Shepherd's Calendar*. The "dead shepherd" is Christopher Marlowe, who was killed in 1593.

81. From Marlowe's *Hero and Leander*—

> "Where both deliberate, the love is slight.
> Who ever loved that loved not at first sight?"
>
> (*First Sestiad*, line 176.)

(See Introduction, § 4.)

82-84. Observe the change in Phebe's manner to Silvius.

89. Alluding to the precept, "love thy neighbour as thyself". She turns off Silvius's importunities with an ambiguity and a silly jest— not flatly denying him as before, since now she has need of him.

92. 'And even now I do not actually *love* you.'

93. Cf. what Orlando says, iv. 1. 77, "I take some joy to say you are, because I would be talking of her".

98–103. In these melodious lines, Shakespeare has expressed once for all the spirit of the 'old dog'.

102, 103. **loose…A scattered smile.** The metaphor of the gleaner is kept up.

103–134. These lines are the dramatic equivalent of the famous song in Lodge called *Rosalind's Description*—("Like to the clear in highest sphere"). Shakespeare contrives to give at once an exquisite description of Rosalind's person and of the state of Phebe's heart, vacillating as it is between passion and pride. Her resentment is not all assumed, for some of Rosalind's taunts have gone home—cf. 128–130. Observe how the uncomplimentary qualifications gradually sink, and pass into unreserved admiration.

109. **peevish,** forward. See Glossary.

112. **It is a pretty youth.** Observe the contemptuous turn given by the *it*; but in a couple of lines, "*He*'ll make a proper man".

122. **mingled damask.** Shakespeare uses *damask* in two slightly different senses: (1) of blood red, (2) of mingled red and white, as here. In the first sense, he has in mind the damask *rose*; in the second, the varying shades of Damask *silk*. The damask rose is not known to be variegated.

124. **in parcels,** piecemeal. See Glossary.

125. Phebe—unlike the Phœbe of the novel—deliberately deceives Silvius. From this point onwards, Shakespeare treats the pastoral sub-plot more freely, with a half-comic touch that is wanting in Lodge. In Lodge, Phœbe falls sick of love: Montanus carries her letter, though he suspects the contents, and actually intercedes for her with Ganymede.

128. **what had he to do,** what business had he.

130. **I am remember'd,** I recollect. See ii. 7. 189.

132. **omittance is no quittance** : evidently a proverb—'a debt is not cancelled because you omit to exact it'. Cf. Milton, *P. L.*, x. 53, "Forbearance no acquittance".

135. **straight,** immediately.

136, 137. A rhyme is probably intended.

137. **passing** : here an advb. = surpassingly. Shakespeare also uses it as an adj.

Act IV.—Scene i.

This scene continues—after an interval—the wooing proposed in iii. 2, and is conceived in much the same spirit. But the intimacy of the lovers has made progress in the meantime. In Lodge, the mock-marriage, to which this scene leads up, takes place immediately after the wooing eclogue, and at the same meeting.

1. Jaques, as usual, is in search of company.

This is the only direct encounter between Jaques and Rosalind, but it is long enough to mark effectually the contrast between his affected melancholy humour and her natural wit. Jaques' manner towards the disguised Rosalind shows Shakespeare's fine disregard of prosaic likelihood. An old courtier would scarcely take such plain-speaking from a shepherd boy. But even in disguise Rosalind's womanhood secures a certain deference.

5. Salarino expresses the same sentiment, *Merchant of Venice*, i. 1. 51—

"Nature hath framed strange fellows in her time:
   Some that will evermore peep through their eyes
   And laugh like parrots at a bag-piper,
   And other of such vinegar aspect
   That they'll not show their teeth in way of smile,
   Though Nestor swear the jest be laughable".

6. **modern**, ordinary (cf. ii. 7. 156); **censure**, judgment; not necessarily adverse. Shakespeare uses it in the modern sense in line 170 below.

10. Jaques does not meet Rosalind's criticism any more than he met the Duke's (ii. 7. 70); but by way of answer enlarges fondly on his own pet affectation. This passage is decisive as to the nature of his malady. It is not the world-sick brooding of Hamlet, still less the passionate world-hate of Timon. "The melancholy of Jaques is not grave and earnest, but sentimental, a self-indulgent humour, a petted foible of character, melancholy prepense and cultivated" (Dowden).

13. **politic**: *i.e.* out of pretended sympathy for his client.

14. **nice**, finical. See Glossary.

15. **a melancholy of mine own.** Jaques is a thorough egotist. The fact that his melancholy is his own puts it above criticism.

15. **simples**, the ingredients (usually herbs) of a drug.

17. **my often rumination.** F1, *by*. The construction (reading *my*) will be, "My often rumination in which". *Often* is here used as an adj.

18. **humorous.** Dowden's 'prepense' comes very near the meaning.

F

24. To Rosalind's healthy mind it seems that such experience as Jaques' is not worth the price he has paid for it.

28. An interesting line, as showing Shakespeare's consciousness of the difference between prose and verse in dialogue, for which see Prosody 2. Cf. Falstaff's burlesque rise to verse in *1 Henry IV.*, ii. 4. 431; *2 Henry IV.*, v. 3. 105.

29. The *Exit*—not marked in F1—is marked here in the other folios. Rosalind punishes Orlando's unpunctuality by ignoring his presence, and flinging taunts after the retreating Jaques.

30. lisp and wear strange suits. For similar attacks on contemporary affectations cf. *Romeo and Juliet*, ii. 4. 26, "The pox of such antic, lisping, affecting fantasticoes"; and *Merchant of Venice*, i. 2. 79, where Portia says of her English suitor, "How oddly he is suited! I think he bought his doublet in Italy, his round hose in France, his bonnet in Germany, and his behaviour everywhere".

31. disable, disparage: **benefits**, advantages.

33. Shakespeare knew this discontent in himself. Cf. Sonnet 29—
    "Wishing me like to one more rich in hope,
        Featured like him".

34. swam in a gondola: *i.e.* been in Venice. Writers like Ascham denounced Italy as a school of vice: the other side of the question is represented by the vigorous Italian proverb—" *Inglese Italianato è un diabolo incarnato* ", "An Englishman Italianate is a Devil incarnate". *Swam*, past for p. part.—a license not uncommon in Shakespeare.

42. clapped him o' the shoulder. The general meaning is plain: Orlando may be touched, but his passion is not serious. But the exact metaphor is not clear — patted by way of encouragement? or tapped by way of arrest? Perhaps—as Cupid is an archer—it is used as in *2 Henry IV.*, iii. 2. 51, "clapped i' the clout"—a term of archery—meaning that Orlando is 'winged'.

49. jointure, marriage-settlement.

52. beholding, beholden, obliged. See Glossary.

54. prevent: here in the sense of the Lat. *praevenire*, to anticipate.

57. Celia for once puts in a word of her own accord : but it is characteristically addressed to Rosalind.

58. leer, look. See Glossary.

63. you were better: cf. i. 1. 126.

64. gravelled, stuck: now a colloquialism, but used gravely in E.E.

65. out, at a loss.

66. God warn us, God save us. See Glossary under *warrant*.

66. the cleanliest shift, the best way out of it.

73. honesty, chastity, as in iii. 3. 25, &c.

73. ranker, better grown. The meaning is 'If I can't discomfit you, I shall think myself more chaste than witty'.

77. Cf. iii. 5. 94. Orlando says just what he ought to say, and Rosalind dashes into a witty declamation against dying for love.

81. attorney, here in the true legal sense of deputy or proxy. For derivation, see Glossary.

82. there was not, there has not been. Cf. iii. 1. 1. And for the so-called 'omission of the relative', i. 2. 119.

84. Troilus, the lover of Cressida, who was given to the Greek Diomed. He is the hero of Shakespeare's *Troilus and Cressida*. In classic story he was killed by Achilles: the Grecian club, like Leander's cramp, is invented by Rosalind in a spirit of resolute common-sense.

86. Leander, he. This insertion of a pronoun, commonest after a proper name (Abb. § 243), converts the noun into a sort of exclamation—'as for Leander'. Leander lived at Abydos, across the Hellespont from Sestos, and to visit Hero had to swim the strait. Their story is told in Greek by Musaeus (?), translated by Marlowe, and completed by Chapman.

90. chroniclers. Hanmer corrected to *coroners*, because of the verb *found*. But (1) the jest is equally good as it stands; (2) there would only be one coroner; and (3) the Shakespearian form is not *coroner* but *crowner*.

96. Tenderness almost surprises Rosalind out of her part, but she recovers herself.

100. Fridays and Saturdays and all. This is explained as 'fasting-days and all', but it is merely light nonsense to cover real feeling.

107. Observe that it is Rosalind who proposes the mock-marriage. In Lodge, the suggestion comes from Alinda (Celia). The change is typical of the increased prominence which Shakespeare gives to the part of Rosalind.

119. commission, your warrant for 'taking' me to wife.

119. Note the emphatic form of words: Rosalind speaks in all seriousness here. She has plighted her troth.

120. there's a girl goes...: meaning, that she has anticipated what Celia should have dictated.

127. Another coruscation of assumed scepticism, elicited by Orlando's correct "For ever and a day".

131. a Barbary cock-pigeon. The epithet suggests oriental jealousy (Furness).

132. against, before, in expectation of.

134. Diana in the fountain. See Introduction, § 4. But probably Shakespeare has no particular figure in mind. 'Weeping' Dianas were a common ornament of fountains.

135. hyen, hyena, whose bark was thought to resemble a laugh, "He cometh to houses *by night*, and feineth *mannes voyce*" (Bartholomaeus).

138. Another *double entendre*; but Orlando suspects nothing.

141. the wiser the waywarder. Rosalind seems to agree with the wife of Bath, that women love most "dominacioun", and their waywardness is only a contrivance to get their own way.

141. make, shut. Cf. German *machen zu*. The expression survives in Yorkshire and Leicestershire dialect.

146. A proverbial expression: 'What are you after?' Cf. i. 2. 48.

151. her husband's occasion, an occasion against her husband (objective genitive): rather than, occasioned by her husband.

156. This is unguarded tenderness, but Orlando takes it for good acting, and his commonplace reply gives Rosalind time to resume the boy.

165. See Introduction, § 4.

167. pathetical: a word (intentionally or unintentionally) misused by Shakespeare for anything striking, shocking, 'awful'. Armado and Costard use it (*L. L. L.* i. 2. 103; iv. 1. 150). Perhaps Shakespeare had no very definite notion of its meaning himself. See note on *anatomized*, ii. 7. 56.

172. religion, strict observance—the sense of 'binding' is the original one.

174. A literal expansion of the phrase, "Time tries all".

176. misused, abused. In some of their senses ('reviling and 'maltreating') *misuse* and *abuse* have changed places in Modern English. Cf. iii. 2. 338.

177. This is from Lodge—"And I pray you, quoth Aliena, if your robes were off, what mettle are you made of that you are so satirical against women? is it not a foul bird that defiles its own nest?"... "Leave off, said Aliena, to taunt thus bitterly, or else I'll pull off your page's apparel."

181. fathom. For this form of the plural, see note on iii. 2. 303.

183. the bay of Portugal, a name "still used by sailors to denote that portion of the sea off the coast of Portugal from Oporto to the headland of Cintra" (Wright). The water here is 1400 fathoms deep within 40 miles of the shore.

187. **thought**, melancholy brooding.   **spleen**, caprice—another piece of Shakespearian physiology.

188. **abuses**, deceives. Cf. iii. 5. 78. Meaning that love is blind.

191. **shadow**, a shady place.

Scene 2.

This scene is a sylvan interlude, intended to fill up the two hours of Orlando's absence.

3. **like a Roman conqueror**: alluding to the triumphal return of a victorious general. This Roman practice—like everything about that great people—seems to have appealed to Shakespeare's imagination.

5. **a branch of victory.** Jaques probably intends a pun; *branch* is used for the antlers of the deer. Cf. Tennyson, *Princess* (*Conclusion*), " and shook the *branches* of the deer".

11. Cf. Lodge—"What news, forester? hast thou wounded some deer, and lost him in the fall?   Care not, man, for so small a loss; thy fees was but the skin, the shoulder, and the horns."

12. Ff.—"*Then sing him home, the rest shall bear this burthen.* Theobald saw that the latter half of the line was a stage direction.

13. **Take thou no scorn**, be not ashamed.

Scene 3.

This scene falls naturally into two parts, the letter brought by Silvius and the message brought by Oliver. Shakespeare still follows Lodge closely in the incidents; but (1) the order is inverted; (2) Rosalind's reception of Phebe's letter is differently conceived; (3) Oliver is made to narrate his own rescue; and (4) the occasion of his message is transferred (see Introduction, § 9, *e*).

2. **here much Orlando** ! ironical.

4. Celia gives the sentence an unexpected turn (παρὰ προσδοκίαν) —'to sleep' instead of 'to hunt'.

12. **as**, in the capacity of: almost tautologous.

13. Rosalind opens the letter, and finds a declaration.   To cover her surprise, she seizes on Silvius's guess as to the contents, and continues in this strain while reading. The "Well, shepherd, well" of line 19 marks that she has reached the end.

16. **and that she could.**   A verb of saying is to be understood from the preceding "calls": this idiom is common in Greek.

F 2   (M 7)

17. **phœnix**, a fabulous bird of Arabia. There was only one at a time: it lived 500 years, and was re-born from its own ashes.

20. In the novel, Rosalind, after reading the letter, leads Montanus to confess his love, and then shows that it is hopeless. Here, she seems to wish to cure Silvius by rousing his indignation, if possible.

25. **freestone-colour'd**, of a dirty brown.

27. **a huswife's hand**: *i.e.* hard with house-work.

29. **invention**, conception. Cf. ii. 5. 43. **hand**, hand-writing, with a pun.

31–36. Rosalind works up to a climax the picture of Phebe's imaginary scorn, and by the contrast brings out effectively the utter abandon of her surrender.

34. **giant-rude**: one of the compound adjectives freely coined by Shakespeare. The first part of the compound has the force of an adverb.

35. **Ethiope**: not elsewhere used as an adjective.

39. **She Phebes me**, plays the Phebe to me.

48. **vengeance**, mischief, not revenge: in this sense commonly used as a curse, "vengeance on you".

49. Phebe, of course, means that Rosalind is a god.

50. **eyne**, eyes. Shakespeare uses this archaic plural only in rhymed passages, as a conventional poetic form.

53. **in mild aspect**. Here, as in iii. 2. 136–149, the metaphor is astrological: *aspect* = the appearance of a planet. For the accent, see Prosody, 4 *a β*.

59. **youth and kind**, youthful nature—a hendiadys: *kind* here almost = sex.

61. **make**, produce by my work, earn.

65, 66. Celia's pity and Rosalind's indignation are equally characteristic. To Rosalind's vigorous common-sense Silvius's hopeless devotion seems unmanly, she herself being fortunate in love.

67. **an instrument**: in the twofold sense of a tool and a musical instrument. The metaphor is worked out in *Hamlet*, iii. 2. 380–389, "You would play upon me", &c.

69. **a tame snake**. 'Snake' is a common expression of contempt in E.E.

71. **unless thou entreat for her.** This in the novel Montanus actually does. Silvius is now dismissed.

74. **fair ones.** If this is not a misprint, it is a curious slip on Shakespeare's part.

77. By a fine touch, Celia, who was dumb in Orlando's presence, is addressed by and answers Oliver.

77. **neighbour bottom**, neighbouring dell—subst. as adj.

78. **rank**, row.   See iii. 2. 85.

79. **left** is here a participle—being left.

85. **favour**, appearance.   See Glossary.

85. **bestows himself**, behaves.

86. This line has been suspected on account of the halting metre. But the omission of the third stress, though rare, is not unexampled. See Prosody, 3 *b β*.

87, 88. Oliver addresses his question to Celia, in the singular: in her reply she speaks for both.

92. **napkin**, quite equivalent to *handkerchief* in E.E.

96. **handkercher.**   This spelling represents a common pronunciation.

97-155. Shakespeare has two reasons for narrating Oliver's rescue by his own mouth, instead of representing it directly: (1) the lioness and the snake could not have been put on the stage; (2) the effect of the rescue on Oliver's *mind*, its effect in promoting his 'conversion', is what Shakespeare is most interested to show; and this is best ensured by making him the narrator.   This conversion of Oliver's has always been regarded as one of the weakest points in the play: it is made at least more plausible by Shakespeare's indirect rendering.   See Introduction, § 9.

103. **Under an oak.**   Ff. *Under an old oak.*   This is not metrically impossible; but the adjective is worse than superfluous.   The correction is Pope's.   Compare this with the brook-side oak described in ii. 1. 31-32; the two pictures are quite distinct.

105. **A wretched ragged man, o'ergrown with hair.**   These details are added by Shakespeare, not only to excite compassion for Oliver, but also to indicate the length of his wanderings.   See Introduction, § 9.

107. The "green and gilded snake" is another vivid detail added by Shakespeare.

111. **indented glides:** an admirable description of the sinuous zigzag of the serpent's path.

113. Again Shakespeare heightens the effect by making the lion of the novel a lioness, sucked and hungry.

120. Celia's interest in Oliver had already been excited by Orlando's conversation.

121. **render**, describe as.

124. But, to Orlando, but to come to Orlando.   Rosalind is not interested in Oliver's unnatural conduct; she wishes to know whether Orlando has acted nobly or no.

126. This line represents a " meditation" of two pages in the novel.

128. his just occasion, his fair chance of revenge.

130. hurtling, crashing, din of fight.   See Glossary.

131. Oliver's identity is naturally and effectively revealed by the pronoun in the last line of his speech.

133. contrive, plot.   The expression would now mean ' manage to kill him'; but *contrive* in E.E. does not imply success.

134. do not shame, am not ashamed.

137. Again Rosalind recalls Oliver to the subject of Orlando.

138. In the novel, Rosader does not reveal who he is till Saladin has made a full confession of his sins.

139. recountments, narratives: a noun coined from the verb, but not elsewhere found in Shakespeare.

140. As, for instance.   This, and not ' namely', is the true meaning here.   Oliver breaks off with " In brief— ".

146. In the novel, Rosader is wounded in rescuing Alinda from the robbers, and Saladin merely brings word of his convalescence. The transference here enables Shakespeare to introduce the "bloody napkin" and by means of it Rosalind's tell-tale swoon.

149. Brief, to be brief.   **recover'd,** restored him (from his faint).

154. this blood: so F 1.   The other Ff. *his blood.*

156. sweet Ganymede: 158. Cousin Ganymede: Celia almost betrays Rosalind's secret in her alarm.

161. Rosalind's faint thus becomes an excuse for further intimacy between Oliver and Celia.

164. Ah, sirrah.   The form *sirrah* usually implies disrespect; but sometimes, when preceded by *ah*, it forms part of a soliloquy, and is little more than an exclamation.

164. a body, a person.   This use of *body* is now confined to dialect, except in the compounds *somebody, anybody, nobody*; but was good English in Shakespeare's time.

168. a passion of earnest, a real attack.   *Passion* is used more widely in E.E. of any strong and over-mastering feeling.

177. Oliver's significant " Rosalind" seems to show that he suspects something.   Remember that he knew of the princesses' flight. But his suspicions are of no consequence, so long as he does not tell Orlando.

Act V.—Scene I.

One reconciliation has already been effected, that between Oliver and Orlando. Only one more revelation and one more reconciliation are needed " to make all doubts even"; but these are inevitably postponed to the last scene. To this last scene the second is preparatory; the third is another of those short lyrical interludes which here and there relieve the action; the first is a comic, almost farcical, prelude, which comes in aptly after the somewhat grave close of Act IV., and forms a transition to the jubilant and masque-like wedding-scene.

10. **it is meat and drink to me,** 'as good as a feast', we might say. The expression was proverbial.

11. Touchstone's complacent consciousness of his own parts gives an odd cast to his reflections on the same trait in William.

12. **shall,** must. For this sense of obligation which clings to *shall*, see note on i. 1. 119.

14. **God ye good even,** *i.e.* God give you good even; further abbreviated to *Godgigoden, Godden.*

16. Compare Touchstone's manner on the appearance of Jaques in iii. 3.

32. This figure may have been suggested by Lodge: "Phœbe is no latice for your *lips*, and her *grapes* hang so high, that gaze at them you may, but touch them you cannot".

38. Such parodies of learning were evidently a favourite item in the repertoire of the professional wit. The point of Touchstone's figure is that they can't both have her.

41. **ipse:** Lat. 'he himself'.

44. Touchstone suddenly abandons his friendly patronizing air and turns on the oaf with a torrent of high-sounding threats. Several turns of phrase recall Don Armado; cf. *L. L. L.* i. 1. 267, "a female; or, for thy more sweet understanding, a woman".

56. **God rest you merry:** a common wish, especially at parting. *God* is often omitted.

57. **seeks:** singular verb after two subjects; cf. Abbot, § 336.

Scene 2.

This scene is wholly preparatory for the final recognition and denouement in scene fourth. As such, it is somewhat bare and business-like, but at least economical and clear. The composition of the wedding-scene is foreshadowed in the grace and balanced grouping of the close.

3. **wooing:** absolute participle, without noun.

3. **perséver**: so regularly spelt and accented in Shakespeare.

8. The relations of the brothers are now so far inverted that Oliver asks Orlando's consent to his marriage.

10. **estate**, bestow. The offer ignores the Duke's seizure, but serves as earnest of Oliver's conversion.

16, 17. Rosalind calls Oliver 'brother' as Celia's lover; he calls her 'sister' in reference to her masquerade.

27. **I know where you are**, I know what you mean. Afraid, perhaps, that Orlando may ask awkward questions about her swoon, Rosalind dashes characteristically into a humorously exaggerated account of the sudden attachment between Oliver and Celia. This speech of hers is Shakespeare's apology for his treatment of their hasty wooing. In the novel it forms an episode of some length. But Shakespeare probably felt that it would be hard to make it probable or pleasing on the stage; he evades the difficulty, and masks the weak place by the present speech.

29. **thrasonical**, vain-glorious. See Glossary.

29. **I came, saw, and overcome**: *veni, vidi, vici*—Caesar's famous despatch after defeating Pharnaces at Zela, B.C. 47. Shakespeare seems to have been struck with it; he quotes it in three other places, giving the Latin in *L. L. L.* iv. 1. 68, and always translates as here. No character in history interested him so much as "the hook-nosed fellow of Rome".

34. **degrees**: with a play on the literal sense of 'steps'.

35. **incontinent**, without delay. See Glossary.

36. **wrath**, impetuosity, properly of combat—the lovers being humorously represented as trying to get at each other. "Clubs, clubs" was the rallying cry of the London prentices, who used these weapons (they could not carry swords) to keep the peace, or to break it. See Scott's *Fortunes of Nigel*, c. 1.

38. The marriage of Oliver and Celia has been vigorously denounced as an ugly concession to the practice of 'pairing off' the characters. But the true bone of contention must be the reality of Oliver's conversion, of which his marriage is the seal.

39. **nuptial**: so generally, perhaps always, in Shakespeare. This word is properly an adj.

49. **conceit**, intelligence. See Glossary.

50. **insomuch**, inasmuch as, because—only here in Shakespeare.

55. **conversed**, associated. This is the common meaning in Shakespeare, though he also uses it in the more limited modern sense.

55. Orlando in v. 4. 32 identifies this magician with the uncle whom Rosalind had mentioned in iii. 2. 325. This may be a slip of Shakespeare's. In Lodge, the magician is spoken of simply as a 'friend'.

56. See Introduction, § 4. Rosalind's magician is a "white witch".

57. **cries it out**, proclaims. For the use of *it* cf. i. 3. 115.

61. **human as she is**: *i.e.* no phantom but the real Rosalind without any of the dangers which attend magic rites.

63. **tender dearly**, value highly. See Glossary.

67. With the entrance of Silvius and Phebe, the dialogue rises at once to verse.

87-89. **observance**, homage. In one or other of the lines— probably the latter—the word is a misprint, but no convincing emendation has been suggested. Malone's ' obedience' is as good as any.

94. **to love you**, for loving you—the gerundial infinitive. Cf. i. i. 96.

97. **why...too.** So the Folios; corrected by Rowe to *who...to* for the sake of harmony. But no change is necessary.

100. **'t is like the howling of Irish wolves against the moon.** The simile is suggested by Lodge—"thou barkest with the wolves of Syria against the moon". But Lodge's expression means ' to cry for what you can't get '; Rosalind here is merely referring to their discordant clamour. The wolf, though extinct in England, was still found in Ireland, and this may have suggested the epithet; or the point may lie (as Deighton thinks) in the harshness of the Irish language. Ireland was much in men's minds at the time.

Scene 3.

We probably owe this little interlude originally to stage require-ments, but it justifies its insertion by a freshness of its own, and forms a sort of good-bye to the forest life in which the action has moved so long.

4. **dishonest**, immodest. See Glossary under *honest*

4. **to be a woman of the world**=to be married. Shakespeare twice uses the phrase "to go to the world" for ' to be married '— *Much Ado*, ii. i. 331; *All's Well*, i. 3. 20—the idea being that marriage is a woman's start in life.

9. **clap into 't roundly**, set about it straight away. From the sense of ' complete' *round* is used widely for unqualified, straight-forward, without ceremony.

10. **the only prologues**, only the prologues. For the inversion of *only* cf. i. 2. 162.

14-31. In the Folios, the last stanza of this song is printed second. The present arrangement, which is obviously the right one, is given by Morley (see Introduction, § 3), and in a MS. in the Advocates' Library in Edinburgh. The dislocation has not been explained.

17. **the only pretty ring time,** the season for marriage. Ff. *rang time*: corrected from the MS.

20. **acres:** here, and generally in Shakespeare, in its literal sense of 'fields'.

22. **folks:** *fools* in the MS.

28. The MS. reads: *Then pretty lovers take the time.* The moral of the ditty is the same as that of the song in *Twelfth Night*—"Youth's a stuff will not endure".

32-33. Instead of qualifying his condemnation of the sense by praise of the tune, as he leads them to expect, Touchstone παρὰ προσδοκίαν condemns tune and all.

33. **untuneable.** Cowden-Clarke says that *tune* and *time* were once synonymous. At any rate, the pages defend their time, and so lay themselves open to Touchstone once more.

Scene 4.

The conception of this scene is in the main original. The divergence from Lodge in the matter of the usurper's conversion has been noticed in the Introduction. In the novel, the most prominent figure in the scene before the nuptials is Montanus; in the play it is Touchstone. The difference is characteristic. A good deal of unfavourable criticism has been bestowed on the finish of the play: but Shakespeare often prefers to touch in the denouement lightly, though the execution here is scarcely in his best style.

4. 'As those who fear that their hope is only a hope, but know for certain that they fear.' Various attempts have been made to emend this difficult line ; but no change is necessary.

5. **compact.** For the accent, see Prosody, 4 *a β*.

6. The arrangement and declaration on Orlando's part, here presupposed, are first made at this point in the novel.

13, 14. This bargain (also presupposed) is made on an earlier occasion in the novel, but is postponed till this point by Shakespeare, in order to set it off against the similar bargain with Orlando.

22. **or else...to wed.** This is another instance of that absolute use of the infinitive, explained in note to iii. 2. 151.

27. **lively,** life-like.

28-34. This speech of Orlando's should settle at once the absurd idea that he had recognized Rosalind.

32. **desperate,** dangerous, as tampering with forbidden arts.

34. **obscured,** hidden. The expression may have been suggested by the invisibility of magicians within their charmed circles.

35-97. The dramatic purpose of this comic dialogue is evidently to give time for the preparation of the pageant which enters at line 98.

35. toward, approaching.

38. salutation and greeting: bilingualism—see note on i. 1. 59 Touchstone has donned his best vocabulary for the occasion.

42. purgation, proof: properly 'exculpation', as in i. 3. 46; but Touchstone misapplies the word, as does Costard in *L. L. L.* iii. 1. 128, "and now you will be my purgation".

43. measure, a stately dance, somewhat like a minuet.

45. and like, and was likely.

47. ta'en up, settled.

52. Touchstone's remarks have so far been addressed to Jaques, in the independent tone of an equal. Observe the sudden and over-whelming deference with which he 'sirs' the Duke.

52. God 'ild you: cf. iii. 3. 62.

52. I desire you of the like, I wish the same to you. In E.E. it was possible to say, 'I desire you of something', as well as 'I desire something of you'.

53. copulatives, people wishing to be married. Such is the force of the termination here: but the word is coined for the nonce by Touchstone.

55. blood, passion—constantly opposed in this sense to judgment, wisdom, and the like.

58. For this use of *your = iste*, see on iii. 2. 49.

60. the fool's bolt. "A fool's bolt is soon shot", says the pro-verb. A *bolt* was a blunt arrow used for killing birds, &c.

60. such dulcet diseases. Touchstone's vocabulary is too much for him again.

62. Jaques returns to the charge, wishing to exhibit Touchstone in his best vein of fooling to the Duke.

64. a lie seven times removed. Malone's explanation—if it be not pedantic to explain Touchstone—seems the right one. The Lie Direct is the Lie proper: the others are diluted forms of lie, 're-moved' from it in various degrees. In Touchstone's case, the quarrel was found to originate in a mild contradiction—the Retort Courteous —seven times removed from the Lie Direct.

65. seeming, seemingly, adj. for adv.

65. dislike, express my dislike of. For similar changes of mean-ing, from feeling to expression or action, cf. *disable* (line 71 below), to disparage; *defy* (*Epilogue*, line 17), to dislike.

F 3

70. **quip**, a jest at one's expense. Milton's much-quoted "Quips and cranks and wanton wiles" has preserved the word to modern English.

75. **countercheck**, rebuff: the metaphor is from chess (Wright).

80. Swords are measured before a duel, to find if they are of equal length. Touchstone and his adversary measured them—and parted.

82. Shakespeare is usually supposed to be referring here to a treatise on duelling by Vincentio Saviolo (1595), the second book of which deals with *Honor and honorable Quarrels*. But the resemblance between Touchstone's Lies and Saviolo's is not very close: if Shakespeare had any particular book in view it may equally well have been, as Furness thinks, *The Book of Honor and Arms* (1590).

83. **books for good manners**, books of etiquette. There were many such then, as now — *e.g.* Whittinton's *Lytle Booke of Good Maners for Chyldren* (1554).

89. **I knew.** Modern usage would require the perfect.

92. **swore brothers.** The expression alludes to the *fratres jurati* ('sworn brothers') of the days of chivalry—warriors who swore to share each other's fortunes. A relic of the custom survives, says Prof. Herford, in the German custom of *Bruderschaft*.

95. This characteristic observation of the Duke's reminds us of the directly satirical intention of Touchstone's wit. It is a hit at a contemporary affectation.

96. **stalking-horse**, a real or artificial horse, under cover of which sportsmen approached their game.

97. **under the presentation**, under cover, presenting it before him. The word is used in a somewhat different sense, 'show' > < 'substance', in *Richard III.*, iv. 4. 84.

Still Music], soft music.

98. Critics have objected to the introduction of Hymen as on a different level of convention from the rest of the piece. But the pageant, as Dr. Johnson pointed out, is contrived by Rosalind as the magic machinery which restores her to her father.

100. **atone**, are at one. Shakespeare also uses the word transitively, to reconcile. See Glossary.

105. **her bosom.** The Folios and the Globe have *his*, which I do not understand.

114. Rosalind has been the moving spirit of the last three acts, sustaining the dialogue and guiding the various strands of plot. Now that she has made all doubts even, she gives herself to her father and her lover, and says no more.

115. **bar**, prohibit.

120. **If truth holds true contents,** if truth be true. This speech of Hymen's, and the following song, have been suspected, but on no evidence except their general feebleness. It must be admitted that the execution of this scene is not up to the level of the earlier acts, at least in the verse part.

124. **to,** for, as still in 'have to wife'.

125. **sure together,** a sure match.

127. **wedlock-hymn.** In Shakespeare's days music formed a regular part of wedding-ceremonies. Wright compares the similar pageant in the *Tempest*.

131. **Juno's crown.** Juno, the queen of the gods, presided over wedlock.

134. **high,** solemn.

138. **Even daughter,** my daughter equally with Rosalind. The sense of *equally*, *likewise*, is more in place here than the ordinary 'corrective' sense—"my niece, nay, my daughter"—though this is possible.

140. "Thy fidelity knits my love to thee". For this sense of *combine*=to bind, cf. *Measure for Measure*, iv. 3. 149, "I am combined by a sacred vow".

141-156. Attention has been called in the Introduction to this important departure from the novel. The action has been steeped so long in the atmosphere of Arden that an incursion of the evil passions which dominate the first act would be felt as a grave breach of harmony. One of the evil principles has already been reconciled by the conversion of Oliver, and Shakespeare now eliminates the other by similar means. The Duke's conversion is narrated, because it does not admit of dramatic treatment. Moreover, by being presented thus indirectly, the fact is kept remote, and felt only as a cloud that has passed away. Jaques de Boys merely discharges the function of the ἄγγελος of Greek tragedy.

146. **Address'd a mighty power,** prepared a great force. See Glossary.

147. **in his own conduct,** under his own leadership.

151. **question,** conversation.

151. **was converted.** A subject is supplied from line 149.

154. **all their lands restored.** 'Were' may be supplied, but the construction is probably nom. absol.

156. **engage,** pledge. See Glossary.

156. The elder Duke accepts the return of fortune in the same philosophic spirit in which he endured adversity.

157. **offer'st fairly,** makest a handsome present.

160. do those ends, accomplish those purposes.

162. every, every one. Cf. *any* as pronoun, i. 2. 119.

163. shrewd, hard. See Glossary.

165. states, fortunes—'estates' in the wider sense.

170. by your patience, by your leave. This sentence is addressed to the Duke.

172. pompous, ceremonious.

174. In this way Jaques, like the usurper, though for a different reason, is eliminated from the 'better world' which the Duke's return inaugurates.

174. convertites: the E.E. form of 'converts'.

176. The real courtesy which prompts these good wishes forbids us to take too harsh a view of Jaques. He is a gentleman spoiled. His sarcasm is reserved for Touchstone, who is fair game.

176. You to your former honour I bequeath. Schmidt cites this as an instance of a phrase in which the whole relation of ideas is inverted = I bequeath your honour to you. Such inversion is naturally most common in verbs of joining and separating.

177. deserves: cf. note on v. 1. 57.

EPILOGUE.

Spoken in his own person by the boy-actor who played Rosalind.

1. It is not the fashion, &c. Not before the Restoration was it common to assign Prologue or Epilogue to characters in the play: in the *Tempest*, however, the Epilogue is spoken by Prospero, and in *All's Well* by the King. For a female character to speak the Prologue was a novelty in 1609: "A She-Prologue is as rare as a usurer's alms", Prologue to *Every Woman in Her Humour*. (From G.S.B., *The Prologue and Epilogue*.)

2. unhandsome, in bad taste.

3. Good wine needs no bush. An ivy bush was the sign of a vintner—ivy being sacred to Bacchus, the god of wine. The custom still survives in parts of Germany; and in this country 'The Bush Inn' is still no uncommon name for a tavern. The proverb means that good things don't need to be advertised.

7. insinuate, ingratiate myself.

10-14. The sense of this nonsense seems to be: let each one like what pleases him or her, and so among you all the play will please everybody.

11. as please you. *Please* is subjunctive, used indefinitely after relatives = *as may please*.

15. **If I were a woman.** Women's parts, on the public stage, were not regularly taken by women till after the Restoration, though they had acted before in masques and private theatricals. "The innovation had been made tentatively, and with some secrecy, and the practice was formally legalized by Royal Patent in 1662" (Ward, *English Drama*, ii. 422). The tables have been turned at last. On Feb. 27th of this year, *As You Like It* was played in London by a company consisting entirely of women. "The general effect," said the newspapers, "was less unpleasant than might have been expected."

16. **liked,** pleased. Originally impersonal, *hit lícaδ me*, a usage which lasted into the 16th century. Hence two others (1) personal —other subjects instead of *it*; but in Shakespeare in the sense of *please* the impersonal use is common; (2) 'I like it', *i.e.* find it pleasing—a change of meaning helped by French. Cf. *please.*

defied, disliked. See note on v. 4. 65.

APPENDIX A.

HAD SHAKESPEARE READ THE COKE'S TALE?

Most critics think not. "The old bard", says Farmer, "was no hunter of MSS.", and the Tale is not known to have been printed till 1721. It is no argument that Lodge had read it: Lodge was a man of university training; he had been a servitor at Trinity College, Oxford, and may there have acquired habits of research.

On the other side, Knight argues that Lodge's novel was written *at sea*. Yet he follows the Tale so closely that we can hardly help thinking (urges Knight) that *he must have had a copy of it before him*. If this were so, then the Tale must have been more widely diffused (in MS. or broadsheet) than is commonly imagined. We may, therefore, give up our prejudice on that head, and judge the question by the evidence.

The following are the chief points of comparison, and of these I attach most importance to 3 and 6:—

1. Sir Johan is at first advised to leave all to his eldest son.
2. Johan "*feeds*" Gamelyn "*yvel and eek wrothe*". So Orlando says that Oliver's horses "are fair with their *feeding*": "he lets me *feed* with his hinds" (i. 1. 10, 16).
3. When called a "gadelyng" Gamelyn retorts:

> "Cristes curs mot he have that clepeth me gadelyng.
> I am no worse gadelyng, ne no worse wight,
> But born of a lady, and geten of a knight."

So Orlando: "I am no villain; I am the youngest son of Sir Rowland de Boys; he was my father, and he is thrice a villain that says such a father begot villains" (i. 1. 49).

4. Johan prays that Gamelyn may *break his neck* in the wrestling; Oliver tells Charles—

> "I had as lief thou didst *break his neck* as his finger" (i. 1. 125).

5. In the Tale, as in the play, the Franklin bemoans his sons; in the novel he is stoical.

6. When the wardens of the wrestling tell Gamelyn that the fair is over, he replies—

> "I have not yet halvendel [half] sold up my ware"

So Orlando—

> "I am not yet well breathed" (i. 2. 184)

178

To sum up: (1) In the absence of evidence, it would be antecedently improbable that Shakespeare had read the Tale. (2) The resemblance between the Tale and the novel is not strong enough to support Knight's conclusion. It is confined to points of incident, and proves no more than that Lodge had a good memory. (3) The resemblance between the Tale and the play, on the other hand, is mainly in points of expression. Some of those are plainly accidental; and though the coincidence in Nos. 3 and 6 is striking, it is no more than might naturally happen when two poets are treating the same incident independently.

APPENDIX B.

ON SOME SUPPOSED INCONSISTENCIES IN ACT I.

In support of his view that the play was hurriedly finished, Mr. Wright adduces the following 'marks of hasty work':—

(1) The name of Jaques de Boys. When he comes in in act v. he is called "Second Brother", to distinguish him from the melancholy Jaques.

(2) In i. 2. 70, 71, the First Folio has—

> "*Clo.* One that old *Fredericke* your Father loues.
> *Ros.* My Father's loue is enough to honor him."

From i. 2. 200 and v. 4. 144 it appears that Frederick is the name of the usurping Duke.

(3) In i. 2. 238, the First Folio has—

> "But yet indeed the taller is his (*i.e.* the usurper's) daughter",

whereas in i. 3. 108 Rosalind says *she* is "more than common tall".

(4) In i. 2. 255, Orlando exclaims, "But heavenly Rosalind", though he has just been asking Le Beau which was which.

(5) "Nor is Touchstone", says Mr. Wright, "at all what we are prepared to expect from the early description of him as 'the clownish fool' and the 'roynish clown'."

(6) In i. 3. 68, the swan which belongs to Venus is given to Juno.

Such are Mr. Wright's points. (1) and (6) we may at once concede (see note *ad loc.*). (2) is probably a printer's error—*Ros.* for *Cel.* Walker has a list of 60 such mistakes in the First Folio—two others from our play. (4) proves nothing; Orlando would know Rosalind's name though he did not know her by sight. Oliver knows the name—"Can you tell (he asks) if Rosalind, the duke's daughter, be banished with her father?" (i. 1. 92).

Nor is there much force in (5). It must not be forgotten that

Touchstone is Shakespeare's first essay in treating the professional fool. He is a court jester, and in i. 2 he is still at court and labouring in his vocation. It is not till he finds himself among rustics that he begins to air his manners. "It is meat and drink to me to see a clown." Mr. Furness actually suggests that Shakespeare based *As You Like It* on an older play, which crops out (he thinks) in this scene (i. 2). But the scene is undoubtedly Shakespeare's, though not perhaps in his best manner; and I can see no radical difference between the humour of "pancakes and mustard" and the humour of "batlets and peascods".

It is not so easy to explain away (3). "Taller" can hardly be a printer's error. The remarkable thing is that Shakespeare should have contradicted himself within 150 lines without noticing it. It should be observed that all these (real or supposed) inconsistencies occur in the first act, and all but two in the second scene of that act. It is possible that Shakespeare may here have laid down his pen, and resumed his work at a later date. No such careless touches mar the forest scenes. It is on "the airy column", not on "the massive pedestal" that he has lavished his care. In any case, he cannot have revised the play for the press. Other indications—remarked on the notes—seem to show that the text of 1623 was printed from a stage copy.

NOTE ON SHAKESPEARE'S PROSODY.

Orl. Good day and happiness, dear Rosalind!
Jaq. Nay then, God be wi' you, an you talk in blank verse.

1. Definitions—Verse, Prose, Blank Verse.—In reading any composition, a certain *stress* is laid on syllables at various intervals. The succession of these stresses constitutes the *rhythm*, or flow, of the composition: when they succeed each other at (more or less) regular intervals, they constitute *metre*, and the composition is called *verse.* Ordinary Shakespearian dialogue is written in a metre which consists of 5 stressed alternating with 5 unstressed syllables, in rising rhythm (*i.e.*, opening on an unstressed syllable), and without rhyme. Hence the name, Blank Verse.

2. More than half of *As You Like It*, however, is written in prose. Shakespeare's choice of these two modes of expression is noteworthy. It is mainly determined by two considerations: (*a*) the characters speaking; (*b*) the dominant sentiment or interest of the situation. Since prose is nearer to the language of ordinary life, it is used (*a*) by clowns, servants, and women in familiar conversation; (*b*) whenever the interest is mainly comic, intellectual, or commonplace. Verse is a more ceremonious and conventional mode of speech, and so is used (*a*) by noble persons; (*b*) wherever the interest is mainly emotional, passionate, or imaginative. In the present play, observe that (*a*) the two dukes and the lords generally talk verse, the servants and rustics prose. Rosalind and Celia talk prose when alone, except in i. 3. 83 to end, where see note. (*b*) Silvius and Phebe, the idyllic characters, always use verse; Touchstone, Audrey, and William always prose. Corin uses verse to Silvius and prose to Touchstone. Rosalind's witty flights are all in prose; Jacques moralizes in blank verse.

3. Variations.—The normal blank verse, then, has 10 syllables, 5 stresses, rising rhythm, no rhyme—

Good day' and hap'piness', dear Ro'salind'.

All variations will fall under the head of (*a*) more or fewer syllables; (*b*) more or fewer stresses; (*c*) falling or level rhythm; (*d*) rhyme.

(*a*) (*a*) *Extra syllables.* An additional (unstressed) syllable may be inserted anywhere in a line. It is commonest immediately before a pause, and so is most frequently found at the end of the line. Such endings are called *feminine* endings, and, properly used, impart a peculiar softness and beauty—cf. v. 4. 8–34 with the

181

first lord's speech ii. 1. 25–43. Two extra syllables are rarely found at the end: perhaps iii. 5. 42—

> I see no more in you than in the ord | inary.

But (when there is no slurring) such instances should be classed as 6-stress lines. Within the line, the extra syllable usually comes at the *caesura* (see below), *e.g.*

> And we will mend thy wa | ges. I like' | this place (ii. 4. 88).

or with a change of speakers: *e.g.*

> And faints for suc | cour.
>   Fair sir', | I pity her (ii. 4. 69).

Extra syllables are also common in proper names; thus, perhaps,

> If there be truth in sight, you are my Ros | alind (v. 4. 109).

Indeed, Shakespeare sometimes treats proper names as altogether extra-metrical.

(β) *Syllables omitted.* An unstressed syllable is sometimes, though rarely, omitted. This generally takes place after an emphatic mono-syllable, usually an imperative; *e.g.*

> Peace', | I say'. | Good e' | ven to' | you, friend' (ii. 4. 63).
> Bring' | us to' | this sight', | and you' | shall say' | (iii. 4. 52).
> Some scar' | of it'; | — lean' | upon' | a rush (iii. 5. 22).

In all these cases there is a marked pause: hence this omission is commonest in the first foot—compare the monosyllabic first feet in Chaucer—and after that in the third. In our last instance, modern editors read 'lean but upon a rush'.

(*b*) (*a*) *Extra stresses.* Lines with 6 stresses ('Alexandrines') are occasionally found; *e.g.*

> Besides', I like' you not'. If you' will know' my house' (iii. 5. 73).

This is the usual type of 6-stress line, with a pause after the third foot.

So also ii. 1. 49 and 52 (note that half of each line is Jacques' reflection, half Amiens' description), iii. 3. 25, iii. 5. 117, &c.

(β) *Stresses omitted.* Lines with 4 stresses, not being exclamatory or broken lines, are very rare. But cf.—

> Like a | ripe sis | ter :—' | the woman low (iv. 3. 86).

This may be a true 4-stress line, with extra syllable at the mid-line pause, as (*a*) (*a*) above ; or the omission may be compensated by the strong pause. But genuine 4- and 6-stress lines can hardly be regarded as mere variations of the ordinary pentameter. They are new metres, interspersed somewhat arbitrarily at impressive turns of the dialogue.

(γ) But Shakespeare makes abundant use of *short* or *broken* verses. They occur usually at the beginning or end of a speech, when a speaker leaves off in the middle of a verse or interrupts another without regard to the metre. They sometimes occur in the middle of a speech, when the speaker breaks off and resumes anew.

Exclamations, interjections, and asides belong to this class of broken lines, and present no difficulty.   In ii. 4. 32, 35, 38, Silvius breaks off each time at 'Thou hast not loved': in v. 2. 76–81, 82–85, 90–93, Silvius's broken line 'And so am I for Phebe' is taken up by the others in a sort of round.

Many apparent 4-stress lines are to be explained as two broken lines; *e.g.*

> *Ros.* I have more cause.
> *Cel.*   Thou hast not, cousin (i. 3. 86).
> *Cel.* Are you his brother?
> *Ros.*   Was't you he rescued? (iv. 3. 132).

Sometimes a part line seems to do double duty; *e.g.*

> And let him feed.
> *Orl.* I thank you most for him.
> *Adam.*   So had you need (ii. 7. 168–9).

Here *Orl.* caps the Duke's line, and is in turn capped by *Adam.*[1] So ii. 3. 15–16.

(δ) In the preceding sections, I have spoken merely of 'stressed' and 'unstressed' syllables, as if this classification were exhaustive. But stress is obviously a matter of degree; every syllable has some stress, and between the faintest and the strongest there are many shades.   Hence, without actual omission of stress, a foot may be weakened by the substitution of a *weak* or *intermediate* for the normal strong stress.   This variation is exceedingly common—not more than 1 line in 15 having the normal 5 full stresses—but is exercised under the following laws—

(1) The weak stress (') is commonest in the fifth foot; *e.g.*

> And high top bald with dry antiq | uity' (iv. 3. 104).

(2) There are never more than two weak stresses in a line.

(3) Two weak stresses rarely come together.

(4) The loss of weight is generally made up for (except in the fifth foot) in one of two ways.   Either, the other syllable in the foot has also a slight stress—

> I fly | thee', for' | I would not injure thee (iii. 5. 9).

or, one of the neighbouring feet has two stresses—

> Will you' | go' sis' | ter? Shepherd ply her hard (iii. 5. 76).

(c) **Rhythm.**—(a) The order of stressed and unstressed syllables may be inverted in any foot, thus changing the rhythm (for that foot) from rising to falling; *e.g.*

> (1) Sweet' are | the uses of adversity (ii. 1. 12).
> (2) Than that | mix'd' in | his cheek (iii. 5. 121).
> (3) Such Ethiope words, | black'er | in their effect (iv. 3. 35).
> (4) Afflict me with thy mocks, | pi'ty | me not (iii. 5. 33).

---

[1] This is Abbot's "Amphibious Section".   König would treat Adam's words as an ordinary broken line at the opening of his speech; but the instances of lines which thus cap each other are too numerous to be accidental.

Stress-inversion like stress-weakening is practised within certain limits.

(1) It is commonest after a pause—*i.e.*, in the first and after that in the third and fourth feet. It is not often found in the second.

(2) It is very rare in the last place—there is no clear case of such inversion in *As You Like It*—because a change of rhythm in that place produces a halting effect. Hence the name *scazon* ('limping') given to this metre in Greek.

(3) There are never more than two inversions in a line,—a majority of inversions would alter the character of the rhythm, not merely of the foot, but of the line.

(4) Two inversions rarely come together.

(β) Under the conditions recorded above (*b* δ) the two syllables of a foot may have approximately equal stress, thus giving a level or 'spondaic' rhythm. This is occasionally found even in the fifth foot; *e.g.*—

> More than your enemies. *Cel.* Will you | go', coz'? (i. 2. 221).
> 'Tis but a peevish boy; yet he | talks' well' (iii. 5. 109).

(*d*) **Rhyme.**—Shakespeare is very sparing of rhyme in *As You Like It*. He employs it only in two closely related ways. (1) To *close* a scene or speech. (2) To *clinch* an argument. Thus (1) *scenes* i. 2, i. 3, ii. 3, ii. 4, ii. 7, iii. 4, iii. 5, v. 4 end with rhymed couplets; as also do *speeches* in ii. 3. 67, 68, iii. 5. 78, 79, v. 4. 166–169. In the last of these cases, as also in v. 4. 185–188, and ii. 3. 69–end, we find sequences of two and four couplets. The first two instances are appropriate to the closing scene; the last is a series of sententious reflections put into the mouth of old Adam, and is connected with the second use of the rhymed couplet, (2) to clinch a point. This naturally coincides very often with the end of a speech, but is also found in other places, *e.g.*, Rosalind's

> Cry the man mercy; love him; take his offer;
> Foul is most foul, being foul to be a scoffer (iii. 5. 61–2),

the proverbial turn of which may be compared with the rhyme in i. 2. 253, 254.

APPARENT VARIATIONS.

4. Apparent variations, due to difference of pronunciation then and now, are (*a*) Accentual (*b*) Syllabic.

(*a*) **Accentual Variations.**—There has been little change in the accentuation of *simple* words; but E.E. shows greater laxity in the case of *compounds*.

(α) **Germanic Compounds.**—If the word is felt as compound it is naturally accented on the important part. Thus verb-compounds are regularly accented on the verb, *e.g.*, *outface* (i. 3. 115); whereas compounds of two prepositions, and pronominal compounds, in which the parts are of nearly equal importance, show no fixed rule: *e.g.*, *unto'* (iv. 3. 143), but also *un'to*; *therein'* (ii. 7. 71) and *there'in* (ii. 7. 81); *there'by* (ii. 7. 28) and *whereby'*; *there'fore* and *therefore'*, &c. Possibly *where'in* (ii. 7. 83).

Older compounds, on the other hand, which have ceased to be felt as compounds, follow the rule of simple words. But the verb part generally keeps the accent even when compounded with an inseparable prefix. *Un-* is sometimes accented before the p. part.; rarely before any other part of the verb.

(β) **French and Latin Compounds.**—The struggle in M.E. between the French and English systems of accentuation ended in the victory of the latter. But the influence of Latin quantity has preserved or restored the original accent in the case of many compounds, and by analogy in simple words as well. Thus in Shakespeare we sometimes find the English accent, *e.g.*, *an'tique* (always) (ii. 3. 57), *quint'essence* (iii. 2. 136) where we have returned to the Latin. On the other hand we find *exile'* (ii. 1. 1) and *exiled'* (v. 4. 155), but also *ex'ile*; *confines'* (ii. 1. 24), but also *con'fines*; *contents'* (iv. 3. 8), but also *con'tents*; *aspect'* (iv. 3. 53) (and so always); *compact'* (v. 4. 5), but also *com'pact*; *allies'* (v. 4. 179) (always). *Miscon'strues* (i. 2. 231) was pronounced, as it was often spelt, *miscon'sters*. Probably also *ex'ceeded* in the difficult line i. 2. 210—

But jus | tly, as | you have ex' | ceeded | all pro | mise.

(*b*) **Syllabic Variations.**[1]—(*a*) A vowel may be lost before a consonant in prefixes and monosyllables: *e.g.*, *'gainst* (i. 2. 244); *'mongst* (iv. 3. 122); *'tis*, *'twas* (*passim*), *was't* (iv. 3. 132); *were't* (i. 3. 107); *mark't* (iii. 4. 50); *write't* (iv. 3. 22). This will present no difficulty, and is often indicated in printing.

(β) Short *e* is almost always mute in *-es* of genitives and plurals. In the 3rd pers. sing. of verbs *-es*[2] (mute) *-eth* (sonant) is the rule. In *-ed* and *-est* there is much variety, but Shakespeare favoured the short form as he grew older. *E.g.*, *markéd* (ii. 1. 41); *livéd* (ii. 3. 72); *promiséd* (v. 4. 2); *be'st* (i. 3. 36); *diest* (i. 3. 38); *frail'st* (iii. 5. 12), &c. Here, too, the printer is a guide.

(γ) An unaccented vowel is sometimes lost before a consonant in the middle of a word of more than two syllables; *e.g.*, *residue* (ii. 7. 196); *covetousness* (iii. 5. 90); *medicine* (ii. 7. 61); but in such a case it is not always easy to say whether the vowel is lost or an extra syllable inserted.

(δ) Two adjacent vowels may be run into one, in the same or in adjacent words.

---

[1] In this section I have followed the order adopted by Prof. Herford in his *Richard II.*, in preference to the artificial nomenclature of König. And I would take this opportunity of acknowledging my great obligations to Prof. Herford; his *Richard II.* has supplied me with countless suggestions, both as to form and matter.

[2] The mark (.) under vowel shows that it is mute.

(1) In the same word—*envious* (i. 2. 207), *Amiens* (ii. 1. 29), *effigies* (ii. 7. 193), *executioner* (iii. 5. 3), *Silvius* (iii. 5. 84), but also *Silvi-us* (iii. 5. 82); *piteous* (ii. 1. 40), *being* (ii. 7. 143, &c.), but also *be-ing*; *lineaments* (iii. 5. 56), *virtuous* (i. 3. 74), *sinewy* (ii. 2 14), *power* (iii. 5. 29), *voyage* (ii. 7. 40 and v. 4. 181), &c.

(2) In adjacent words—*thou hadst* (i. 2. 196), *you have* (i. 2. 208, &c.), *I have* (v. 4. 18), *know it* (ii. 7. 38), *to it* (iii. 1. 4)—pronounced *thou'dst, know't*, &c. (prodelision); *the extremest* (ii. 1. 42), *the embossèd* (ii. 7. 67), *the extremity* (iv. 3. 23), *she urged* (i. 2. 224) pronounced *th' extremest, sh' urged*, &c. (elision); *do all* (i. 3. 45) (slurred); *follow her* (iii. 5. 49)—pronounced *foll'w'er*.

It will be seen that slurring is commonest, in both cases, when the first vowel is *i* or *u*, which readily assume a consonantal power = *y* and *w*.

(3) On the other hand, the terminations *-ion*, *-ience*, &c., now universally contracted, are frequently open in Shakespeare, *e.g.*, *conditi-on* (i. 2. 230), *intermissi-on* (ii. 7. 32), *observati-on* (ii. 7. 41), *reputati-on* (ii. 7. 152), *acti-on* (iv. 3. 9), &c; *pati-ence* (i. 3. 71). In all these cases, except the third, the open *i-on, i-ence* is at the end of a line.

(ε) One of the most characteristic differences between Elizabethan and modern pronounciation is the fluid state of the semi-vowels, or 'vowel-likes', *l, m, n, r*, and perhaps *-ng*. These letters may exercise the function either of vowels or consonants, *e.g.*, in *little* the first *l* is consonantal, the second vocalic. The sign (͜) under the letter is used to indicate the sonant (vocalic) value.

(1) A sonant liquid (*ļ, m̥, ņ, ŗ*) may form a new syllable; *e.g.*, *wrestļer* (ii. 2. 13).

(2) A liquid may cause the loss of a syllable at the end of a word, either by becoming consonantal before a following vowel, or by being slurred before a following consonant. *E.g.*, *given him* (=*givnim*) (i. 2. 204), *sudden and quick* (=*suddnand quick* (ii. 7. 151), *complexion and* (=*complecshnand*) (iii. 5. 115), *brother his* (=*brothris*) (iv. 3. 119), *hither I* (=*hithri*) (ii. 7. 195)—but see below (ζ); perhaps too *weeping into* (3 syllables) (ii. 1. 46).

Instances of slurred liquids are more numerous; *e.g.*, *heaven* (i. 3. 97 and iii. 5. 58), *bitter with him* (3 syllables) (iii. 5. 138) *father the* (2 syllables) (ii. 7. 196), *newfall'n dignity* (5 syllables) (v. 4. 166), *victuall'd so* (2 syllables) (v. 4. 182). This rule probably applies to ii. 4. 69—

> And faints for succour. Fair sir, I pity her—

where there is a change of speakers (but see 3 (*a*) (*a*) above). So too I would scan i. 3. 35—

And get | you from | our court | .

Me', un' | cle?

You', | cousin—

where *me* and *you* are clearly emphatic, and *cousin* is an extra mono-syllable. Cf.

We do | debase | ourselves | , cousin, do | we not?

Rich. II., iii. 3. 127.

(3) Syncope of an unaccented vowel in the middle of a word, rare before a consonant, is very common before a liquid. *E.g.*, *humorous* (i. 2. 232), *natural* (i. 2. 242), *unnatural* (iv. 3. 121), *sovereign* (i. 3. 59), *reference* (i. 3. 120), *difference* (ii. 1. 6), *flattery* (ii. 1. 10), *butchery* (ii. 3. 27), *boisterous* (iv. 3. 31), *murmuring* (iv. 3. 78), *desperate* (v. 4. 32), *Frederick* (v. 4. 144), *every* (v. 4. 162); *animals* (ii. 1. 62), but trisyllabic in ii. 1. 36; *countenance* (iv. 3. 36). It will be seen that contraction before *r* is far the most common. Even when it comes before the vowel, a liquid seems to make contraction more easy; *e.g.*, *forest* (i. 3. 100), *innocent* (ii. 1. 39).

(4) A long vowel or dipthong is sometimes resolved into two syllables before the liquid *r*; *e.g.*, *hour* (2 syllables) (v. 4. 12); so *prayers* (iv. 3. 55) remains uncontracted.

(5) In *other, whether,* &c., *over, ever, even, seven,* &c., contraction results after suppression of the consonant; *i.e.,* *whe'er* (not *wheth'r*), *e'en, se'en* (not *ev'n, sev'n*). *E.g.,* *other* (1 syllable) (i. 2. 239), *seventeen* (2 syllables) (ii. 3. 71). Cf. Scotch *loe* for *love.* Add *ta'en* for *taken* (i. 2. 244).

5. **Pauses.**—In § 3 I have enumerated the variations possible within the limits of the single line. But, when we come to consider a sequence of lines, or verse-paragraph, a new source of variation is disclosed in the disposition of the pauses. Naturally there is a pause at the end of each line, with a slighter pause (caesura) within the line. Such is the regular structure of the primitive English pentameter (*e.g.*, in *Gorboduc*); the caesura falling commonly after the second foot. This monotony Shakespeare breaks up (1) by varying the position of the caesura; (2) by dispensing now and then with the end-line pause, thus producing what are called *enjambed* or run-on lines. There is enjambement in some degree wherever the end of a line goes more closely *in reading* with what follows than with what goes before. But the closeness of an enjambement depends upon the grammatical connexion, the importance, and the order of the parts. The enjambements in *As You Like It*, though numerous, are not bold. There are more of those 'light' and 'weak' endings—lines closing on a conjunction, a preposition, a relative, or a copula—which may be found on every page of the *Winter's Tale* or the *Tempest.*

6. **Metre as a Test of Date.**—Three of the variations mentioned above are occasionally of use in helping to determine

the chronology of Shakespeare's writings:—(1) Rhyme, which he affected less and less; (2) double-endings, and (3) enjambement, which he affected more and more. Their value as chronological tests is not equal; it is lowest in the case of rhyme, which we ha˙ˉe seen that Shakespeare uses consciously and for a special purpose; highest in the case of enjambement, where it denotes a gradual growth of the rhythmical sense. More valuable than any, perhaps, is (4) the speech-ending test, based on the coincidence of speech-endings with verse-endings, a coincidence which Shakespeare came gradually to avoid.

The versification of *As You Like It* has the general characteristics of the middle period—rhymes are scarce, double-endings common, &c., but the various tests yield no definite result. I give the percentages for *As You Like It*, *Love's Labour's Lost* (a typical early play), and the *Tempest* (a typical late play):—

	L. L. L.	A. Y. L. I.	Temp.
Rhyme	62·2	6·3	·1
Double-endings	7·7	25·5	35·4
Enjambements	18·4	17·1	41·5
Speech-endings	10	21·6	84·5

By the first test, *As You Like It* stands 14th in the list of plays; by the second, 24th; by the third, 12th; by the fourth, 21st. We can only say that, like *Twelfth Night*, it falls somewhere between *Romeo and Iuliet* and *Troilus and Cressida.*[1]

---

[1] The figures in this section are taken from König, *Der Vers in Shaksperes Dramen*, pp. 130–138. Under the third test König reckons only the more marked enjambements, *i.e.*, those in which enjambement is heightened by close syntactical connexion or otherwise.

GLOSSARY.

a, an, the indefinite article. O.E. *án,* one, differentiated into *oon,* numeral, and *an,* article. Note these uses: (1) *a*=a certain (i. 1. 106); (2) *a*=one, the same (i. 3. 67; v. 3. 12).

addressed (v. 4. 146), prepared, F. *adresser;* late Lat. *addirectiāre,* to make straight, < *directum,* straight. Hence (1) to put in order; (2) to direct one's speech to; (3) to direct one-self to.

adventure (ii. 4. 41), chance. O.F. *aventure,* Lat. *adventura* (*res*), a thing about to happen, fut. part. fem. of *advenīre,* to arrive. The spelling went back to the Latin. For the meaning cf. *peradventure*=perhaps.

allottery (i. 1. 63), share. Probably an English formation on *allot; -ery* being added direct to the verb. Only here.

an (i. 2. 175), if. Probably the same as *and* co-ordinate. Skeat refers it to Norse *enda,* but the use probably arose independently in English. Spelt *and* before 1600.

any (i. 2. 119); still used as a noun in E.E. O.E. *aenig* is noun or adj.

argument: O.F. *argument,* Lat. *argumentum,* < *arguere,* to prove. Hence (1) Proof, reason (i. 2. 245). (2) Debate, arguing (i. 2. 41). (3) Subject of debate—*Henry V.,* ii. 1. 21, "And sheathed their swords for lack of argument". (4) Object of debate or action in general (iii. 1. 3). In modern English the word has been confined to the original Latin sense; but we still speak of the 'argument', *i.e.* subject of a play, &c.

assayed (i. 3. 122), ventured. Properly *essay.* O.F. *essai,* Lat. *exagium,* weighing, < *exigere,* to try. Hence, to put to the test, to attempt.

The spelling *assay* is now confined to testing metals.

atone (v. 4. 100), come into unity. From *at-one* (pronounced *oon*). Generally transitive—short for 'set at one'. The verb is a 16th century formation, and comes from the use of 'at one' in adverbial phrases; cf. the use of *further,* and other adverbs as verbs (Wright). The true sound of 'one' has also been preserved in *alone.* .

attorney (iv. 1. 81), proxy. O.F. *atourné,* p. part. of *atourner,* to turn to, appoint. Here in the correct legal sense.

bandy (v. 1. 52), fight; lit. to strike a ball at tennis. Origin obscure. F. *bander,* "to bandie at tennis" (Cotgrave); perhaps f. *bande,* a side.

bastinado (v. 1. 51), cudgelling. Spanish *bastonada,* f. *baston,* a cudgel. Now generally of the Eastern punishment of beating the soles of the feet.

batlet, or **batler** (ii. 4. 45), a 'beetle' for beating clothes. The first form is the diminutive of *bat;* the second comes from *battle* (to beat), + *er* of the instrument.

beholding (iv. 1. 52), obliged. A common E.E. corruption of p. part. *beholden,* from O.E. *behealdan,* 'to hold, behold'. From the sense of 'holding' comes that of 'obligation', which is confined to the participle. The curious substi-

183

tution of the present part. for the past "may have been due to a notion that it meant 'looking to', *e.g.* with respect or dependence".

bid (v. 2. 38), invite. O. E. *biddan*. Not the same word as 'bid', to order, which is from O.E. *beddan*.

bob (ii. 7. 55), a jest. Lit. a rap. Probably an onomatopoetic word, from the sound of a smart tap. Cf. the verb *bob*=strike with the fist.

bonny (ii. 3. 8), big. Connected with O. F. *bon*, good; but the formation is unexplained. Generally means beautiful, but see note.

bravery (ii. 7. 80), finery. From *brave* (F. *brave*) in the sense of fine: cf. Sc. *braw* and *braws*.

brawls (ii. 1. 32), runs noisily. Not much before 1400. The origin is unknown: it is not connected with F. *branler*, which may, however, be the source of the noun 'brawl', *i.e.* a dance: "The grave Lord Keeper led the brawls" (Gray).

burden (iii. 2. 227), bass, undersong, accompaniment. O.E. *byr-ðen*, < *beran*, to bear. This peculiar sense comes from confusion with M. E. *burdoun*, F. *bourdon*, bass [Lat. *burdon-em*, drone]—from the notion that the bass is 'heavier' than the air. Hence the sense of theme.

butchery (ii. 3. 27), shambles. M.E. *bocherie*, O.F. *boucherie*; *-y* denotes place. The word is still used of the slaughter-houses in barracks or aboard ship.

capable (iii. 5. 23), perceptible —through O.F. from Lat. *capabil-em*, < *capere*, to catch. See note.

carlot (iii. 5. 107), peasant. A diminutive — probably coined by Shakespeare—of *carl* < O.E. *carl*, man. From the soft form *ceorl* comes *churl*, with a depreciation

of meaning like that observed in *villain*, *q.v.*

cater (ii. 3. 44), provide. Short for *acater* (cf. '*gainst*, '*mongst*, &c.), O.F. *achater* (F. *acheter*), to buy: late Lat. *ac-captare*, to acquire, < *ad*+*captare*, to catch.

chanticleer (ii. 7. 30), the cock. Originally a proper name. O. F. *Chantecler* (F. *Chanteclair*), the name of the cock in the famous *fabliau* of *Reynard the Fox*: meaning the clear-singer, < *chanter*, to sing; +*cler* (F. *clair*), clear.

character (iii. 2. 6), write. Through Lat. from Gk. χαρακτήρ, a mark. Shakespeare uses the verb always, and the noun generally, in the literal sense of writing; even when metaphorically used, 'character' is never applied(as now) to inward qualities, but always to outward expression.

cicatrice (iii. 5. 23), mark. Properly, the scar of a wound; Lat. *cicatric-em*.

civil (iii. 2. 115), civilized; **civility** (ii. 7. 93), courtesy. These words have a finer meaning in E.E. than now, when they indicate merely external politeness, the absence of rudeness. From O.F. *civil*, *civilité*, Lat. *civilis*, *civili-tatem*, of the qualities proper to a citizen, *civis*.

conceit (ii. 6. 7), thought. An English formation from *conceive*, on the analogy of *deceit* f. *deceive*, &c. Meaning (1) conception, (2) private opinion, and so (3) an overweening opinion of one's self. The last meaning, the common one now, never attaches to the word in Shakespeare.

conned (iii. 2. 251), learned by heart. Same word as *can*. O.E. *kunnan*, to know or to be able, had two forms in the present, *ic can* and *ic con*. These forms differentiated (1) in meaning — *can* being limited to power, *con* to knowledge; (2) in inflexion — in

M.E. *con* becomes a regular verb, the past *could* being reserved to *can*. Meaning (1) to know, (2) to get to know, (3) to learn by heart.

cony (iii. 2. 311), rabbit. O.F. *conil*, pl. *coniz*, whence Eng. *conys*, *cony*: < Lat. *cuniculus*, a rabbit. The name 'rabbit' was originally applied to the young only.

cote (ii. 4. 77), cottage. O.E. *cote* (fem.), a parallel form to *cot* (neut.).

countenance (i. 1. 15), bearing. Late Lat. *continentia*, mien, carriage; hence (1) deportment, (2) the face itself. From a similar transference and limitation of meaning, compare *favour*, *complexion*, &c. [On Walker's view, that the word is here used in the sense of 'allowance', it would come from, or represent, the Lat. *contenement-um*. But see note.]

courtesy (i. 1. 39), customary usage. O.F. *cortesie*. It. *cortese*, courteous. The expression "courtesy of nations" (*jus gentium*) recalls the legal sense of the word, usage not fixed by statute, *e.g. courtesy of Scotland*, &c.

coz (i. 2. 1), short for 'cousin'. F. *cousin*; Late Lat. *cosinus*, *cossofrenus*, < Lat. *consobrinus*, cousin by the mother's side (*con* + *soror*). But the word was often used to translate *consanguineus*, and so was extended to other blood-relations, especially uncle, nephew, and niece, (cf. i. 3. 35), and finally used as a mere term of courtesy (cf. ii. 7. 173).

curtle-axe (i. 3. 110), cutlass. The form is a popular corruption of cutlass, which in the 16th century was spelt *coutelase*, whence the forms *courtleace* and *cuttle-ax*; both parts of the word getting corrupted, as if from *curtal*, short, and *axe*. Really it comes from F. *coutelas*, from *couteau*, Lat. *cultell-um*, knife.

dole (i. 2. 110), lamentation. O.F. *duel* (Fr. *deuil*), < L. *dolēre*, to grieve. Cf. Scotch *dule*.

embossed (ii. 7. 67), protuberant. In E.E. there are two distinct words of this spelling, with some inevitable confusion of meaning: (1) from *en* + *boss* = bulged, as here; (2) from *en* + O.F. *bos*, *bois*, a wood —a term of hunting, 'driven to the wood', brought to bay, and so by influence of sense (1) foaming at the mouth. Cf. Milton, *Samson Agonistes*, 1700, "In th' Arabian woods embost"; and *Taming of the Shrew*, Ind. i. 17, "The poor cur is emboss'd".

emulator (i. 1. 123), envious rival. Lat. *aemulari*, f. *aemulus*, a rival. Shakespeare uses this word and its cognates in a bad sense. In E.E. the mental emotion is prominent, in Md. E. the active effort (Bradley).

engage (v. 4. 156), pledge. F. *engager*, < *en* + *gage*, to offer as a guarantee.

entreat (i. 2. 125, i. 3. 62), to induce, implore. O.F. *en-traiter*, < Lat. *tractare*, to handle. Hence (1) to treat, (2) to treat with, and so (3) to ask, implore—the modern sense (i. 3. 71), and (4) to ask with success, to induce (i. 2. 159).

envious, envy. O.F. *envie*, Lat. *invidia-m*. The meaning fluctuates between the general sense of 'spiteful', 'malicious' (i. 2. 207), and the more special sense of 'painfully jealous' in which we now use it (i. 1. 123).

erst (iii. 5. 94), formerly. Superlative of *ere*.

expediently (iii. 1. 18), promptly. Lat. *expedire* (*ex* + *pedem*), to disentangle the feet, remove obstacles. "Thence, a course which *tends to remove or avoid obstacles* is 'expedient': a sense also common in E.E., now exclusive" (Herford).

extent (iii. 1. 17). M.E. *extente*, O.F. *extente*, p. part. fem. of *extendre*, used as substantive. See note.

extermined (iii. 5. 88), ended. F. *exterminer*, Lat. *exterminare*. Shakespeare does not use *exterminate*, which is an English formation from the Lat. p. part.

fancy, fantasy. M.E. and O.F. *fantasie*, through Low Lat. from Gk. φαντασία, imagination. Shakespeare uses both words indifferently for (1) the faculty of imagination and its objects (iv. 3. 100); (2) love (ii. 4. 27, v. 2. 85). If there is a distinction, in *fantasy* the element of thought is prominent, in *fancy* that of taste. The sense of 'liking' is confined to *fancy*.

favour (v. 4. 27), appearance. Norm. F. *favor*, Lat. *favor-em*, kindliness. Transferred, like *countenance* (*q.v.*), from feeling to expression. Hence *ill-favouredly* (i. 2. 41)=ugly. The verb is still used colloquially in the sense of 'resemble'; and this may mark the transition (incline to; look like; look).

feature (iii. 3. 3), make, appearance. O.F. *faiture*, Lat. *factura*, < *facere*, to make. Applied in E.E. to shape in general, now confined to the face (cf. *countenance* and *favour*). [There seems to be another word, *feature*, in E.E., from Lat. *fetura*, offspring, which has been thought to be the meaning here. But it is always used with a consciousness of the physiological metaphor, *e.g.* in Latimer's "some *ingendred* one some other such *features*". There is no evidence for the meaning 'composition', '*literary* production'.]

foil (i. 1. 112), defeat. O.F. *fouler*, to trample on, Low Lat. *fullare*, to full cloth by beating.

Cf. *defile*, from *defouler*. Spenser uses *fyle* for to dirty.

fond (ii. 3. 7), foolish. M. E. *fonned*, p. part. of *fonnen*, from *fon*, a fool. From meaning "to be infatuated" about anything, it has come to mean simply "to care for".

gamester (i. 1. 141), gamesome fellow. From *game*+*ster*, a suffix conventionally confined in O.E. to female agents. In E.E. the word has a contemptuous sense, but is not definitely restricted to mean 'gambler'.

gentle (i. 1. 38), (1) of good birth, (2) of good nature. M.E. *gentil*, Lat. *gentilis*, belonging to one of the *gentes*, or original clans.

gracious (i. 2. 159), popular. It. *gratioso*, Lat. *gratiosus*, < *gratiam*, favour. Now generally transitive=showing favour.

graff (iii. 2. 104), graft, O.F. *graffe*, a pencil, Lat. *graphiolum*, Gk. γραφίον, < γράφειν, to write. The form *graft*, which Shakespeare also uses, is corrupt, due to being confused with the p. part. *graffed*.

hinds (i. 1. 16), farm-servants. M.E. *hine*, O.E. *hína*, a gen. pl.; so that *hína* stands for *hína man*, one of the domestics. The *d* is an excrescence, as in *sound*, &c. The meaning 'farm-servant' is still common in Scotch.

holla (ii. 2. 224), stop! F. *holà*, ho, there!=*ho* + *là*, there. Not the same as Eng. *halloo*, which calls attention. Confusion has produced the intermediate *hollo* and *halloa*.

honest (i. 2. 33, &c.), chaste. O. F. *honeste*, Lat. *honestus*, honourable, < *honos*, honour. In Shakespeare note the meanings (1) upright, hence *honesty*=fairdealing in ii. 4. 85; (2) chaste, modest—very common.

hooping (iii. 2. 177), shouting.

M.E. *houpen*, to shout; a variant of *whoop.*

humorous (i. 2. 232, &c.), see notes. O.F. *humor*, Lat. *humorem*, moisture. Applied specially to the fluids of the body.

hurtling (iv. 3. 130), dashing together. M.E. *hurtlen*, frequentative of *hurten*, in the sense of 'to dash'.

'ild (iii. 3. 63), reward. Short for *yield*, in its original sense of 'pay', M.E. *yelden*, O.E. *geldan*, to pay. Cf. Ger. *gelten*, to be worth.

incontinent (v. 2. 35), instantly. F. *incontinent*, lit. without holding one's self in; Lat. *in+continēre*, to restrain.

kind (iii. 2. 90; iv. 3. 59), nature. M.E. *kind*, O.E. *cynd*, nature. A noun formed from the adj. **kind**, cf. *kindly* (ii. 3. 53). (O.E. *ge-cynde*, native), which in E.E. still retains something of its original sense of 'natural'.

kindled (iii. 2. 311), brought forth. M.E. *kindlen*, to produce, from *kindel*, diminutive of *kind*: generally of a litter, *e.g.* of rabbits, as here.

learn (i. 2. 4), teach. M.E. *lernen*, O.E. *leornian*, to learn; a neuter form sometimes confused with the causative *leren*, *laeran*, to teach. (Cf. Ger. *lernen* and *lehren*). The confusion is reciprocal, *leren* being sometimes used reflexively = to learn.

leer (iv. 1. 58), look. M.E. *lere*, O.E. *hlēor*, cheek, look. At first used in a good sense, but twice in Skelton (time of Henry VIII.) of ugly looks. In Shakespeare (1) look in general, (2) a winning look. Now a sly look.

lief (i. 1. 125), gladly. M.E. *lief* (adj.), O.E. *lēof.* dear (adj. and subst.); cf. Ger. *lieb.* In Shakespeare only in "I had as lief". ["My liefest liege", *2 Henry VI.*, iii. 1. 164, need not be Shakespeare's.]

liege (i. 2. 133; i. 3. 57), sovereign. M.E. and O.F. *lige, liege*, <Old High German *ledic*, 'free': hence properly of the feudal suzerain or *liege-lord*, who alone was free; but also applied to his vassals ("the Queen's lieges"), by supposed derivation from Lat. *ligare*, to bind.

lieu (ii. 3. 65), return. Fr. *lieu*, Lat. *locum*, place. See note.

limned (ii. 7. 194), drawn. Properly 'illuminated'. M.E. *limnen*, for *luminen*, short for *enluminen*, O.F. *enluminer*, Lat. *illuminare.*

manage (i. 1. 11), training of a horse. O.F. *manège*, lit. handling (esp. of horses), Lat. *manum*, hand.

mettle (ii. 7. 82), spirit. Same word as *metal*, the metaphor being from the temper of the *metal* of a sword.

misprised (i. 1. 146), undervalued. O.F. *mespriser*, to contemn (Spenser has *mesprize* = contempt) <O.F. *mes-* = Lat. *minus*, less, and Lat. *pretiare*, to value, from *pretium*, price.

modesty (iii. 2. 135), chastity. F. *modeste*, Lat. *modestus*, measurable, from *modus*, measure. For the special sense, cf. *honest* above.

moe (iii. 2. 241); **more** (iii. 2. 239), more. *Moe* is from O.E. *ma* (advb.), *more* from *māra* (adj.) = greater. *Ma* was used as neut. noun followed by gen., *i.e.* more of so and so. Hence Alexander Gil's dictum that *moe* is comp. of 'many', *more* of 'much'. In Shakespeare's usage *moe* is always followed by a plural.

mortal (ii. 4. 50), excessive. Johnson suggests a connection with the vulgar *mort* = a large quantity.

mutton (iii. 2. 50), sheep. O.F.

moton (F. *mouton*), a sheep. In M.E. after a time the French name came to be reserved for the dead meat, the English for the live animal—cf. *boeuf*, *beef*.

necessary (iii. 3. 42), unavoidable. O.F. *necessaire*, Lat. *necessarius*. This is the proper Latin sense; but Shakespeare also uses the word in the looser modern sense of 'needful'—useful, but *not* indispensable.

new-fangled (iv. 1. 132), fond of what is new. The *d* is an excrescence. M.E. *newe-fangel*, O.E. *newe* + *fangel*, < *fang-*, to seize = ready to seize what is new. In Md.E. the word is commonly used of things, and simply = 'novel'.

nice (iv. 1. 14), finical. O.F. *nice*, simple, Lat. *nescius*, ignorant. The regular M.E. meaning is 'foolish'; in E.E. (1) of persons, 'fastidious', (2) of things, 'fine-drawn'—whence the ordinary modern meaning of pleasant. The curious change of meaning may be due to confusion with *nesh*, soft, delicate, dainty—a word still preserved in Lancashire dialect.

owe (iii. 2. 66), possess—*i.e.* bear (hate to no man). O.E. *ág*, *áh*, possess. The modern sense of 'obligation' may be paralleled by the sense of 'compulsion' which attaches to *have* in "I have to do so and so".

pageant (ii. 7. 138, &c.), show. M.E. *pagent*, lit. scaffold, stage < Lat. *pagina* ('page'), in the sense of 'platform'.

pantaloon (ii. 7. 158), dotard. An Italian loan-word, late 16th century. In Italian it was applied (1) to Venetians as a nickname— it was a common baptismal name in Venice, the patron saint of the city being St. Pantaleone (cf. 'Paddy' for Irishman); (2) in Italian comedy the *pantalone* was an amorous old dotard who was the butt of the piece.

parcels (iii. 5. 124), small parts. The original sense is simply 'portions'. F. *parcelle*, Lat. *particella*, dim. of *pars*, a part.

pathetical (iv. 1. 167). O.F. *pathetique*, through Lat. from Gk. παθητικός, passionate < πάθος, suffering. For Shakespeare's curious use of it, see note *ad loc.*

peevish (iii. 5. 109), forward. M.E. *peuisch*, ill-natured. In M.E. and E.E. the meaning ranges from 'childish' to 'wayward', even 'witty'. (Derivation obscure; probably echoic).

point-device (iii. 2. 348), precise. Short for *at point-device* (Chaucer has "with limmes wrought at point device": *Rom. of the Rose*, 830); a translation of O.F. *à point devis*, according to a point devised, *i.e.* in the best way imaginable.

power (v. 4. 146), force. < O.F. *povoir*, Late Lat. *potere = posse*, to be able. The inf. is used as a *concrete* noun; cf. M.E. *maegen*.

practise (i. 1. 128), plot. F. *practiquer*, from *practique*, experience, through Lat. from Gk. πρακτική, practical (science) < πράττειν, to do. The verb always has a bad sense in Shakespeare.

priser (ii. 3. 8), prize-fighter or wrestler. In either case from F. *prise*, seizing, p. part. fem. of *prendre*, Lat. *prehendere*, to seize.

promise (i. 2. 118), assure. F. *promesse*, Lat. *promissa*, p. part. of *promittere*. In this sense only in the phrase, "I promise you".

proper (i. 2. 102, &c.), handsome. M.E. and F. *propre*, Lat. *proprium*, one's own. Hence 'suitable', 'just', and (externally) 'comely'.

puisny (iii. 4. 37), unskilful. O.F. *puisné*, (F. *puîné*, younger)

< Lat. *post-natum*, born after. Same word as *puny*. For the spelling, cf. "*puisne* judge".

puke (ii. 7. 144), vomit. Perhaps for *spuke*, cf. *spew*, and Ger. *spuken*, to spit.

purchase (iii. 2. 312), acquire. M.E. *pourchasen*, to acquire, O.F. *purchaser*, to pursue. Now of acquiring by payment; but in law all land other than inherited is still said to be acquired by 'purchase'.

purgation (i. 3. 46; v. 4. 42), exculpation. F. *purgation*, Lat. *purgation-em*, < *purgare*, to cleanse. A legal word, used properly by the Duke, and improperly by Touchstone: see note.

purlieus (iv. 3. 75), borders of a forest. O.F. *puralee*, part of a royal forest disforested by *perambulationem*. The form is due to corruption with *lieu*, place, but also appears as *purley*. Shakespeare's use of it is correct: it is now used of precincts in general.

quail (ii. 2. 20), flag. M.E. *quelen*, O.E. *cwelan*, to die (properly, by violence), then to pine. Confused by Shakespeare with *quell*, to kill (O.E. *cwellan*), in *Antony*, v. 2. 85.

quintain (i. 2. 217), see note. F. *quintaine*, Low Lat. *quintana* —probably from the street of that name in a Roman camp; the market-place stood in the *quintana*, and sports would naturally be held there.

ranged (i. 3. 61), roved. F. *ranger*, < *rang*, a rank. The sense of 'roving' comes from scouring the country with 'ranks' of soldiers.

rascal (iii. 3. 47), a deer out of season. M.E. *raskaille*, the common herd, as if from O.F. *rascaille* (F. *racaille*), offscouring, Lat. *rasum* < *radere*, to scrape. See note.

roynish (ii. 2. 8), scurvy. M.E. *roignous*, *royne*, O. F. *roineux*, *roigne*, the mange.

sad (iii. 2. 135), serious. O. E. *saed*, sated. In M.E. and even in E.E. the sense is much wider than now, ranging from 'serious' to 'solid'.

sans (ii. 7. 166), without. A French word, borrowed about 1350, and originally used in French phrases only— *sans faille*, *sans doute*, &c. Quite Anglicized at one time, but now gone out.

savage (ii. 6. 6), wild—without any notion of 'ferocity'. Lit. 'living in the woods', M.E. *sauvage*, *salvage*, O.F. *salvage*, Lat. *silvaticum* < *silva*, a wood.

shrewd (v. 4. 163), hard, bitter. Properly p. part. of *shrewen*, to curse, < *schrewe*, bad. The fundamental sense is 'biting', as in 'shrew-mouse', and this is still felt in E.E.

smirch (i. 3. 105), smear. A weak form of *smerk*, extended from M.E. *smeren*, O.E. *smerien*, to smear.

smother (i. 2. 253), suffocating smoke. M.E. *smorthen*, < O.E. *smorian*, to stifle, Scotch *smore*.

sooth (iii. 2. 364), truth. In E.E. also an adj., and this is the original sense: M. E. *sôth*, O. E. *sôð*, true; the neuter being used as a subst. = a true thing.

speed (i. 2. 177), good fortune. O.E. *spêd*.

squandering (ii. 7. 57), haphazard. A nasalized form of the echoic *squatter* (Sc.), originally to scatter. Now confined to scattering money.

stanzo (ii. 5. 16), stanza. An Italian loan-word, still new to Shakespeare's ear; Low Lat. *stantia*, an abode, < *stare*, to stand: hence, a pause in verse.

suit (i. 2. 212), see note. F

suite, "a chase...also the train, attendants, or followers of a great person" (Cotgrave); Lat. *secta* < *sequi*, to follow.

swashing (i. 3. 113), swaggering. Probably echoic, from the sound of a noisy blow.

synod (iii. 2. 147), council. Through F. and Lat. from Gk. σύνοδος, meeting, < σύν + ὁδός, way. The word is now confined to ecclesiastical councils, and in Shakespeare, five times out of six, it is used of councils of the gods.

taxation (i. 2. 72); **taxing** (ii. 7. 86), censure, satire. O.F. *taxer*, to assess, Lat. *taxare*=*tactare*, to handle < *tactum*, touch. From meaning 'to charge' it passes to the sense of 'charging' with crimes, &c., and so of satirizing.

tender (v. 2. 63), value. A verb formed without change from the adj. *tender*. F. *tendre*, Lat. *tenerum*.

thrasonical (v. 2. 34), boastful. An E.E. coinage, from Thraso, the braggart in the *Eunuchus* of Terence.

traverse (iii. 4. 37), cross-wise. F. *traverse* (fem.), Lat. *transversa*, turned across, < *trans* + *vertere*.

trow (iii. 2. 163), know. O.E. *treówian*, to have trust in, < *treówa*, trust. Properly, to suppose true.

umber (i. 3. 105), brown ochre. F. *ombre*, short for *terre d'ombre*, earth for shading, It. *terra d'ombra*, < Lat. *umbra*, shade. [The usual derivation from Umbria, where it

is supposed to be found, is only a guess of Malone's.]

uncouth (ii. 6. 6), strange. Lit. 'unknown', O.E. *uncúð* < *un* + *cúð*, p. part. of *cunnan*, to know, cf. Sc. *unco*.

vents (ii. 7. 41), utters. Probably < Fr. *vendre*, Lat. *vendere*, to sell; but affected by (1) *vent*, to breathe < Lat. *ventum*, wind; (2) *vent*, a hole < Lat. *findere*, to split.

videlicet (iv. 1. 83), namely. A Lat. loan-word, used with affected precision by Rosalind, and familiar in the contraction *viz*.

villain (i. 1. 50, 49), (1) a base-born person, (2) a scoundrel. O.F. *vilein*, servile, Low Lat. *villanus*, farm-servant, < *villa*, farm-house, For the degradation of meaning cf. *churl*.

warp (ii. 7. 187), see note. M.E. *warpen*, a derivative weak verb, not the same as *werpen*, to throw, but of Scandinavian origin.

warrant (i. 2. 173), assure, < O.F. *warant*, *guarant*, protector; cf. Ger. *wehren*. Audrey misuses the word: "Lord warrant us" (iii. 3. 5) = "God warn (*i.e.* protect) us" (iv. 2. 77). *Warn* and *warrant* are ultimately cognate.

wind (iii. 3. 86), turn and go. < O.E. *windan*, to turn; connected in sense and etymology with *wend*, which is the causal verb.

yond (ii. 4. 58), yonder. In O.E. *geond* is adv., *geon* is adj. The confusion came from supposing that *yon* was a shortened form of *yond*.

INDEX OF WORDS.

(The references are to the Notes *ad locc.* Other words will be found in the *Glossary*.)

GENERAL INDEX.

SHAKESPEARE'S STAGE IN ITS BEARING UPON HIS DRAMA

§ 1. The structure and arrangements of the Elizabethan theatre are still under discussion, and many points of detail remain unsettled. A very extensive and highly technical literature on the subject is available, chiefly in England, America, and Germany. It is based especially on the new evidence derived from (1) the original stage directions, (2) contemporary illustrations and descriptions. The following summary gives the conclusions which at present appear most reasonable, neglecting much speculative matter of great interest.

§ 2. When Shakespeare arrived in London, soon after 1585, theatrical exhibitions were given there in (1) public theatres, (2) private theatres, (3) the halls of the royal palaces, and of the Inns of Court.

Of the 'public' theatres there were at least three: The Theater, the Curtain, both in Shoreditch, and Newington Butts on the Bankside or Southwark shore. About 1587, the Rose, also on the Bankside, was added. All these were occasionally used by Shakespeare's company before 1599, when their headquarters became the newly built Globe, likewise on the Bankside. Of the 'private' theatres the principal, and the oldest, was the Blackfriar, on the site of the present *Times* office. It was also the property of the company in which Shakespeare acquired a share, but being let out practically his whole career, does not count in the present connexion. At court, on the other hand, his company played repeatedly. But his plays were written for the 'public' theatre, and this alone had any influence in his stage-craft.

§ 3. The 'public' theatre differed from the other two types chiefly in being (1) dependent on daylight, (2) open overhead, and (3) partially seatless; and from the court-stages also, in (4) not using painted scenes. While they, again, had the rectangular form, the typical 'public' theatre was a round or octagonal edifice, modelled partly on the inn-yards where companies of players had been accustomed to perform, prior to the inhibition of 1574, on movable stages; partly on the arenas used for bear-baiting and cock-fighting;—sports still carried on in the 'theatres', and in part dictating their arrangements.

The circular inner area, known thence as the 'cock-pit', or 'pit', had accordingly no seats; admission to it cost one penny (6*d.* in modern money), and the throng of standing spectators were known as the 'groundlings'. More expensive places (up to 2*s.* 6*d.*) with seats, were provided in tiers of galleries which ran round the area, one above the other, as in modern theatres; the uppermost being covered with a thatched roof.

§ 4. **The Stage** (using the term to describe the entire scenic apparatus of the theatre) included (1) the *outer stage*, a rectangular platform (as much as 42 feet wide in the largest examples) projecting into the circular area, from the back wall, and thus surrounded by 'groundlings' on three sides. Above it were a thatched roof and hangings but no side or front curtains. In the floor was a trap-door by which ghosts and others ascended or descended. At the back were (2) two projecting wings, each with a door opening obliquely on to the stage, the *recess* between them, of uncertain shape and extent, forming a kind of inner stage. Above this was (3) an upper room or rooms, which included the actors' 'tiring house', with a window or

i

windows opening on to (4) a *balcony* or gallery from which **was** hung
(5) a *curtain*, by means of which the inner recess could be concealed or
disclosed.

§ 5. The most important divergence of this type of structure from
that of our theatres is in the relation between the outer stage and the
auditorium. In the modern theatre the play is treated as a picture,
framed in the proscenium arch, seen by the audience like any other
picture from the front only, and shut off from their view at any
desired moment by letting fall the curtain. An immediate consequence of this was that a scene (or act) could terminate only in one
of two ways. Either the persons concerned in it walked, or were
carried, off the stage; or a change of place and circumstances was
supposed without their leaving it. Both these methods were used.
The first was necessary only at the close of the play. For this reason
an Elizabethan play rarely ends on a *climax* such as the close of
Ibsen's *Ghosts*; the overpowering effect of which would be gravely
diminished if, instead of the curtain falling upon Osvald's helpless
cry for " the sun ", he and his mother had to walk off the stage.
Marlowe's *Faustus* ends with a real climax, because the catastrophe
ipso facto leaves the stage clear. But the close of even the most over-
whelming final scenes of Shakespeare is relatively quiet, or even, as
in *Macbeth*, a little tame. The concluding lines often provide a motive
for the (compulsory) clearing of the stage.

In the *Tragedies*, the dead body of the hero has usually to be borne ceremoniously
away, followed by the rest; so Aufidius in *Coriolanus*: "Help, three o' the chiefest
soldiers: I'll be one". Similarly in *Hamlet* and *King Lear*. In *Othello*, Desdemona's bed was apparently in the curtained recess, and at the close the curtains
were drawn upon the two bodies, instead of their being as usual borne away.
The close of the *Histories* often resembles the dispersing of an informal council
after a declaration of policy by the principal person; thus *Richard II*. closes with
Bolingbroke's announcement of the penance he proposes to pay for Richard's
death; *Henry IV*. with his orders for the campaign against Northumberland and
Glendower; *King John* with Falconbridge's great assertion of English patriotism.
In the *Comedies*, the leading persons will often withdraw to explain to one
another at leisure what the audience already knows (*Winter's Tale*, *Tempest*,
Merchant of Venice), or to carry out the wedding rites (*As You Like It*, *Midsummer-
Night's Dream*); or they strike up a measure and thus (as in *Much Ado*) naturally
dance off the stage. Sometimes the chief persons have withdrawn before the close,
leaving some minor character—Puck (*Midsummer-Night's Dream*) or the Clown
(*Twelfth Night*)—to wind up the whole with a snatch of song, and then retire
himself.

§ 6. But the most important result of the exposed stage was that it
placed strict limit upon dramatic illusion, and thus compelled the
resort, for most purposes, to conventions resting on symbolism, suggestion, or make-believe. It was only in dress that anything like
simulation could be attempted; and here the Elizabethan companies,
as is well known, were lavish in the extreme. Painted scenes, on the
other hand, even had they been available, would have been idle or
worse, when perhaps a third of the audience would see, behind the
actors, not the scenes but the people in the opposite gallery, or the
gallants seated on the stage. Especially where complex and crowded
actions were introduced, the most beggarly symbolic suggestion was
cheerfully accepted. Jonson, in the spirit of classical realism, would

have tabooed all such intractable matter; and he scoffed, in his famous Prologue, at the "three rusty swords" whose clashing had to do duty for "York and Lancaster's long jars". Shakespeare's realism was never of this literal kind, but in bringing Agincourt upon the stage of the newly built Globe in the following year (1559) he showed himself so far sensitive to criticisms of this type that he expressly appealed to the audience's imagination—"eke out our imperfections with your thoughts"—consenting, moreover, to assist them by the splendid descriptive passages interposed between the Acts.

It is probable that the Elizabethan popular audience did not need any such appeal. It had no experience of elaborate 'realism' on the stage; the rude movable stages on which the earliest dramas had been played compelled an ideal treatment of *space* and a symbolic treatment of *properties*; and this tradition, though slowly giving way, was still paramount throughout Shakespeare's career. Thus every audience accepted as a matter of course (1) the representation of *distant* things or places simultaneously on the stage. Sidney, in 1580, had ridiculed the Romantic plays of his time with "Asia of one side and Africa of the other", indicated by labels. But Shakespeare in 1593–4 could still represent the tents of Richard III. and Richmond within a few yards of one another, and the Ghosts speaking alternately to each. Every audience accepted (2) the presence on the stage, in full view of the audience, of accessories irrelevant to the scene in course of performance. A property requisite for one set of scenes, but out of place in another, could be simply ignored while the latter were in progress; just as the modern audience sees, but never reckons into the scenery, the footlights and the prompter's box. Large, movable objects, such as beds or chairs, were no doubt often brought in when needed; but no one was disturbed if they remained during an intervening scene in which they were out of place. And "properties either difficult to move, like a well, or so small as to be unobtrusive, were habitually left on the stage as long as they were wanted, whatever scenes intervened" (Reynolds).

Thus in Jonson's *The Case is Altered* (an early play, not yet reflecting his characteristic technique), Jaques, in III. 2, hides his gold in the earth and covers it with a heap of dung to avoid suspicion. In IV. 4, he removes the dung to assure himself that the gold is still there. The intervening scenes represent rooms in Ferneze's palace, and Juniper's shop; but the heap of dung doubtless remained on the stage all the time. Similarly in Peele's *David and Bethsabe*, the spring in which Bethsabe bathes; and in his *Old Wives' Tale*, 'a study' and a 'cross', which belong to unconnected parts of the action.

It follows from this that the *supposed locality of a scene could be changed* without any change in the properties on the stage, or even of the persons. What happened was merely that some properties which previously had no dramatic relevance, suddenly acquired it, and *vice versa*; that a tree, for instance, hitherto only a stage property out of use, became a *tree* and signified probably, a wood. The change of scene may take place without any break in the dialogue, and be only marked by the occurrence of allusions of a different tenor.

Thus in *Doctor Faustus*, at v. 1106 f., Faustus is in "a fair and pleasant green", on his way from the Emperor's Court at Wittenberg; at v. 1143 f., he is back in his house there. In *Romeo and Juliet*, I. 4. 5, Romeo and his friends are at first in the street; at I. 4, 114, according to the Folio, '' they march about the stage and serving-men come forth with their napkins ''; in other words, we are now in Capulet's hall, and Capulet presently enters meeting his guests. This is conventionalized in modern editions.

§ 7. The Inner Stage.—An audience for which the limitations of the actual stage meant so little, might be expected to dispense readily with the concessions to realism implied in providing an actual inner chamber for scenes performed ' within ', and an actual gallery for those performed ' aloft '. And the importance and number of the former class of scenes have, in fact, been greatly exaggerated.

Applying modern usages to the semi-mediæval Elizabethan stage, Brandl (*Einleitung* to his revised edition of Schlegel's translation) and Brodmeier (Dissertation on the stage conditions of the Elizabethan drama), put forward the theory of the ' alternative ' scene; according to which the inner and the outer stage were used ' alternately ', a recurring scene, with elaborate properties, being arranged in the former, and merely curtained off while intervening scenes were played on the outer, or main stage. But while this theory is plausible, as applied to some of Shakespeare's plays (e.g. the intricate transitions between rooms at Belmont and piazzas at Venice, in the *Merchant*), it breaks down in others (e.g. *Cymbeline*, II. 2. 3; *Richard II.*, I. 3, 4), and especially in many plays by other dramatists.

It is probable that the use of the ' inner stage ' was in general restricted to two classes of scene: (1) where persons ' within ' formed an integral though subordinate part of a scene of which the main issue was decided on the outer stage; as with the play-scene in *Hamlet*, or where Ferdinand and Miranda are discovered playing chess in *The Tempest*; (2) where a scene, though engaging the whole interest, is supposed to occur in an inner chamber. Thus Desdemona's chamber, Prospero's cell, Timon's cave, Lear's hovel, the Capulet's tomb.

§ 8. The Balcony.—There is less doubt about the use of the balcony or gallery. This was in fact an extremely favourite resource, and its existence in part explains the abundance of serenade, rope-ladder, and other upper-story scenes in Elizabethan drama.

From the balcony, or the window above it, Juliet discoursed with Romeo, and Sylvia with Proteus (*Two Gentlemen of Verona*, IV. 2); Richard III. addressed the London citizens, and the citizen of Angers the rival Kings. From the window the Pedant in *Taming of the Shrew*, V. 1, hails Petruchio and Grumio below; and Squire Tub, in Jonson's *Tale of a Tub*, I. 1, puts out his head in answer to the summons of Parson Hugh. But whole scenes were also, it is probable, occasionally enacted in this upper room. This is the most natural interpretation of the scenes in Juliet's chamber (IV. 3, 5). On the other hand, though the Senators in *Titus Andronicus*, I. 1, '' go up into the ' Senate House ' '', it is probable that the debate later in the scene, on the main stage, is intended to be in the Senate-house by the convention described in § 6.

For further reference the following among others may be mentioned:
G. F. Reynolds, *Some Principles of Elizabethan Staging* (*Modern Philology*, II. III.); A. Brandl, *Introduction* to his edition of Schlegel's translation of Shakespeare; V. E. Albright, *The Shakespearian Stage* (New York); W. Archer, *The Elizabethan Stage* (*Quarterly Review*, 1908); W. J. Lawrence, *The Elizabethan Playhouse and other Studies* (1st and 2nd series); D. Figgis, *Shakespeare, a study*.

From one or other of these, many of the above examples have been taken.

C. H. H.